THE GARDEN BIBLE
Designing your perfect outdoor space

Barbara Ballinger and Michael Glassman

THE GARDEN BIBLE
Designing your perfect outdoor space

Published in Australia in 2015 by
The Images Publishing Group Pty Ltd
ABN 89 059 734 431
6 Bastow Place, Mulgrave, Victoria 3170, Australia
Tel: +61 3 9561 5544 Fax: +61 3 9561 4860
books@imagespublishing.com
www.imagespublishing.com

Copyright © The Images Publishing Group Pty Ltd 2
The Images Publishing Group Reference Number: 1

All rights reserved. Apart from any fair dealing for the purposes of private study, research, criticism or review as permitted under the Copyright Act, no part of this publication may be reproduced, stored in a retrieval system or transmitted in any form by any means, electronic, mechanical, photocopying, recording or otherwise, without the written permission of the publisher.

National Library of Australia Cataloguing-in-Publication entry

Creator:	Ballinger, Barbara, author.
Title:	The garden bible: designing your perfect outdoor space / Barbara Ballinger, Michael Glassman.
ISBN:	9781864706185 (hardback)
Subjects:	Gardens—Design.
	Landscape design.
	Landscape gardening.
	Vegetable gardening.
	Gardens—United States—Case studies.
Other creators/contributors:	Glassman, Michael, author.
Dewey Number:	712.6

Production manager: Rod Gilbert
Senior editor: Gina Tsarouhas
Graphic designer: Ryan Marshall

Printed on 140gsm GoldEast Matt Art paper by Everbest Printing Co. Ltd., in Hong Kong/China

IMAGES has included on its website a page for special notices in relation to this and our other publications. Please visit www.imagespublishing.com.

Every effort has been made to trace the original source of copyright material contained in this book. The publishers would be pleased to hear from copyright holders to rectify any errors or omissions. The information and illustrations in this publication have been prepared and supplied by the the authors. While all reasonable efforts have been made to ensure accuracy, the publishers do not, under any circumstances, accept responsibility for errors, omissions and representations express or implied.

THE IMAGES PUBLISHING GROUP INTERACTIVE APP

Step 1: Scan the QR code to download the free IMAGES Interactive App onto your mobile device via our website.

Step 2: Browse through the book and keep an eye out for imagery marked with our icon.

Step 3: Using the app, scan the marked images to view additional digital content.

CONTENTS

6 Foreword

10 Introduction

14 **Chapter 1**
Understand Your Site and Climate

20 **Chapter 2**
Develop a Budget and Stick to It

30 **Chapter 3**
Hire the Best Professionals

38 **Chapter 4**
Find Your Garden Style

56 **Chapter 5**
Design Principles for a Functional and Aesthetic Outdoor Environment

72 **Chapter 6**
Recognize Problems Before You Start

78 **Chapter 7**
Great Gardens to Inspire

81 Zen Garden

85 The Eclectic Outdoor Room

89 Adios Snakes

93 Artist's Retreat

97 Savoring a View

101 Reclaimed Haven

105 Design Is in the Details

109 Bucolic Farm Redo

113 Waterfall Fantasy

117 Experimental Lab

121 Look: No Lawn

125 Spanish Colonial Revival Muse

129 Water Right

133 Serenity Evolved, Water Banished

137 Multitiered Maximizer

141 Evolved Landscape, from Barren to Mature

145 Staycation Showcase

149 Cohesive Clarity

153 Trifecta of Delights

157 Hip Revival

161 Natural Wildness Balances Cultural Turf

165 Woodlands Star

169 Historic Inspirations for Food, Flowers, Company

173 Rule No 1: Bag the Master Plan

177 Celebrating the Land

181 Family Fun

185 Water Times Three

189 Minimalist Signature

193 Nuts Inspire a Home Resort

196 **Chapter 8**
Find Inspiration—Garden Tours, Community Gardens, and Gardens Around the World

208 **Chapter 9**
Dig into Garden Blogs and Books

212 **Afterword**
A Personalized Garden Teaches a Final Lesson: Remember to Pick up Clues

214 Authors

216 Acknowledgments

222 Photography Credits

FOREWORD

The craft of designing and building a garden is not necessarily an easy thing to define, or to do. Throw in something as intimate as a personal home and the factors multiply exponentially. No two gardens are exactly the same. No two homes are exactly alike.

Each and every space requires its own set of solutions to various factors: Is there a lot of harsh afternoon sun? What is the condition of the soil? Do I have a Homeowners Association (HOA) that restricts certain elements in a garden such as a fence? Which types of azaleas will flourish in the garden, and how big will they grow? How should the drainage be handled to avoid erosion? These questions only scratch the surface of all the factors involved in designing and planting a garden and outdoor space.

Garden design is a multi-disciplinary field. A little bit of horticulture, some light engineering, minor geology, carpentry, masonry, and the list goes on. That's why it can be so hard to define exactly what it is.

Over the last 16 years of my career as a landscape designer, I can't pinpoint exactly when I felt I had mastered the craft and art. To be honest, I'm still learning and hope I never get to the point of feeling like I've totally learned it all. There is always something new to discover. Each year, I set out intentionally to learn a new skill set. I constantly research new materials and plant species. I attend as many conferences and education sessions as my schedule will allow. Many Friday afternoons, you can find me hunkered down in my office reading a trade magazine or favorite garden blog. The more I learn, the more I realize there is so much I don't yet know.

One thing that I do know, and I convey to my clients regularly, is that garden design is quite possibly one of the most rewarding tasks on earth. We take the surrounding environment as it is, and create a new space as we want it to be. It's quite a powerful feeling. It's also infinitely rewarding as gardens mature and tend to change over time. Each passing season brings new color and growth. Local wildlife can and will make a home in the garden. If you've never seen a family of finches bathe in a fountain, then you are in for a real treat when you do! Even more enjoyable is when they return each year with a new set of young to introduce to the world.

Many people find the task of designing and building a garden space intimidating or to be more work than they can handle, so they hire professionals. Others relish the task and jump right in as a hobby and labor of love they can tackle themselves. Wherever you fall on the spectrum, I sincerely hope that your reading of this beautifully presented and informative book, *The Garden Bible: Designing your perfect outdoor space*, inspires you and points you in the right direction to the joys and possibilities of garden design. *The Garden Bible* is a book written by people who have a true appreciation and love for good garden design and sharing that information. Whether you are a seasoned professional, experienced hobbyist, novice, or anywhere in between, there is always something more to discover within these pages, and in the wonderful outdoors.

James Hughes

Affiliate ASLA, American Society of Landscape Architects

Owner/Principal, James Hughes Landscaping

Tallahassee, Florida

2014–2016 Co-Chair of ASLA Residential Landscape Architecture Professional Practice Network (PPN)

Opposite: Landscape designer James Hughes constructed a natural water feature to bring peace to a garden in Havana, Florida. The use of large boulders and tree branches enhances the natural quality of this water amenity.

Above: Landscape designer Morgan Washburn of Botanical Decorators designed a "sun" spot in front of a house in Alexandria, Virginia, which is largely wooded, adjacent to the front porch where the owners can relax with coffee in the morning. "This was the first step in the design of the site before we added patios and a pool in back," Washburn says.

Above: This urban terrace in Chicago's Wicker Park neighborhood was designed by its owner Jill Maremont to savor views of downtown and provide areas to cook, garden, entertain, and meditate with comfortable seating, lush plantings, and a shade structure equipped with curtains to block wind.

FOREWORD 9

INTRODUCTION

Consider us your garden doctors, here to make a house call, even if only metaphorically, but with varied prescriptions for your landscape's health. We wrote *The Garden Bible: Designing your perfect outdoor space* to be a clear, concise and invaluable resource for everyone—from the neophyte to seasoned gardener. Whether you landscape yourself or hire experts, this book will help you maximize your site's potential in numerous ways based on topography, size (large, small, or in between), location, soil, amount of sunlight and shade, climate, orientation to other houses and the street, budget, and special challenges such as wildlife, drought, and building codes and requirements.

The outdoor environment is not just a place for planting material such as trees and shrubs, but it can also improve natural resources, your physical and mental well-being, and your home's value, just as your indoor rooms do.

A well-designed site isn't just one component either, but a series of parts that should in the end look cohesive, well tended, and most of all, loved. Each should have its own special function, or sometimes multiple ones, and reflect your personal style. Front yards offer a first impression of your style and personality and can affect the value of your property, hence the term "curb appeal." Your back yard usually provides more private space and is typically the better site to satisfy your wish list for how you want to use your outdoors. Your home also requires practical service areas—often in your side yard where you can keep and conceal such items as trash cans, tools, storage sheds, air-conditioning condensers, and pool pumps.

Sounds like a steep challenge? Yes, but with proper planning, it becomes a major success. This book will inspire you to dream and see different possibilities. Its prime purpose is to give you the information you need to enjoy time outdoors and identify what works and what does not.

Our content features a wide variety of gardens, sometimes with before and after photographs. They range from small, tranquil Zen-style gardens, to large traditional designs with formal beds, clipped hedges, and stately trees, with numerous variations in between. Many are presented in Chapter 7: Great Gardens to Inspire (page 78) as case studies of how landscape designers and architects solve common site challenges with creative solutions. From these studies, you can identify ideas that reflect your own landscape dilemmas and choose the best choices to fit your needs financially, functionally, and visually.

We walk you through the entire process, whatever your goals, in the proper order to make it all less daunting and more successful:

- Heighten your understanding of your site and climate.
- Develop a budget that is comfortable, takes into account how long you plan to stay in the property, and reflects your home's value and neighborhood prices and styles.
- Hire the right professionals to advise you, make some or all of the installations, and continue to improve and maintain them.
- Create a master plan that maps out your entire yard's needs from the start, which you can install all at once or in stages, depending on your funds.
- Learn to analyze and solve problems that are indigenous to your site and climate, or that crop up as conditions change.

Opposite: A narrow shade garden on Buffalo's Bidwell Parkway during the annual Garden Walk Buffalo tour.

- Understand the hardest garden lessons to master:

Plants in a garden need time to fill in and evolve. A finished design can't be ordered from a catalog and delivered overnight. The first year it sleeps, the second year it creeps, and third year it (finally) leaps!

There are no "throw-away" spaces. Property isn't always just about the front and/or back yards. Side yards can be transformed, as can rooftops and garages; these spaces sometimes offer the best views and privacy.

Design is in the details. Specialized lighting, focal-point artwork, sweet-sounding water features, special tiles, architectural-style trees, and manicured shrubs can personalize and create drama or serenity in a landscape.

Not everything works out as planned. Unlike interior rooms that sometimes remain static, gardens are living and breathing entities. Plants and trees mature, erosion occurs, bugs and animals visit and feast on what's growing, and climate continues to change. Results can rarely be guaranteed.

By using this book to solve the problems of your outdoor spaces, we want you to be able to focus on the joys of your garden.

We both continue to be inspired by public gardens, arboretums, community gardens, and private garden tours all around the globe that offer the fun of being welcomed to peer nosily into other homeowners' yards, which are usually off-limits.

Our advice will not produce a beautiful garden for you by snapping your fingers, but will set you on the right course to tailor your landscape to your needs and enjoy your outdoors more without digging a financial hole. In so doing, you will also help improve your community, add value to your home, and become a good steward of the environment for planet earth, yourself, and native wildlife. This kind of "paying it forward" is tough to beat!

Barbara Ballinger & Michael Glassman

Left: Amber Freda, whose landscape and design firm is based in New York City, designed a wrap-around roof garden in the city's West Village neighborhood with a 15-foot by 30-foot (4.6-meter by 9.1-meter) custom planter of red cedar that she filled with a lush mix of evergreens and flowers, including boxwoods, spiral junipers, Alberta spruce and gold mop cypresses. Two big challenges were the weight restriction of 35 pounds per square foot (15.9 kilograms per 0.9 square meter) and lack of a building elevator. To resolve these, Amber used lightweight potting soil and had everything on the deck carried up five flights of stairs. "Who needs a gym membership when you have a roof garden to install," she says. **Top left:** "When one door closes, another door opens" is a popular adage, and in this garden, designed by Howard Roberts, an opening from his clients' driveway to their rear terrace became more of a ceremonial adventure with a handsome arbor, climbing roses, and fencing. **Top right:** Every garden needs a passage…why not irregularly shaped stepping stones lined with hostas for an historical Tudor in Westfield, New Jersey, says its designer, landscape architect Marc Nissim.

INTRODUCTION 13

Chapter 1

UNDERSTAND YOUR SITE AND CLIMATE

In the dead of winter, you peruse the garden catalogs that begin arriving. It's inspiring and fun to dream about what can grow come springtime. When the weather is warmer, you're ready to transform all or part of your outdoor space into your perfect garden. To achieve success, be sure you take into account your site and climate.

First, take a look, literally, at the lay of your land. Does it slope dramatically, subtly, or is flat? If you have a very steep grade that's good for planting grapes, it might not be the ideal site to install a pool. A level lot is preferable, though land can be built up, rocks removed, and pool cantilevered. However, beware the extra labor and material costs.

Second, take note of the amount of sun and shade at various times of the day and during different seasons. If you want to grow roses or sun-loving perennials, and you have many mature trees that serve as a huge canopy to block sunlight, you may need to have those trees pruned. Or, a smarter choice might be to select plantings that require less light. Consider shade-loving azaleas, impatiens, hosta, or ferns. Also, find out what trees and shrubs grow native in your area and be sure companion plants like the same sun and soil conditions.

Next, know your soil's pH and content. Most garden soils have a pH level between 5.0 and 8.0. The pH level lets you know whether your soil is acidic or alkaline. If the soil level is below 6.0, the soil is too acidic and it is important to add ground limestone, which will raise the pH level. If the soil is above 7.5 it's too alkaline, so you need to add sulfur. The alkaline soil will be problematic for vegetables but good for roses and certain perennials. Acidic soil would be good for growing azaleas, rhododendrons, camellias, gardenias, and Japanese maples. Soil is made up of different contents. Clay particles are the smallest and are high in nutrients but slow to drain. Loam has larger particles and is easier to work with, offering better drainage. Sandy soil has the largest soil particles but water drains right through it and so do nutrients. Sandy soil may need to be augmented with organic matter to grow sea-thrift or native grasses; clay soil may work best for roses and lavender but not for rhododendrons and daphne. Don't forget to check drainage on the larger scale: be sure water drains away from your house and neighbors' yards into proper drainage lines. If not, it may collect near the foundation of your house or flow into your basement. Note that your community may also have rules about stormwater runoff and where it can and can't flow.

There may be other city, town or regional setback requirements that could limit your wish list and determine the placement of landscape elements such as shade structures, gazebos or swimming pools. These usually have to be a certain number of feet from street and property lines. There may also be rules regarding the height of fences and storage units. In some master-planned communities, a series of landscaping rules called Covenants, Codes and Regulations (CC&Rs) dictate additional guidelines, even sometimes specifying the species of trees, shrubs and groundcover permitted, and the look of all structures including colors, construction materials, lighting placement, and whether you may have fire pits and fireplaces. In addition, many of these CC&Rs specify watering schedules, which should influence landscape choices. If strict, xeriscaping materials that require little or no water are smarter. Fortunately, most communities require a homeowner to submit a landscape design plan for approval. This avoids having the association levy violations and fines against the homeowner. Some also require homeowners to post a bond so that if there is damage to the existing landscape there will be money to cover the repair.

Don't forget about wildlife. They will share your outdoor space. Birds, bees and butterflies can enhance the beauty of your garden and even help pollinate your plantings. On the other hand, deer,

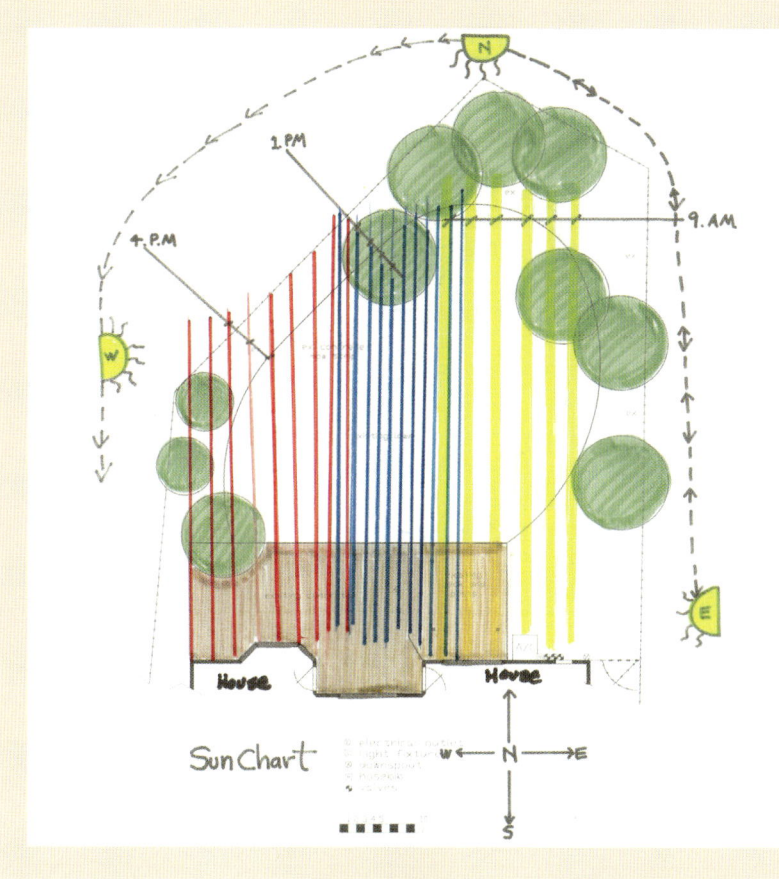

How to Create a Sun Chart

This process will tell you what areas get full sun and at what time of the day.

Step 1. Draw an outline of your house or back yard, including any existing trees, patios or structures. Scale is not important. Also mark where north, south, east, and west are located in relation to your yard. Show by arrows the path of the sun on your drawing.

Step 2. Go out to your yard at 9:00 am and look where the sun is shining. Then draw in yellow lines where the morning sun is on your chart.

Step 3. Go back out to your yard at 1:00 pm and note where the sun shines on your yard at midday and draw blue lines on your chart.

Step 4. Go back outside in the afternoon around 4:00 pm to see where the sun is in your yard. Then note this with red lines on your chart.

There will be areas that get sun at all times of the day, and areas under trees and next to fences and walls that will get little to none, so you can use your sun chart to map out the best locations for plantings. For example, roses need at least four to five hours of full sun to thrive. Ferns and hostas need morning sun but burn in afternoon sun. Vegetable gardens thrive with four to six hours of sun, while patios for dining are best to get morning sun and afternoon shade. Swimming pools should get the maximum amount of sun exposure for heating and solar benefits.

Above left: Landscape designer Michael Glassman designed this entry for a shade garden using Japanese maples, azaleas, and dwarf boxwood hedges. **Above right:** Michael Glassman transformed this dining patio with a custom water feature to block neighborhood noise, and planted timber bamboo to provide privacy.

rabbits, wild turkeys, and voles can disturb and destroy your handiwork by eating your carefully planted vegetables, herbs, and fruits. You may want to avoid temptation by installing a fence for your vegetables, building raised planters with heavy-duty wire mesh bottoms, or planting flowers and shrubs that repel or don't appeal to these unwelcome visitors. While dealing with this part of the animal kingdom, you want to ensure the safety of your family pets as well. Avoid using plants such as foxglove, oleander, and sago palms that are poisonous to dogs and cats. And don't forget to consider your family's health needs. Some members may be allergic to certain or all grasses, Scotch broom, olive trees, or pine pollen. There are many things to consider, so make a point of knowing before you spend time on materials and labor.

Climate, too, should dictate the types of plants you choose to add, and possibly the ones you remove if they are not doing well. Drought-prone Californian landscape specialists now favor succulents and low or no-water plants like crepe myrtles, flax, yuccas, trailing rosemary, and manzanita rather than water-loving ferns, hosta, hydrangeas, and poplar, willow and cottonwood trees. In long-wintering Chicago, spring comes late, and citrus and roses will not typically do well, but dogwoods, rose of Sharon, birches, sugar maples, Japanese maples, and peonies will thrive. Blue flag iris, yellow canna lilies, viburnum, maples, and wax myrtle will grow best in Florida's wettest areas. And sea thrift, echium, Monterey cypress, ice plant, and native grasses and lupines will do better by an ocean location with salt water, spray, and wind.

Having or retaining rainfall is another key concern as droughts continue worldwide. There are different sources to check your annual rainfall such as books like the Farmer's Almanac and its online version; the weather channel where you live; and other on-site resources such as www.weather.com. You may want to consider storing rainwater as well as runoff drainage in cisterns and underground storage tanks. And installing a hardscape that allows water to percolate back into the ground is smart; consider for this purpose permeable pavers atop a sand base rather than mortar. In addition, more municipalities are beginning to encourage the use of greywater systems that recycle water from the home for use outdoors in the landscape.

Opposite: Interior designer Sarah Barnard and landscape architect Scott Martin collaborated on a design for a luxury estate garden with a saltwater pool, vintage waterwheel and teak furnishings with custom upholstery. **Above left:** Michael Glassman designed rusted steel planters to terrace a steep-sloped front entry into this home. Drought-tolerant, colorful plantings accent the contemporary hardscape design. **Above right:** Landscape designer Laurie Van Zandt designed a summer vacation home on a tight site in northern Utah. Because of the property's size, she maximized space by constructing a fire pit on a side facing a fabulous view. Both the pit and seat wall were built from local stone.

UNDERSTAND YOUR SITE AND CLIMATE 17

And while you're blooming with inspiration about how your outdoor space is emerging, remember your home's architectural style should factor into your landscape's look. Keep in mind that there should be some cohesiveness and similarities between house and garden through complementary materials, color palette, and scale. They don't have to be exact clones, so long as they complement one another. A mid-century, modern house can look great paired with a Japanese garden, whereas an overflowing English cottage garden would not look as compatible since it is far more casual. Also, how your house is oriented in relation to your neighbors' houses should also factor into your landscaping plans. For example, you won't want a private, meditation garden to abut your neighbor's driveway, or one that is blocked from sun by a neighboring home's overhanging roof.

All these challenges point to one major caveat: research in advance! Looking for inspiration on the internet, in books, or by driving around your neighborhood and favorite areas will help you learn the different architectural as well as garden styles that are most compatible with one another. Stop into your favorite nursery and ask questions if you're unsure. Know your climate zone and whether there are microclimates on your site. Do a sun map on your property to determine when and where there is sun and shade, how much, and at what times of the day. Factor in how often it rains, or doesn't, remembering that that can easily change. Get your soil tested for its pH level from a local community extension service, sometimes affiliated with a college, or from a nursery that offers that service. Be mindful of what wildlife frequents your area and look for signs on your property of their impact and minimize harmful effects on both wildlife and your garden environment. You need to co-exist.

All this information will help you pick the right plant materials for your region and site, and know those to avoid, even if you love them. By planning ahead, you will save time and money. For more detailed strategies on avoiding pitfalls, see also Chapter 6: Recognize Problems Before You Start (page 72).

Above left: The landscape design of this New York City terrace by Gunn Landscape Architecture extends interior living areas outdoors; cozy furnishings and plant materials—evergreens, native grasses and perennial blooms—work in most seasons. **Above right:** The view through foliage near a pool house in New York shows off purple clematis growing up columns. Designer John Cowen used the same plant groupings of hosta, peony, phlox, nepeta, miscanthus and hydrangeas in clusters around the property to link planting groups and produce a unified feeling. (Pool house: Farrell Building Company, Bridgehampton, New York.) **Opposite:** Located in the middle of a walnut orchard, raised planters and a decorative fountain wall now provide privacy and create a separate entertainment space on a flat, sunny site; design from Michael Glassman.

Chapter 2

DEVELOP A BUDGET AND STICK TO IT

Your ideas unfold like petals in spring. You think, "Wouldn't it be great to create an outdoor room for cooking, dining and relaxing? Or, a glassed-in conservatory perfect for a winter retreat with a magnificent terraced rose and vertical garden?" Fabulous ideas, but what about the cost?

The sky is the limit with how much you spend on outdoor improvements, just as it is with interior decorating and remodeling projects. Your budget may be very generous, but while your ideas add up faster than potential debts, you don't want to spend more money and time than you allotted because you didn't understand all the costs that go into a good landscape design.

It's time to budget. How long and detailed the budget is depends on the scope of your project. Before you come up with a dollar amount for your landscaping, avoid unwanted costs by setting aside a specific amount and dividing it into components that fulfill your wish list. Some areas may already exist in your outdoor space and won't need to be replaced, while other hardscape and plantings you'll want to purchase new.

For all these categories, most landscape designers and architects advise spending anywhere from 5 to 30 percent of the value of your home, which you may then increase or decrease. So much depends on the size and characteristics of your site, existing hardscape elements, complexity of your desired plan, elaborateness of your material choices, available funds, neighborhood aesthetics, and how long you think your stay may affect how much you want to spend. Prioritize and put in your favorite essentials first, with the view that any major construction work, be it that elaborate deck or adding your much-wanted hot tub, for example, will be of benefit to the overall value of the property should your circumstances change and you wish to sell.

Pare Costs

There's good news when it comes to cutting costs; for most costly choices, there are more conservative alternatives. For example, with softscaping, you can buy smaller, less exotic plants, when they are out of bloom, or start with bare root specimens. You can plant perennials, which will return yearly and will save you money over time compared to annuals that will need to be replaced each spring. Of course, prices will depend on how many you buy and where you shop. A discount superstore or most farmers' markets will set you back less for your plantings than if you shop at a one-of-a-kind nursery or certain online sources.

> **The Four Key Elements of a Strong Budget**
> 1. Include the **softscape**—the plants, mulch, irrigation, soil, and drainage.
> 2. List the **hardscape**—walks, decks, patios, fencing, pergolas, awnings and gazebos.
> 3. Compile the **main amenities** such as a pool, outdoor kitchen, furnishings, sound system, lighting, and outdoor TV.
> 4. Add in **labor for installation and initial maintenance**, which will vary greatly depending on where you live. Ongoing care will be a separate cost to consider.

Typically, flowers are just the beginning of your expenses. You may want to install sod, which is more expensive than planting seed, but offers the payback of immediate lawn and easier care. Seeding is labor-intensive and requires weeding and frequent re-seeding. Irrigation is necessary to keep your landscape thriving. A drip system is less

Opposite: Howard Roberts of Liquid Inc. wanted his clients' home to be a place where they'd have years of memories for gathering. During the day they can dine under the pergola and watch TV, and at night the sky twinkles with lighting draped through the pergola, and they can warm themselves by the fireplace.

Stone Choices

Today you have a choice of natural or artificial products. Base your choice on size, price, and other materials in your yard:

- **Tumbled stone** exudes a soft, weathered appearance and older age stability and patina.

- **Rock facing stone** adds a more rugged character, depth, and dimension.

- **Brick** introduces color and texture and can be layed in different patterns such as basket weave, herringbone, or running bond.

- **Crushed gravel** offers a wonderful sound when walking on it, helps control weed growth, and comes in various natural colors and even sizes for terraces, walks, and driveways.

- **Slate** and **quartzite** are natural stones that will last indefinitely and add warmth and substance to any landscape. They come in tile or larger flagstone sizes and are a dramatic addition to a garden.

- **Interlocking pavers** are permeable and allow water to drain through. They come in different patterns, sizes and colors.

- **Decomposed granite** is a natural material in a golden or gray color that can be stabilized to give a hard surface. Used in natural walkways, on trails, and in state parks, it can be an inexpensive surface to use instead of a more expensive hardscape. Use it at least 4 inches (10 centimeters) thick, so it compacts well when wet.

Top: Blue Adirondack chairs surround a fire pit in a garden landscape by John Algozzini of K&D Landscape Management, Inc. designed to go with a farmhouse from 1887. **Bottom:** Landscape architect Carrie Stanker worked to make access from a family's driveway to their entertaining spaces accessible and attractive. She added a meandering curved path accented with pockets of color. **Opposite top:** For a small lot in an urban setting, the homeowners wanted a place to entertain without grass. Landscape architect Stephen Wlodarczyk of Botanical Decorators Inc. designed a cedar pergola with fiberglass columns, which provides shade and definition. **Opposite bottom:** Designer Amber Freda redesigned a rooftop terrace in New York City to enhance an existing wood deck and painted fence without having to replace these features. She picked lightweight planters that can be moved around and filled them with a mix of evergreens, birch trees, soft grasses and colorful chrysanthemums.

expensive to add than a conventional underground system, but involves a lot more maintenance, especially when you have animals that may chew through pipes or you live in places where well-water deposits might clog the valves. You may simply go with a hose and sprinkler and move it about your yard. (It is good exercise after all.) If your site already features an appealing inventory of healthy, mature trees, bushes, and flower beds, you may be able to trim your overall budget. And, if you want to enjoy your outdoor space both day and night, good lighting is a must—it's also essential for nighttime safety.

When it comes to your hardscape, there are ways to save money, most of which reflect simpler, more commonplace materials. For example, pouring a concrete patio will be less expensive up front than using bluestone, slate, or travertine, and instead of stamped concrete for your driveway consider asphalt. Prices do, however, vary greatly by area. In California, we've found a stamped or salted colored concrete patio will run about half the cost installed versus slate or bluestone. Take into account too that certain elements of your hardscape are more important than others. A patio represents the bones of many outdoor designs and "rooms", and should be built for function and durability for the long haul. Materials like bluestone, slate, and travertine don't wear out, and look as handsome in years to come as when you installed them. Although cheaper, concrete can crack after seven to 10 years, and commonly in very cold climates if not installed properly. Be extra careful in your choice if you have a driveway or walk lined with gravel that you don't want destroyed with a snowplow. You will then have to replace much of those surfaces come spring. And don't be short-sighted in terms of best use overall. Too many homeowners reduce the size of their patio and find themselves without enough space for their planned functions, furnishings, and number of users. Bigger is usually better here, though it should be in proportion with the house and its site. Usually, the differential costs are minimal and again, planning is essential.

DEVELOP A BUDGET AND STICK TO IT   23

Introduce Amenities

The amenities you want to include can take another big bite of your budget. An overhead structure for shade such as a pergola is a good way to block strong sun and offer weather protection, but it may require engineering expertise and a building permit, versus installing an already-assembled pergola from a hardware store or simply buying and opening a large umbrella.

A rollaway barbecue is another way to cut costs versus constructing a built-in outdoor kitchen with refrigerator, sink, dishwasher, beer tap, pizza oven, granite counter, and storage. A portable metal fire pit will be less expensive than a built-in, stone-faced fireplace, and allows you to still enjoy a warm glow and sit outdoors on chillier days and nights. A screened-in porch is less costly than adding on a room, but can still extend the use of your outdoor areas. Constructing a concrete pool on a wooded area or in very hilly rocky terrain are both much more labor intensive and expensive than building a vinyl-lined pool on a flat, barren lot. In fact, building an in-ground pool of almost any kind can be the most expensive hardscape amenity that also requires periodic and often costly repairs. Fiberglass pools or above-ground pools and portable spas are more economical alternatives initially, though they may not last as long with lifespans of 10 to 15 years.

Outdoor Kitchen Staples

When thinking about incorporating amenities for your outdoor kitchen, consider the following elements. For tips on good outdoor kitchen design principles, see Designing Your Outdoor Kitchen (page 60).

- **Grill.** You have two prime options—gas or charcoal. Gas is quick, clean, and easy to control. Charcoal is messier and takes longer to get going, but offers a barbecue flavor unmatched by gas. Some manufacturers produce hybrid units. A grill is a necessary fixture in an outdoor kitchen, whether freestanding or incorporated into a built-in kitchen countertop.

- **Pizza oven.** These appeal as a separate freestanding oven that can be used, yes, for cooking pizza, but also baking bread or cooking any meal one might do in an oven. Be prepared for the steep cost when they're built of stone and are freestanding, but newer, portable models that are less expensive are also available.

- **Kegerator.** These beer taps are built in under a counter and are refillable.

- **Refrigerator.** Outdoor fridges come in all shapes and sizes depending on bells, whistles, and size desired.

- **Sink.** If you run hot water, you need to tie it into your sewer line. If you plan on just cold water, you may be able to dump it into the existing drainage system of your town or village, or even as greywater for the garden. Inquire what the situation is with your local authorities.

- **Counters.** The most popular choices are granite, tile, and poured concrete, but some favor porcelain or travertine tile. Depending on how many cooks, include enough counter space for at least two to work comfortably.

- **Storage.** You may want to stash plates, cups, cutlery, and utensils outdoors during the season, so fabricate your storage units with stainless steel for best cold-weather upkeep.

- **Lighting.** Don't forget good low-voltage, energy-efficient LED lighting so you can use your outdoor kitchen at night.

Right: This outdoor kitchen by Arterra Landscape Architects is the ultimate in alfresco dining. Its generous size lets guests gather at the island while the hosts prep and cook at the grill. The thick green granite counter and wide ipe boards make a strong modern statement.

DEVELOP A BUDGET AND STICK TO IT 25

Contractor Bids, Site Plans and Budgeting

Here we show a sample of a contractor's bid and an example of a site plan along with general estimates on the range and types of variations in plantings and amenities to expect when reviewing your budget, for example, for more affordable, midrange or more costly landscape work.

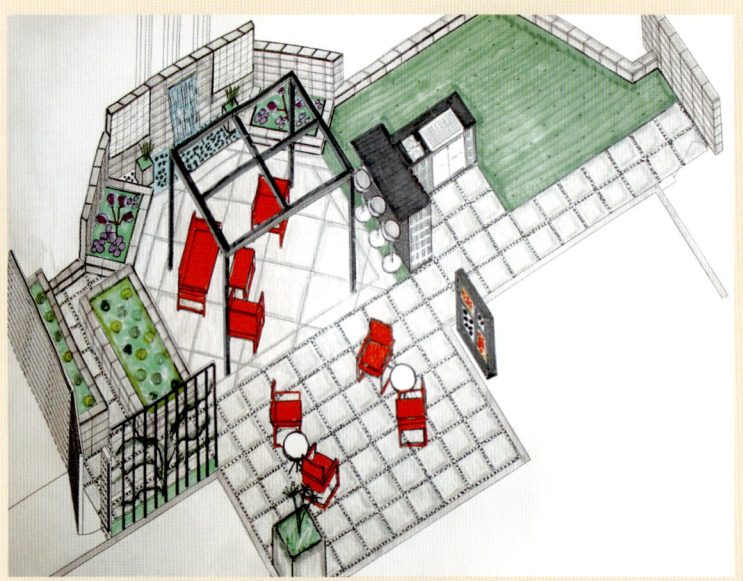

Sample Estimate

DATE	ESTIMATE NO.
12/2/2014	1139

NAME / ADDRESS

DESCRIPTION	QTY	TOTAL
1. PURCHASE AND INSTALL 1/8" STEEL SHEETING IN A PAINTED DTM BRONZE FINISH MOUNTED WITH DECORATIVE NUTS AND BOLTS TO 4X4 PRESSURE TREATED WOOD POSTS SET IN CONCRETE FOOTINGS. THE SHEETING IS TO BE IN FRONT OF THE EXISTING FENCE AND AT THE HEIGHT OF THE EXISTING FENCE.	330	6,237.00
2. FACE THE EXISTING GATE WITH 1/8" STEEL SHEETING IN A PAINTED DTM BRONZE FINISH MOUNTED WITH DECORATIVE NUTS AND BOLTS. MATCH SIZE OF EXISTING GATE.	24	453.60
3. PURCHASE AND INSTALL 1/8" STEEL SHEETING IN A PAINTED DTM BRONZE FINISH GATE/ENCLOSURE TO ENCLOSE THE A/C UNIT. MATCH HEIGHT OF EXISTING FENCE.	48	907.20
4. EXTEND EXISTING OVERHEAD STRUCTURE AT BACK PATIO LOCATION WITH 2" X 4" LEDGER BOARD, CORRUGATED METAL AND FLASHING AT HOUSE CONNECTION WITH A 2' SECTION OF GUTTER AND A RAIN CHAIN.	2	1,039.50
5. GROUND LEVEL PLANTER WITH TWO 6'-0" WIDE IRON LATTICE SCREENS INSTALLED IN THE GROUND IN REMOVABLE METAL SLEEVES AT BACK OF GARAGE	1	787.50
6. NEW ENLARGED PATIO OVER LAID WITH PERUVIAN 16"X16" TRAVERTINE TILE ON THE DIAGONAL. PATIO CONSTRUCTED OF 4" MIN. THICKNESS OF POURED CONCRETE OVER 4" MIN. THICKNESS OF COMPACTED GRAVEL WITH #3 REBAR 24" O.C..	450	6,468.53
7. PURCHASE AND INSTALL 28 LINEAR FEET OF SINGLE SIDE 2" THICK CUSTOM RADIUS SINGLE SIDE BULLNOSE TRAVERTINE CAP FOR THE TOP OF EXISTING CONCRETE WALL.	28	2,352.00

TOTAL $18,245.33

SIGNATURE

Budget contract

- Stained deck the same color as the house;
- Stained railing trim color;
- Added three brightly colored ceramic pots that were planted with flax and trailing red geraniums;
- Added drip irrigation to pots; and
- Added new furniture with colorful cushions.

Total Cost: U.S. $5,000

Midrange contract

- Poured colored concrete patio;
- Built overhead shade structure;
- Installed prefabricated fireplace and faced it in ledgestone;
- Ran new gas line to fireplace; and
- Added table and chairs.

Total Cost: U.S. $27,000

Top-end contract

- Installed travertine tiled patio on raised steel patio;
- Built custom stone-faced fireplace;
- Installed custom wrought-iron railing; and
- Furnished with high-end outdoor furniture.

Total Cost: U.S. $75,000

Assemble Your Team

A good budget should also include the funds to hire professionals: a landscape designer or architect who can develop your overall plan, a contractor to install your hardscape, or a maintenance company to maintain your garden on a weekly or monthly basis. And then, if you live in a snowy or cold climate, you may want someone to plow.

Analyze Costs

Costs add up quickly so try not to get discouraged. Many homeowners tend to spend the largest amounts of money on their indoor spaces while neglecting their outdoor areas. Look at it this way. How does the interior of your home look after 10 years? Probably, a bit worn and in need of some significant redecorating. Paradoxically, at 10 years or longer, a well-designed landscape has come into its own and looks full and lush. In that time, shade trees have matured, groundcover has filled in, and patios have aged to a handsome patina, a better match for the home's façade in most cases. See also Maintaining Your Landscape (page 54).

The result is a new outdoor living environment with greater curb appeal and more personal enjoyment. You may never want to leave home but instead enjoy a "staycation." Additionally, installing a well-planned, functional landscape is sustainable and environmentally friendly because it could last a lifetime.

Master Plan

Your garden is starting to come together. By taking into account all these factors, you start to draw a big picture of the design for your entire yard, including all four sides if you have a freestanding, single-family home, hard- and softscapes, and amenities; what your professionals will put together in an overall master plan. These changes can be phased in over time. You don't have to spend your entire budget in one lump sum and do all the installations at once. Sometimes, it works better to focus on one section at a time since you may change your mind as you see results. (For example, you may have installed a serpentine flower bed in the back yard and nearby a large vegetable garden in raised redwood planters surrounded by gravel, only to discover you miss the sound of water. You decide to install a small, recirculating feature the next spring.) By following our approach of careful planning well before excavating or planting, you will also save money because you will avoid the hidden costs of tearing out unsustainable or non-functional elements and replacing them.

See also Chapter 4: Find Your Garden Style (page 38) for more ideas on consolidating your master plan and amenities with your personal style.

Below left: Interior designer Sarah Barnard collaborated with the landscape design firm Jones & Potik to create a lush arrangement of succulents in Asian ceramic pottery for a Manhattan Beach, California, residence. **Below right:** Michael Glassman designed this rustic covered outdoor room for dining and relaxing adjacent to a free-form pool surrounded by shade-loving dogwoods, Japanese maples and azaleas.

Pools

The sky's the limit with pools. Most above-ground pools are the affordable option, followed by in-ground pools with vinyl liners, gunite in-ground pools, and lastly, natural swimming pools, the most costly. Because of a site's topography, trees and bushes, and all the bells and whistles you might include such as steps, boulders, slides, decking, lights, cleaning pumps, heaters, and more, it's impossible to provide cost estimates. The key is to be sure you compare apples to apples when you shop for the pool, plus take into account the excavation and installation costs.

Top: This Connecticut site had an existing pond that BioNova Natural Pools transformed into a natural pool. **Bottom:** For a vacation home in Maine, BioNova Natural Pools rooted the plants in gravel in the regeneration zone, which clarifies and purifies water for the swimming zone. **Right:** In New Jersey, BioNova Natural Pools designed a pool in collaboration with pond designer Anthony Archer Wills. Big boulders were trucked in from Pennsylvania and carefully placed as if they'd always existed.

Natural Swimming Pools Make a Ripple

The classic rectangular or oval pool with stone coping and complementary deck, diving board or slide, and metal steps, still holds appeal for many who are adding or remodeling a pool. But natural pools that resemble ponds or swimming holes have become increasingly popular, with their interiors plastered dark blue, gray, or even black; popular features include clusters of rock, waterfalls spilling over outcroppings, a diving boulder, water-loving plants, and salt water.

But, an even newer generation of natural swimming pools has started to gain attention, after first making a splash in Europe. Their look can be similar, or resemble more traditional designs. What differentiates this latest version is that water is cleansed without using chlorine. Instead, beneficial bacterial and micro-organisms, in conjunction with aquatic plants rooted hydroponically in gravel and rocks, filter water in an adjacent pool, known as a "regeneration" zone. Then, the water is pumped back clean to the swimming pool, so it's safe for swimming. It's similar to how wetlands treat water more benignly than chemicals can do.

Consider all the pros and cons before you wade in:

- **Great design flexibility.** While natural swimming pools can be integrated seamlessly into a site, they can also be designed in any style—even a formal Grecian or Roman pool.

- **General health benefits.** They are a good alternative for those with skin allergies, or who don't want to be subjected to chlorine. Know, however, that there still may be minute algae particles.

- **Need for extra land.** They require a larger site because of the regeneration zone. If you design a 700-square-foot (65-square-meter) pool, for instance, you need another pool of equal size. With community rules about setbacks and how much impervious surface you can have on a property, your yard may not be large enough to accommodate it. Don't install a pool smaller than a total of 535 square feet (50 square meters).

- **Higher initial cost.** They cost more to build than conventional pools because of the need to construct two, though per-square costs are similar. They typically cost less to operate because of the absence of chlorine and other chemicals, and their ability to use a smaller pump and less energy.

- **Less than perfectly clear water.** The color of the water isn't always crystal clear, but it is safe for swimming. Color varies, based on such factors as nutrient balance, temperature, and precipitation. Some algae and sediment will always be present.

Chapter 3

HIRE THE BEST PROFESSIONALS

You're ready to begin; you have an idea of what you want in your garden, and a ballpark figure of what you can afford. Now what?

If you just want to plant some flowers to add pizzazz or more curb appeal, or start a simple vegetable garden, you probably can do this on your own by visiting a local nursery or big-box store for supplies, planting materials, and advice that you take home. When you go, take along your sun chart of the area you are planting, so you make the right choices for the location (in other words, put plantings in the right spot where they'll be more apt to thrive). Measure the space so you can calculate how many plants you want and bear in mind that plants need room to grow. Finally, decide on your favorite color palette—a riotous mix, all white, or blue and purple, for instance. See also Chapter 4: Find Your Garden Style (page 38) for further information.

On the other hand, if you are looking to gain an outdoor living environment, for example, construct a swimming pool, raised vegetable garden, Japanese tea house, koi pond, patio, shade structure, or outdoor kitchen, you may want to hire experts who will perform the work, First develop an overall master plan so you understand the design as a whole. This drawing provides a cohesive design, and functions as a road map, so you systematically phase in your landscape installation as your budget permits and as plantings grow. You don't have to do everything at once.

The plans can be drawn up by a residential landscape designer or landscape architect, each an expert in plant selection, irrigation, drainage, lighting, and good landscape design principles, such as scale, balance, structure, color, and sustainability. Many have resources and connections with other professionals, such as landscape contractors, arborists, horticulturists, and engineers for possible water or land challenges.

How to Find the Right Landscape Professional

How do you find the right professionals? As with other home-improvement projects, ask friends, family members, and co-workers for recommendations. You can also go online and check out the websites of the American Society of Landscape Architects (www.asla.org) or The Association of Professional Landscape Designers (www.apld.com).

And who do you choose? What's a landscape architect versus a designer? Generally, architects tackle commercial and industrial projects. They must have formal schooling and be licensed. Designers usually specialize in residential design, have a variable amount of formal schooling, and do not have to be licensed. While there are some professionals that design and construct landscapes, others focus simply on design and recommend independent contractors for the installation. In either case, you want to get references, eyeball their finished work and get estimates before you sign a written contract.

If your site has existing trees, consulting a licensed arborist might be a good idea to learn about their health (see Why You Should Hire an Arborist, page 36). If your property has serious erosion problems, possibly because of a steep slope, your architect or designer may recommend you consult a structural engineer during the design phase.

Be sure the professionals you hire understand you and your site. For this reason, insist you meet your designer, architect, arborist, engineer,

Opposite: This hidden formal garden with a central cast-iron three-tiered fountain accented by trimmed boxwood and iceberg roses on a large, traditional estate was designed by Michael Glassman.

and/or contractor at your home face-to-face so you outline in person the scope of your project. This meeting is also a good test to see if your aspirations and tastes jibe, and if there is chemistry. Getting the professional to understand what you truly want can be tricky because not everyone can pinpoint or verbalize their desires when they begin the process. That's why when you do meet, have your wish list available, possibly accompanied by photos from magazines and/or bookmarked pictures in garden books, and your budget clearly in mind. Ask what they see as the plusses and conversely the main problems with the lot, orientation of the house and yard, climate, and location. Discuss how you can phase in the project depending on available funds. And be upfront and discuss whether your budget is realistic for your goals.

Fee Schedules

Landscape architects and designers have different fee schedules. Many design experts charge by the hour (starting with an initial consultation) to give you design ideas. Others charge by the job. Some supervise construction projects while others just do the master plan drawings and turn the work over to a contractor. Some professionals may take you shopping for plants, trees, and hardscape materials at their hourly rate. Others may include this time as part of their design contract. Ask the right questions. Make sure the professional is available and has time to focus on your project. It is important to find out what services they provide and how they charge for all of them, so you are not surprised later with a much higher bill. What if you make a change? Be sure the written contract specifies the work to be done, how long it will take, how much it may cost, and how you will resolve any difference if unexpected problems arise during construction.

Design Ideas to Turn Your Back Yard into an Oasis

Whether your summer plans include graduation parties, neighborhood barbecues, a back-yard wedding, or just dinner on the deck, the season for outdoor entertaining often comes after a long cold winter in many regions of the United States and abroad. And with it comes a desire to spend as much time outside as possible. Here are four tips to help do so from architect Elissa Morgante of Morgante-Wilson Architects in Chicago:

1. These spaces rarely feel intimate. Define your space with garden walls of brick, stone, or wood, and enclose a portion of your yard. The walls may be tall and vine-covered, low and capped with stone for impromptu seating, or left open at the top to function as planters. Garden walls can also be formed by foliage such as boxwood hedges. Another way is by incorporating a trellis, sail shade, or oversized umbrella. These offer respite from the sun's glare, as well a protection if there's a rain sprinkle. Trellises can be integrated into the architecture of your house and garden by repeating materials, shapes, and scale.

2. Add comfortable furniture with cushions that are weatherproof or all mesh that allows water to flow through and dry quickly.

3. Light up any area for living to create a more inviting outdoor ambience. Just be sure light is soft, not bright, and tuck sources inside your landscaping so you see the light, not the fixture.

4. Incorporate a fan, which moves hot air, adds cooler breezes, and helps keep bugs away.

Opposite top left: The Pond Guys rehabilitated a 20-foot by 20-foot (6-meter by 6-meter) pond in St. Charles, Missouri, making it 3 feet (90 centimeters) deep and adding an island, then filling the pond with lilies, koi, gold fish—and "lots of frogs," says designer Arthur Ruebel. **Opposite top right:** Elissa Morgante, AIA, of Morgante-Wilson Architects in Chicago, Illinois, designed a woven vinyl sail cloth, which was custom-made by an awning company, to provide shade and create a more intimate feeling for an outdoor space. The sofa fabric looks like linen but is polyester that can remain outdoors all year, even in harsh winters. **Opposite bottom:** The topography of the site sloped and was completely blank. This required creativity on the part of landscape architect Brian Hahn to design and construct the resort-style back yard his clients desired. The result included a curved pergola, pool, adjoining spa, and outdoor kitchen. **Above:** Designer Amber Freda added plantings, flowers and pots to soften and add a Mediterranean sensibility to an existing garden on two levels of a New York City apartment. She kept most plantings low because of wind.

Preliminary Drawings vs. Working Drawings

Different levels of detail can be included in your master plan. Whether you agree to preliminary or working drawings, one set of revisions should be included in the fee. In fact, many professionals specify in their contracts how many changes to the plans will be included. If you keep changing your mind, it will probably cost you more to make the extra changes.

Preliminary drawings are carefully measured drawings at a scale that specifies where each hard- and softscape element will go. They may not contain specifications for drainage, lighting, and irrigation. However, a good landscape contractor can still interpret and apply the drainage, lighting, and irrigation to your site based on these drawings. Costs will vary, but preliminary drawings are less expensive than working drawings. They may range in price, but know that so much depends on the complexity, area of the country, and years of experience of the professional.

Working drawings provide more details for construction and should include separate plans for grading, drainage, lighting, irrigation, electrical, and details for hardscape construction and soft plant materials, sometimes in color and with images of the specific choices. If you plan to do the work yourself, if your homeowners association requires this level of drawing, or if your project is very complicated with steep slopes or major drainage problems, you will want this level of detail to proceed. Working drawings may be 50 percent higher in cost than preliminary drawings.

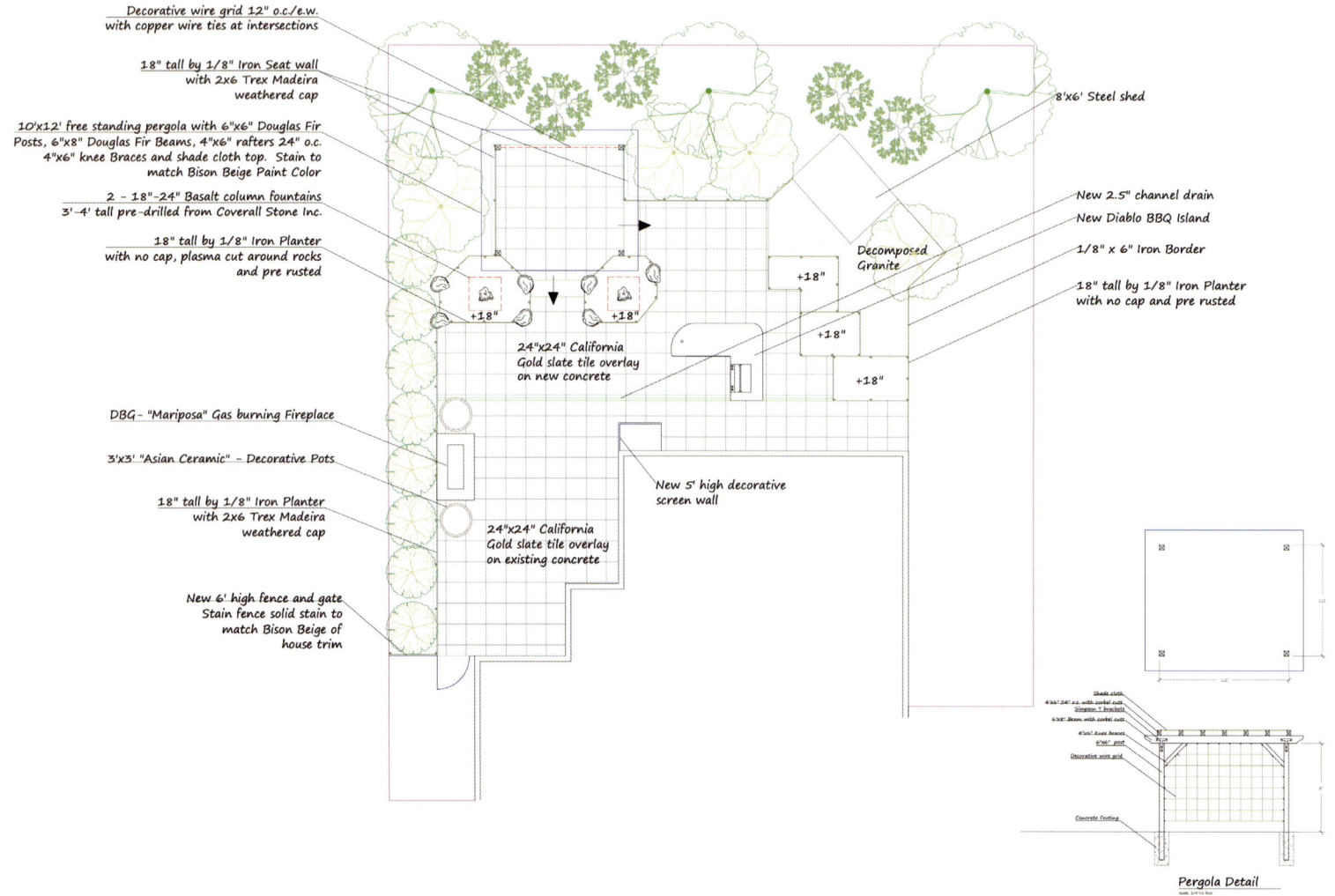

Above and opposite: Plans and details designed by Michael Glassman, Michael Glassman & Associates.

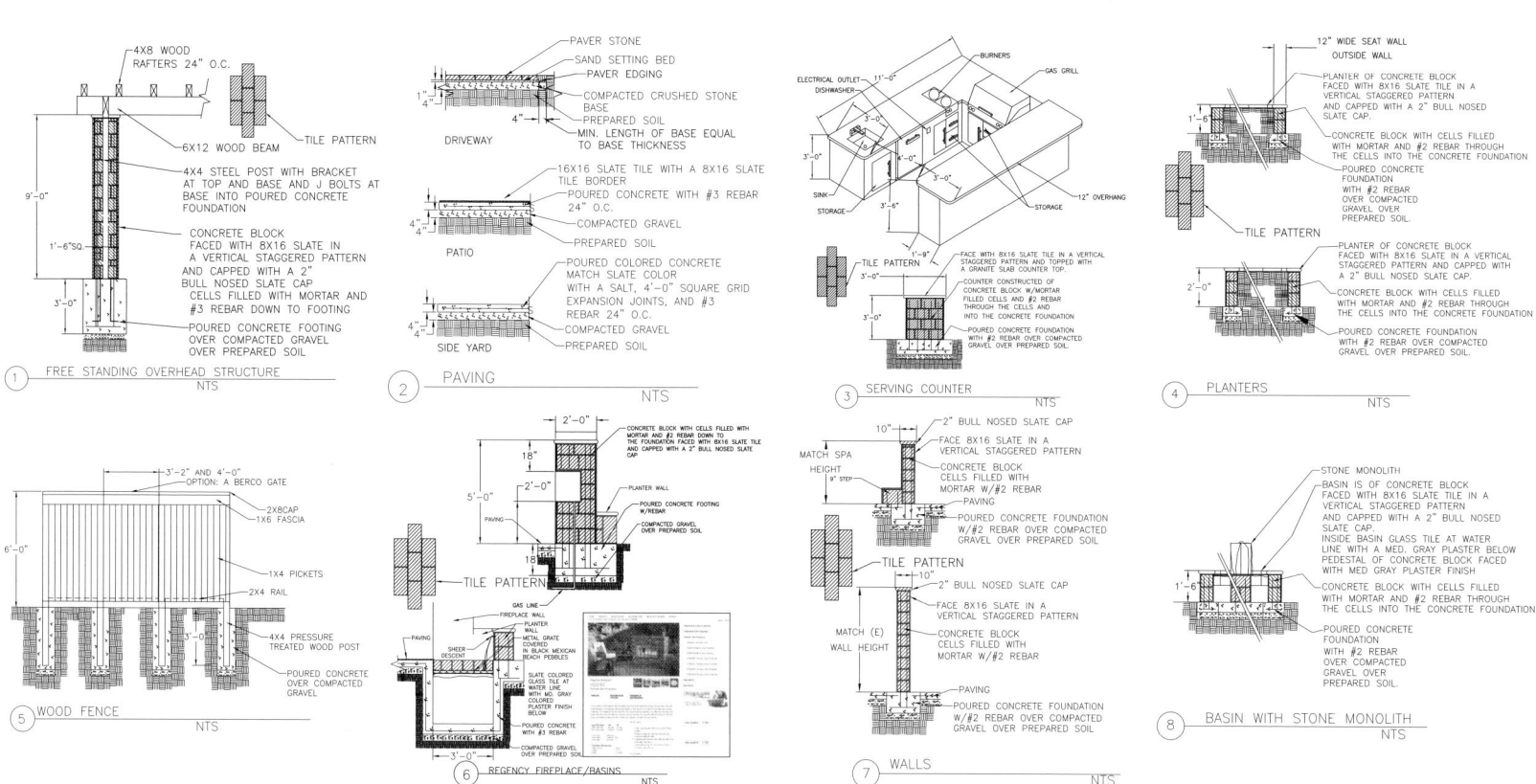

HARDSCAPE NOTES

1. ADD NEW FREE STANDING OVERHEAD STRUCTURE THAT CANTILEVERS OVER THE EXISTING ROOF. THE NEW OVERHEAD STRUCTURE IS TO HAVE SIX POSTS, TWO FANS, AND A CHANDELIER. THE THE OVERHEAD POSTS ARE TO BE 9'-0" HIGH AND 18" SQUARE CONSTRUCTED OF 4x4 STEEL POSTS FACED WITH CONCRETE BLOCK AND 8X16 SLATE TILE IN A VERTICALLY STAGGERED PATTERN. THE OVERHEAD IS TO BE CONSTRUCTED OF 6X12 DOUG FIR BEAMS WITH 4X8 DOUG FIR RAFTERS 24" O.C. COVERED WITH A PERMEABLE PATIO BRA. PROVIDE ELECTRICAL FOR THE FANS, CHANDELIER AND DOWN LIGHTING. PROVIDE SPEAKER WIRE FOR SPEAKERS. WOOD IS TO BE STAINED THE HOUSE COLOR. ON THE EXISTING POSTS CHANGE TO MATCH THE NEW POSTS AND MOVE ONE POST TO LINE UP WITH NEW POST. INCREASE THE SIZE OF THE EXISTING BEAM OR CHANGE TO STEEL IF NEEDED FOR THE CHANGE OF POST LOCATION. SEE DETAIL #1
2. REPLACE EXISTING PAVING WITH NEW PAVING AT ONE LEVEL 6" BELOW THE F.F.E. WITH A STEP DOWN TO THE SIDE YARD. THE NEW PAVING IS TO BE OVERLAID WITH SLATE 16X16 IN A RUNNING BOND PATTERN WITH A 8X16 SLATE TILE BORDER. PATIO CONSTRUCTED OF 4" MIN. THICKNESS OF POURED CONCRETE OVER 4" MIN. THICKNESS OF COMPACTED GRAVEL WITH #3 REBAR 24" O.C. OPTION: RADIANT HEAT UNDER THE TILE. SEE DETAIL #2
3. 4" WIDE CHANNEL DRAIN WITH REMOVABLE GRATE TIED INTO A SOLID DRAIN LINE TO DRAIN TO THE STREET.
4. LARGE POTS – PROVIDE AREA DRAINS AND DRIP IRRIGATION FOR THE POTS.
5. MOVE EXISTING GARAGE DOOR TO THE SIDE YARD.
6. 36" HIGH COUNTER WITH GAS GRILL, BURNERS, SINK, REFRIGERATOR, DISHWASHER, WARMING DRAWER, BAR STOOLS, AND STAINLESS STEEL DOORS AND DRAWERS FOR STORAGE/GARBABE CAN. BAR COUNTER IS TO BE 42" HIGH. COUNTER CONSTRUCTED OF CONCRETE BLOCK FACED WITH 8X16 SLATE TILE IN A VERTICAL STAGGERED PATTERN AND TOPPED WITH A GRANITE SLAB. PROVIDE A GAS LINE FOR THE GRILL AND BURNERS AND ELECTRICAL FOR OUTLETS AND REFRIGERATOR. SEE DETAIL #3
7. 36" SUNBRIGHT FLAT SCREEN TV MOUNTED TO HOUSE WALL. PROVIDE ELECTRICAL AND TELEVISION SERVICE FOR THE TV.
8. 18" HIGH RAISED PLANTER WITH A SEATWALL ALONG THE PATIO EDGE OF THE PLANTER. PLANTER CONSTRUCTED OF CONCRETE BLOCK FACED WITH 8X16 SLATE TILE IN A VERTICAL STAGGERED PATTERN AND CAPPED WITH A BULL NOSED SLATE CAP. PROVIDE AREA DRAINS FOR THE PLANTER AND A FRENCH DRAIN ALONG THE INSIDE LOWER EDGE OF THE PLANTER WALL. SEE DETAIL #4
9. NEW 6'-0" HIGH FENCE WITH NEW GATES STAINED THE HOUSE COLOR TO ENCLOSE THE NEW ENLARGED SIDE YARD. PENDING APPROVAL BY THE CITY OF PALO ALTO. CHANGE THE SWING OF THE GATE TO SWING INTO THE SIDE YARD. THE NEW FENCE IS TO BE CONSTRUCTED OF 4X4 PRESSURE TREATED WOOD POSTS WITH 2X4 WOOD RAILS, 1X4 WOOD PICKETS, 2X8 WOOD CAP, AND A 1X6 WOOD FASCIA UNDER THE CAP. THE GATES ARE TO BE BERCO GATES. THE PAVING IS TO BE REPLACED WITH NEW PAVING OF POURED COLORED CONCRETE TO MATCH THE SLATE COLOR WITH SALT FINISH AND 4'-0" SQUARE GRID DEEP GROOVE EXPANSION JOINTS. PAVING CONSTRUCTED OF 4" MIN. THICKNESS OF POURED CONCRETE OVER 4" MIN. THICKNESS OF COMPACTED GRAVEL WITH #3 REBAR 24" O.C. SEE DETAILS #2 AND #5
10. REGENCY FIREPLACE. HZ042 FACED WITH CONCRETE BLOCK AND 8X16 SLATE TILE IN A VERTICAL STAGGERED PATTERN WITH A BULL NOSED 2" SLATE CAP. PROVIDE A GAS LINE FOR THE FIREPLACE. FLANKING THE FIREPLACE IS TO BE TWO 2'-0" WIDE SHEER DESCENTS MOUNTED UNDER THE CAP OF THE PLANTER WALL THAT SPILL INTO A GROUND LEVEL BASIN 3'-0" DEEP. THE PLANTER WALL IS TO BE FACED WITH GLASS TILE UNDER THE SHEER DESCENTS. INSIDE THE BASIN BE A GLASS TILE THAT MATCHES THE SLATE COLOR UNDER THE PAVING LEVEL WITH A MEDIUM GRAY COLOR PLASTER FINISH BELOW THAT. PUMP TO BE LOCATED WITH THE POOL EQUIPMENT. PROVIDE AUTO FILL FOR THE BASINS. THE BASINS ARE TO HAVE A HEAVY DUTY WIRE MESH WITH A CUT OUT OPENING WHERE THE SHEER DESCENT SPILLS INTO THE BASIN AND COVER WITH BLACK MEXICAN BEACH PEBBLES. SEE DETAIL #6
11. 7.5'X7.5' PORTABLE SPA WITH A WALL AROUND THREE SIDES UP TO THE HEIGHT OF THE SPA. THE WALL IS TO BE CONSTRUCTED OF CONCRETE BLOCK FACED WITH 8X16 SLATE TILE IN A VERTICLE STAGGERED PATTERN CAPPED WITH A 2" BULL NOSED SLATE CAP. PROVIDE A DEDICATED 220 CIRCUIT FOR THE SPA. PROVIDE SPACE ALONG THE BACKSIDE OF THE SPA FOR ACCESS TO THE SERVICE PANEL. THERE IS TO BE A 9" HIGH STEP ALONG THREE SIDES OF THE SPA IN FRONT OF THE WALL OVERLAID WITH SLATE TILE. SEE DETAIL #7
12. COVERED BIKE STORAGE
13. WORK BENCH
14. ART WALL
15. ADD PLUMBING FOR SHOWER TO THE FACE OF THE HOUSE WALL AND COVER THE HOUSE WALL WITH 8X16 SLATE TILE IN A VERTICAL STAGGERED PATTERN.
16. REMOVE THE POOL HEATER AND THE EXISTING ENCLOSURE. REPLACE THE POOL EQUIPMENT AND ADD NEW WALL WITH SINGLE GATE. THE NEW WALL IS TO BE CONSTRUCTED OF CONCRETE BLOCK FACED WITH 8X16 SLATE TILE IN A VERTICAL STAGGERED PATTERN AND CAPPED WITH A BULL NOSED SLATE CAP. THE NEW GATE IS TO BE A BERCO GATE STAINED THE HOUSE COLOR. SEE DETAIL #7
17. POOL IS TO HAVE THE SPA AND STEPS REMOVED TO CREATE A RECTANGLE POOL WITH AN AUTO COVER. THE NEW POOL COPING IS TO BE 18" WIDE 2" BULL NOSED SLATE COPING WITH A GLASS TILE UNDERNEATH THAT MATCHES THE SLATE COLOR. THERE IS TO BE A MEDIUM GRAY PLASTER FINISH BELOW THE TILE. ADD NEW STEPS AND A SWIM OUT TO THE CORNERS OF THE POOL AND CHANGE THE DIVING BOARD TO A SPRING BOARD.
18. 18" HIGH PLANTER WITH A SEAT WALL ON THE POOL SIDE OF THE PLANTER. PLANTER CONSTRUCTED OF CONCRETE BLOCK FACED WITH 8X16 SLATE TILE IN A VERTICAL STAGGERED PATTERN AND CAPPED WITH A 2" BULL NOSED SLATE CAP. FLAKING THE CENTER PLANTER IS TO BE TWO 4'-0" WIDE SHEER DESCENTS MOUNTED TO THE PLANTER WALL UNDER THE CAP THAT SPILL INTO THE POOL. PROVIDE A SEPARATE PUMP TO BE LOCATED WITH THE POOL EQUIPMENT. PROVIDE AREA DRAINS FOR THE PLANTER AND A FRENCH DRAIN ALONG THE INSIDE LOWER EDGE OF THE PLANTER WALL. SEE DETAIL #4
19. 24" HIGH PLANTER WITH A 6'-0" WIDE SHEER DESCENT THAT SPILLS INTO THE POOL MOUNTED UNDER THE CAP. THE PLANTER IS TO BE CONSTRUCTED OF CONCRETE BLOCK FACED WITH 8X16 SLATE TILE IN A VERTICAL STAGGERED PATTERN AND CAPPED WITH A 2" BULL NOSED SLATE CAP. PROVIDE AREA DRAINS FOR THE PLANTER AND A FRENCH DRAIN ALONG THE INSIDE LOWER EDGE OF THE PLANTER WALL. PROVIDE A SEPARATE PUMP FOR THE SHEER DESCENT TO BE LOCATED WITH THE POOL EQUIPMENT. SEE DETAIL #4
20. REPLACE THE EXISTING FENCE WITH A NEW 6'-0" HIGH FENCE STAINED THE HOUSE COLOR. THE FENCE IS TO BE CONSTRUCTED OF 4X4 PRESSURE TREATED WOOD POSTS WITH 2X4 WOOD RAILS, 1X4 WOOD PICKETS, 2X8 WOOD CAP, AND 1X6 WOOD FASCIA UNDER THE CAP. SEE DETAIL #5
21. PAINT THE HOUSE A TONY TAUPE COLOR.
22. REMOVE THE EXISTING DRIVEWAY AND REPLACE WITH A NEW DRIVEWAY OF BELGARD PAVERS DUBLIN COBBLE IN VICTORIAN BLEND. SEE DETAIL #2
23. COVER PLANTER AREA WITH BLACK MEXICAN BEACH PEBBLES.
24. ADD NEW BATHROOM AND NEW DOOR WITH 16X16 SLATE TILE IN RUNNING BOND WITH A 8X16 SLAT TILE BORDER. MATCH HOUSE DESIGN AND COLOR. SEE DETAIL #2
25. 18" HIGH BASIN WITH A SINGLE MONOLITH IN THE CENTER THAT SPILLS INTO THE BASIN COVERED WITH BLACK MEXICAN BEACH PEBBLES. THE BASIN IS TO BE CONSTRUCTED OF CONCRETE BLOCK FACED WITH 8X16 SLATE TILE IN A VERTICAL STAGGERED PATTERN WITH A 2" BULL NOSED SLATE CAP. PROVIDE AUTO FILL AND THE PUMP AND FILTER ARE TO BE LOCATED WITH THE POOL EQUIPMENT. MOVE HOSE BIB. SEE DETAIL #8

HIRE THE BEST PROFESSIONALS

Why You Should Hire an Arborist

Trees are as important as any planting in your outdoor space. They can improve air quality, provide food and harbor wildlife, according to the International Society of Arboriculture (ISA), one of the country's main tree-oriented associations. But too often homeowners take trees for granted. They focus instead on taking care of their lawn and flowers but neglect two of the most important parts of their landscape—trees and shrubs. Many think they take less maintenance, yet both require the same tender loving attention to remain a healthy part of a garden and community.

The work involved can be as simple as watering and fertilizing (see Maintaining Your Landscape, page 54) or as complex as pruning, removing diseased or dead limbs, branches and leaves, transplanting them to another part of the site, or removing them totally. Proper tree and bush care isn't just about good looks as you stroll to your front door or peer out your window and enjoy your front yard. Healthy specimens can add value to your property, particularly when you want to sell. Poorly maintained trees may not just distract visually from the rest of the yard, but cause potential buyers concern: they may jump to the conclusion that if you haven't cared for your trees and bushes, you may also not have cared for the interior parts of your home, whether it's appliances or mechanical systems, and they may be right.

Typical care for trees and shrubs involves sufficient watering, fertilizing, aeration and spraying to control "bad" insects and prevent diseases. But too much watering and fertilizing can also do damage and is likely to happen if the trees are surrounded by grass that is regularly watered. Grasses tend to require more water than trees do, so you have to find the right balance for each. Spraying should be done on a case-by-case basis with the right pesticide that won't kill beneficial insects such as some ladybugs that eat bugs harmful to trees.

But where to start if you just moved in or ignored your trees and bushes for a few years? A prudent beginning is to hire an arborist, a specialist who is knowledgeable about tree and bush care. You can find names of arborists in your area by going online and for one who has been certified by the International Society of Arboriculture (ISA; www.isa-arbor.com) or other similar organizations such as the American Society of Consulting Arborists (ASCA; www.asca-consultants.org/find) and Tree Care Industry Association (TCIA; tcia.org). Before hiring an expert, ask for proof of insurance, licenses, necessary permits, and references.

Other Key Pointers to Heed

- **Overall assessment.** An arborist can perform an assessment on one tree or bush or all on the site, checking for health by spotting abnormalities in foliage such as spotty, wilting or scorched leaves, problems with branches or limbs that may be dead or dying (as evidenced by broken segments or an infestation of insects), or trunks with mechanical damage (as seen in peeling bark). What they look for is anything that's not normal for that specific species. The emerald ash borer is known to go after ash trees, but arborists might also be asked to assess the location of the trees and bushes, for example, if they're in too much shade or sun for their type and the climate. A tree might develop health problems in the future because it was planted in the wrong place. Or, it might conceal too much of the house as it grows, and blocks views and light from entering.

- **Planting.** Arborists will also suggest what trees to plant for the amount of sun, shade, wind, climate zone, space, and soil, since not all trees thrive in every location or climate. Southern magnolias, a favorite in the south, won't fare well, for example, in the colder Chicago area's climate. What does do well in that area and other parts of the Midwest are maples, for instance. Another consideration should be how tall and wide the tree or bush will grow since these measurements vary widely, and they may not have room to grow down the road, therefore requiring transplanting or removing other plant materials to make way. Too many homeowners don't realize how tall certain cypress trees like the bald cypress may grow—up to 40 feet (12 meters) high, for instance; and as they grow, they may thin out at the bottom and become top heavy. Similarly, the saucer magnolia may grow very wide. The same goes for bushes. The best way to avoid such issues is to do research. Look at the fact sheets that come with species when you shop in a nursery or even look online. Or, if you have a favorite type of tree, look it up before you get too infatuated, and also look at the cultivar since certain ones may be bred for being smaller, dwarf versions.

- **Pruning.** An arborist will determine the type of pruning to maintain or improve a tree or shrub's health, appearance and safety. Some limbs, for example, may interfere with wires, gutters, the roof, chimney or windows, or obstruct the house or sidewalk. Other trees or shrubs may be diseased because of pests or be weak from weather problems, and in either case could pose a hazard to the landscape, house and people walking nearby. Or a tree may grow to touch your house, which may attract carpenter ants, who like to feed on your siding or cedar-shingled roof and eventually get inside your home. And sometimes the tree has grown in such a way that its silhouette needs pruning or even bracing to look better or to not camouflage the house or block a favorite view. Pruning atop a ladder is best left to experts; so is any work with a chainsaw. An arborist can also advise how frequently you are likely to need a return visit. For simpler pruning jobs, you may be able to tackle them yourself with practice and help from any number of good books and online sites, such as Edward F. Gilman's *An Illustrated Guide to Pruning* (Thomson Learning, 2002) and the ISA's online articles, "Pruning Young Trees" and "Pruning Mature Trees."

- **Tree and shrub removal.** Although trees should be retained for their beauty, ability to cool the interior of a home, provide shade and add the cachet of patina to a property, that's not always possible. A tree or shrub may need to come down because it's dead or dying, has a disease that can spread to other trees and bushes, presents a hazard to wires, is crowding out other trees or shrubs, was a poor choice for its climate, or is in the way of house construction. Unfortunately, this is a costly process. However, in some cases the trees can be transplanted if they're not too old and the root ball isn't too large. If it's too big, the arborist may not be able to get the entire root mass out, and the tree will lose a lot of its roots and can't adapt to its new setting. If some trees must be taken down for construction, an arborist is skilled to weigh which are less vital and unlikely to survive as construction can be tough on trees and shrubs. An arborist will also know how to protect trees during the construction process.

Ask the Right Questions

We recommend bidding out your job to at least three contractors before you finalize your plans with recommendations on the contractors from the design professional. This way you have an idea of what the elements will cost and can scale up or down to accommodate your budget. You might have to give up slate for gravel for a patio, for example. Going with the cheapest contractor is not always advisable, but going with the most expensive may not always be worthwhile, either. Ask friends for their experiences. See examples of the contractor's work, and listen to your designer or architect to guide you regarding the best companies for your landscape installation.

The six most important questions to ask before hiring a landscape professional:

1. How long have you been working professionally as a landscape designer or architect?
2. Do you have a portfolio or website I can see, and better yet, local landscapes I can visit?
3. Can you provide me with three references for residential work?
4. What kinds of services do you offer—design, installation, maintenance?
5. What is your fee schedule—when do I pay a retainer and how much, and how often after that?
6. Do you think that my budget will work for my wish list or what might we need to scale back from the get-go?

Left: A shady garden path is part of a house on Richmond Avenue in Buffalo, New York. It was enjoyed by many on the city's annual Garden Walk Buffalo tour, the largest residential garden tour in the United States.

Chapter 4

FIND YOUR GARDEN STYLE

Style is defined as a distinctive appearance. Like your clothing and home, landscapes, too, come in different styles that support different ways of living and aesthetics. A garden may complement or serve as an extension of your interior.

Most homeowners are familiar with many of the main architectural styles—Mediterranean, English Tudor, French Country, Contemporary/Modern, to cite a few. Landscapes can also be categorized by different styles. Although matching a garden to the style of the house creates a cohesive whole, there are times when you want your home's architecture and garden style to be a bit different, though still work well together.

The key is to find some common elements: color palette, choice of materials (see also Stone Choices, page 22), scale, accents, or focal points that make your landscape look coordinated with your home rather than something totally separate. Otherwise, visitors might think two people with different visions were involved in the design process. You may also wish to fuse the idea of the traditional pool or pond concept with a natural swimming pool feature or pond. Landscaping is about creating a personal style rather than sticking to rigid rules (see Natural Swimming Pools Make a Ripple, page 29, for details). You want the end result to work best for you and your family, both functionally and aesthetically. Here are some common styles to consider.

Mediterranean

The setting. Brightly colored plaster walls with tile roofs, brightly colored tile accents, and murals. Large comfortable outdoor rooms and a courtyard perfect for outdoor dining and relaxing. This style garden works best in a warm climate. Plantings are big and lush and materials are rustic and natural. Walks may be flagstone, terracotta tile, deco tile, or travertine. Walls may be constructed from indigenous rock or hand-troweled colored or unstained plaster accented with brightly colored decorative tile. Native rocks and boulders may be used as accents. Large glazed or natural pots, fountains, and sculptures can be used as stunning focal points.

Plantings. Drought-tolerant plantings that require minimal water and maintenance because of the hotter climates work best with this style. Fruitless olive trees, crepe myrtles, native oaks, lavender, carpet roses, salvia, sages, flax, coral bells, ferns, and some palms such as Sago palms all work well. The palette generally veers toward orange, red, yellow, green, and grey hues.

Furnishings. Ones that look best are wrought-iron tables and chairs, stone tables and tabletops, and dark-stained natural wood pieces.

Opposite top: Landscape architect Jarrod R. Baumann, principal with Zeterre Landscape Architecture, designed a series of dry-stacked retaining walls, inspired by Scottish artist, Andy Goldsworthy. The clients, from Scotland, celebrate the plants that grow well in California—and their Mediterranean sensibility. **Opposite bottom left:** This outdoor dining room designed by Michael Glassman has a terra-cotta tile patio, hand-troweled custom fireplace, juniper topiaries, and a color palette typical of the Mediterranean style. **Opposite bottom right:** For a garden in Cedarburg, Wisconsin, landscape designer James Drzewiecki of Ginkgo Leaf Studio designed a garden with a southwestern flair for clients who own an art gallery that sells art from that area. The acid-stained concrete patio has an adobe look; the designer also selected plants that provide a desert feeling, yet are able to survive cold Wisconsin winters.

39

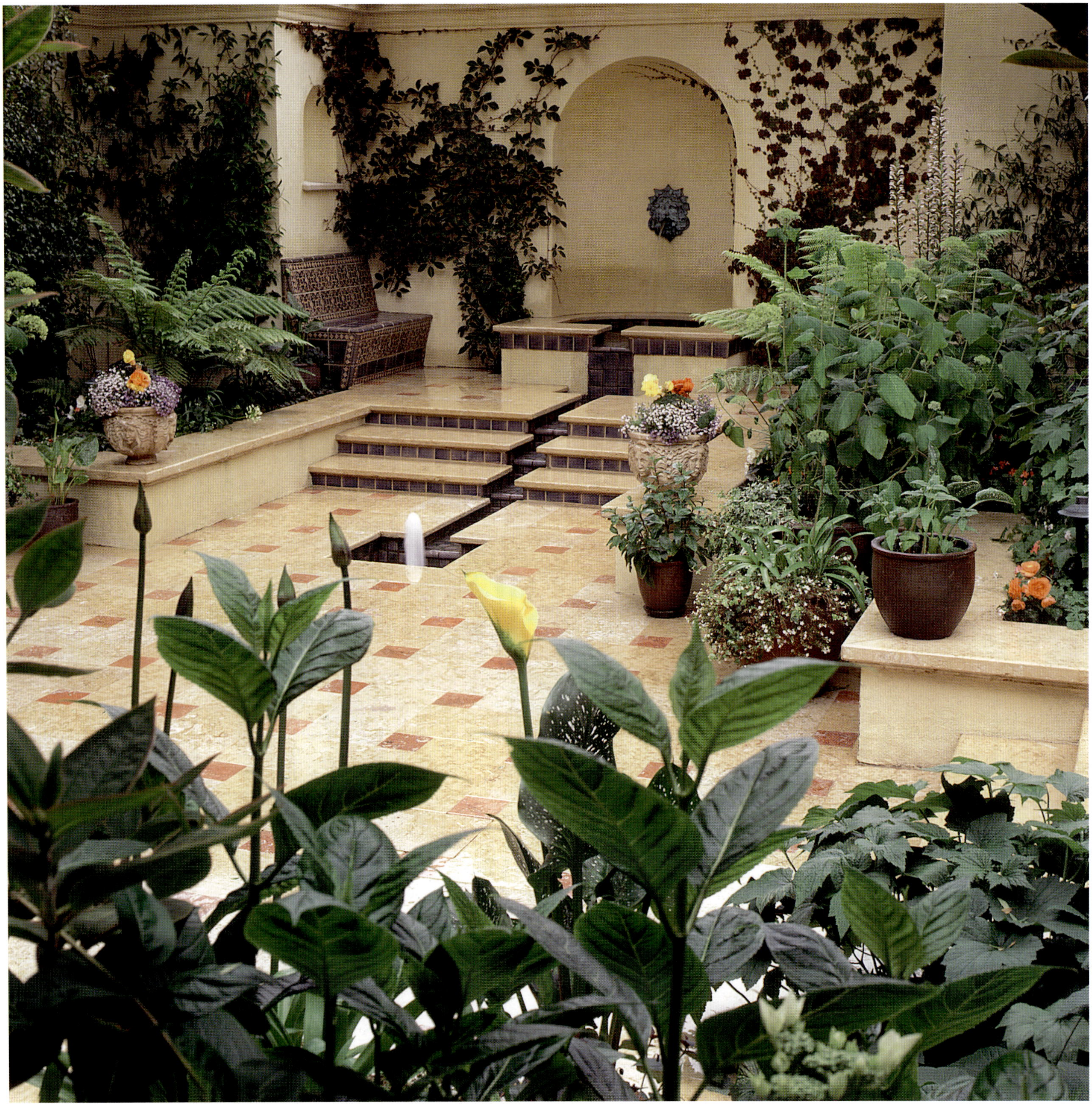

Tropical

The setting. A garden filled with lush, sun-loving, scented plants, big flowers, and colorful floral patterns. In temperate climates, these gardens are designed for year-round pleasure. Flagstone, bluestone, or slate may be used for paving, often with oversized boulders and rocks for accents. Water is an essential element that might show up in the form of a swimming pool, spa, pond, stream, waterfall, or fountain.

Plantings. Popular ones include oversized palms, orchids, gardenias, bananas, cannas, hibiscus, citrus trees, and exotic vegetables. For color, go bold with reds, purples, yellow, and golds, as well as coral and lime green.

Furnishings. Fireplaces and fire pits are common features, often constructed from stucco and rocks. This style uses big urns, umbrellas, *palapas* (small open-sided dwellings with thatched roofs that make you think you've landed in Tahiti), teak furniture, and overstuffed colorful cushions.

Opposite: Landscape designer Stephen Suzman with Zeterre Landscape Architecture planned an outdoor room with a Moroccan flavor by combining two small courtyards. Custom tiles were fabricated from two kinds of marble. **Above left and center:** This tropical paradise designed by Michael Glassman has a natural waterfall and is planted with oversized banana trees, bird of paradise, and giant timber bamboo. The homeowners included a custom carved tikki to give the yard the feeling of Hawaii. **Above right:** A grove of palms frames a serene composition of lawn, black lava rock, and informal pool with waterslide. Naupaka, a tough evergreen shrub native to Hawaii, forms the backbone of the simple planting, design by Stephen Suzman.

FIND YOUR GARDEN STYLE

Traditional

The setting. Whether it's an English Tudor, American Colonial, or French Country house, this garden style has a classic, old-world feeling with much more structure. Edges are more often rectilinear rather than curved, and there is repetition of plants and materials to create hedges and block planting. Traditional style incorporates large expanses of green lawn. English gardens, for example, can also be more natural with large expanses of lush rolling lawns, meandering gravel paths, and brightly colored flowers planted in clusters as borders among trees and shrubs. Terraces can be paved in classic flagstone, gravel, crushed granite, or brick materials, which may be repeated in walks and paths. Garden walls may be built from plaster, ledgestone, or brick, and topped with slate, flagstone, or precast concrete for a precise, finished look. Fountains or water features may be quite stylized and elegant, often in multiple tiers, constructed from concrete or cast iron.

Plantings. These may include iceberg or hedge roses in classic white, pink, or red colors. Other favorites include hedges, clipped topiaries, espaliered fruit trees and annuals such as lobelia, and alyssum. In classic English cottage gardens, brightly colored perennials, annuals, and bulbs are framed with boxwood hedges. Formal rose gardens abound: rose arbors, rose trellises, and rose-covered gazebos. This garden style is more likely to use curves as in knot gardens, an interweaving of hedges filled with aromatic plants and herbs.

Furnishings. Fireplaces tend to be large and structured with carved mantels and columns. They are built from stone, brick, or cast concrete and stucco. Popular options include large pots in terra cotta or cast concrete or limestone filled with topiaries and training vines, teak tables and chairs with monochromatic cushions, marble or cast stone tables and benches, classic weathervanes, and stylized bronze, or cast iron fountains.

Top: In Princeton, New Jersey, landscape architect Marc Nissim of Harmony Design Group went with a traditional garden design and pool to reflect the traditional home and its setting. Pennsylvania fieldstone was used for the dry-stacked retaining walls, which were planted with perennials and boxwood hedges. The patio was paved in Tennessee blue-gray flagstone, which doesn't get as hot as bluestone. **Bottom:** Landscape architect Clara Couric Batchelor of CBA Landscape Architects LLC in Cambridge, Massachusetts, designed a gravel entrance courtyard to a home on Cape Cod in Massachusetts to be a hub that would lead to various destinations. For interest, she designed six bluestone-edged planters, each filled with a different species. **Opposite (clockwise from top left):** Purple candles astilbe grow in a grouping chosen for their ability to survive without much care yet inject a bold color statement, by James Drzewiecki. Informal cascades of old roses and clusters of foxgloves underplanted with lime thyme and isotoma line this romantic flagstone path, by Stephen Suzman. An English cottage with all the typical elements: white picket fence and gate, sinuous brick path, and organized chaos, by John Cowen. A New Dawn Rose crowns a trellis while oak leaf hydrangeas provide a scenic backdrop to this garden vignette in Atlanta, by Jeff Allen.

English Cottage Garden

How do those lush colorful gardens get that look? Years of planting and care, but these three steps offer a key start:

- **Flourish of flowers.** The foundation of the garden is perennials in massed groupings to provide a large-scale wow of color and that return year after year.

- **Colorful choices.** The palette can be complementary, such as mauves, lavenders, magentas, and whites; or contrasting yellows, purples, blues, and reds. The sky's the limit. Try it out with color swatches from a paint store and see what combinations you like. A contrast between adjacent groupings is essential to add interest.

- **Varying heights.** Key elements include layering—shorter in front to taller in back. Be careful that not everything flowers at once but seasonally; also don't forget to consider varying levels of texture and foliage.

FIND YOUR GARDEN STYLE 43

Flowering Arbors and Shade Structures

- **Plants.** Vines are classic arbor accompaniment since you want a plant that climbs and provides color, texture, and fragrant aroma. Good choices are climbing hydrangeas, trumpet vines, wisteria, and tropical annual vine bougainvillea. Also consider star jasmine, honeysuckle or white blooming potato vine.

- **Care.** Many vines require little care, just some plant food and fertilizer. Know specifics, for example, hydrangeas like moistness and shade; wisteria likes sun; and bougainvillea needs to be replanted in colder climates.

- **Paint or stain.** Apply before you add your climbers since once you plant you won't have access through the plantings or you'll damage the vines and other plant materials.

- **Lights.** Add some low-voltage lamps for enjoyment at night; keep the number subtle rather than create the look of a shopping center or airplane runway.

- **Fan.** Install one to help cool the area in summer.

- **Heater.** Add a portable one come crisper days and evenings for extra warmth.

Above: Landscape architect Stephen Suzman showed how a Corten steel and stone pergola could become a bit softer by festooning it with wisteria. **Above right:** Designer Christopher Grubb, owner of Arch Interiors Design Group in Los Angeles, redesigned this landscape with an old-world flavor. There was once just barren lawn and an old pool. He redesigned the pool, introduced pavers on an angle with grass in-between to emphasize the pathway to the pool, installed an outdoor kitchen with comfortable seating, and lighting for nighttime use. **Opposite top:** Classical statuary including a pair of elegant sphinxes, boxwood spheres and iceberg roses grace this formal traditional garden designed by landscape designer Stephen Suzman. **Opposite bottom:** Landscape designer Greg Schaumburg sited a pool, pool house, cabana, outdoor kitchen and spa so all would be centrally located near the main house on a main axis, following a traditional garden plan.

Formal Old-World

The setting. This style applies to large-estate planning or large properties where the architecture is very formal. The hardscape includes natural stone walls, hand-troweled plaster with cast-stone caps, balustrades of cast limestone or concrete, and walkways and terraces surfaced with travertine tile, bluestone or brick. The water features are always structural, whether they are circular lily ponds or rectangular reflecting pools. Ornamentation for this style includes urns, statuaries, tiered fountains, bronze sculptures, and *armalarias* (three-dimensional sundials). This landscape style will often incorporate architectural ruins, such as an old colonnade, fragments of old walls, or a portion of an old arch.

Plantings. This style uses boxwood and privet hedges, topiaries, pollarded and espaliered trees, old-fashioned roses, annual plantings, wisteria, and large expanses of lawn.

Furnishings. Oversized teak tables and chairs, large formal bronze or cast-iron two- or three-tiered fountains, curved stone or large teak benches, sundials or *armillarias*, stone tables with wrought-iron heavy armchairs, large estate–sized urns made of bronze or limestone, iron arches planted with vines.

FIND YOUR GARDEN STYLE

Natural/Meadowland

The setting. The focus here is on recreating the natural environment of the region, thus materials are always indigenous. Boulders and rocks should match the geography of the surrounding area. Water features, such as ponds and waterfalls, are made with natural materials in organic shapes. The hardscape is constructed from natural wood decking or from random patterns of native flagstone, gravel, or decomposed granite. A few rocks, particularly large ones, become a major focal point. Colors tend to be monochromatic, although a bright accent might be included for contrast. Water features are common for the tranquil look and sound they introduce, typically in the form of waterfalls, streams, and fountains.

Plantings. Native or similar species, and their placement should be more random than organized and formal.

Furnishings. Natural styles may incorporate rustic ornaments, such as log furniture, wood or stone carvings, rusted metal, totem poles, rusted metal sculptures.

Above: Kettelkamp & Kettelkamp Landscape Architecture designed a low-maintenance garden outside Chicago with tall and low grasses planted in a ribbon pattern to provide privacy from the street.
Opposite (clockwise from top left): Old Chinese limestone fence posts were repurposed by landscape designer Stephen Suzman of Zeterre Landscape Architecture as sculptures to contrast with the billowy mounds of Pennisetum setaceum grasses. Landscape architect Terrence Parker of Terrafirma Landscape Architecture in Portsmouth, New Hampshire, designed a gravel path to serve two functions: first, as a walkway, and second, to migrate into a dry-stone waterfall that mimics water; he found some boulders on-site and placed others to look natural. A terraced garden wall near a waterfall became a place for Terrence Parker to group plantings with fringe trees in the background with the lower areas composed of asters, blue stem grasses, Russian sage and lavender.

FIND YOUR GARDEN STYLE 47

Edible Landscaping

Imagine stepping out your door into a thriving garden. Plump apples, pears, peaches, and persimmons ripening on every tree, and the shrubs growing under them dripping with juicy red and blue berries. Every herbaceous plant offers sweet fragrances, beautiful flowers and nutrient-rich or medicinal-green leaves and roots. Climbing up trellises and through the nut trees are heavily laden grape or kiwi vines, with clusters of fruit ripening in the sun. Welcome to your yard; welcome to an edible landscape.

Why Edible Landscaping?

Simply put, fresh food tastes better. There's nothing quite like a homegrown tomato, a handful of just-picked blueberries, and the succulent sweetness of a ripe peach. When it comes from your garden, you know it's from your yard to your table, not covered with poisonous sprays or trucked 1,500 miles (2,415 kilometers), the average distance food travels in the US to get into your hands and home.

Furthermore, growing vegetables, herbs, berries, fruits, nuts, and mushrooms in your yard is a great way to engage your friends and family in the garden. Growing and harvesting food with your kids, parents, and neighbors offers meaningful time spent in nature throughout the year—and few gifts are more treasured than a head of fresh lettuce or a punnet of delicious red raspberries.

When you switch to edibles, you and your family will find purpose and meaning in the garden. The labor becomes a labor of love. The oft-dreaded weeding changes from an arbitrary chore to a useful task—help those vegetables grow! Watering is no longer just to keep plants alive—it ensures bountiful yields and nutritious food, some of which might be so abundant you'll want to share it with friends, neighbors or even a local food pantry. And with the right combinations of plants and edible landscaping techniques, you can reduce watering and eliminate weeding altogether.

Delicious and Beautiful

The main types of plants you are likely to use in an edible landscape are vegetables, herbs, flowers, berry shrubs, fruit and nut trees, and vines. Edible plant species come from all over the world, so many are also excellent ornamentals with stunning flowers and unusual foliage. The best plants are multifunctional; they provide beauty, wildlife habitat, beneficial insects, delicious smells, weed control, *and* food. One excellent example is the goumi berry, which has slender silver-green leaves, and honey-sweet white flowers in the spring, makes its own fertilizer by capturing nitrogen out of the air, and produces sweet-tart red berries in the summer, typically June and July.

Edible landscapes often include vegetable gardens and fruit orchards, but can also incorporate more interesting elements like fruit and nut hedgerows, such as hazelnut and Nanking cherry, rainwater gardens with elderberry and highbush blueberry, and forest gardens.

Edible forest gardens include many layers of food production, from: nut trees at the top like chestnut or pecan; fruit trees in the middle such as apples, pears, mulberries, and pawpaws; berry bushes underneath with currants, black raspberries; and wineberries; shade-loving herbs of ramps, violets, sweet cicely; and edible mushrooms, like shiitake, oyster, winecap and stropharia; and finally vines climbing back to the top of akebia, sandraberry, hops and kiwis.

The hardy kiwi is another example of a multifunctional plant: its dense ornamental foliage is sometimes variegated pink; it climbs over arbors and trellises to provide excellent shade in the hot summer months; and its abundant smooth-skinned green kiwis ripen in the fall and have 10 times the vitamin C of oranges!

Edible Means Organic

When growing food for your kids and family, it's very important to use 100 percent organic materials in your garden. Instead of fossil fuel-based chemical fertilizers, try a rich dark compost from cow manure or your own pile from food scraps or organic garden waste. Avoid bio-solids, which is another term for treated sewage from your local municipality, and ask a local farmer for cow or horse manure instead.

Rather than using herbicides to manage weed control, try a nice thick layer of uncolored wood-chip mulch, or natural sugar-cane mulch. Planting perennial groundcovers like white clover or green and gold can totally eliminate weeding under fruit trees and shrubs. And you'll find that growing a variety of herbs and flowers like anise hyssop, yarrow, comfrey, rosemary, and others will reduce your need for pesticide application. As you invite a natural ecosystem into your landscape, the diversity of insects will regulate pests on its own.

Next Step: Get Started

The most important action you can take to begin creating a veritable garden of Eden at your home is simply to *start now*. Many fruit and nut trees take several years to bear their full yields, and once you taste fresh organic produce from your back yard you're going to want more as fast as possible.

Consider working with a local edible landscaper or permaculture designer, who specializes in creating productive ecosystems that take little maintenance for their large yields. Permaculture designers can also help make your edible landscape part of a more sustainable home, integrating renewable energy, rainwater catchment and natural building into your home. They'll also help you find the most appropriate edible-plant nurseries and a local community of people who have planted edible landscapes and are already reaping the harvest.

Did you know that of the 20,000 edible plants in the world, only 150 are being cultivated on a commercial scale? And that 90 percent of the calories eaten by the entire world come from just 20 species? With edible landscaping, you get a chance to rediscover thousands of unique and tasty food plants right outside your front and back doors. So take a step towards diverse, healthy, local food and meaningful fun in your gardens and plant an edible landscape this spring.

Top 10 Edible-Landscaping Nurseries

Oikos Tree Crops, Kalamazoo, Michigan (www.oikostreecrops.com)
One Green World, Molalla, Oregon (www.onegreenworld.com)
Raintree Nursery, Morton, Washington (www.raintreenursery.com)
St. Lawrence Nurseries, Potsdam, New York (www.sln.potsdam.ny.us)
Forest Farm, Williams, Oregon (www.forestfarm.com)
Dave Wilson Nursery, Hickman, California (www.davewilson.com)
Tripplebrook Farm, Southampton, Massachusetts (www.tripplebrookfarm.com)
Edible Landscaping, Afton, Virginia (www.ediblelandscaping.com)
Burnt Ridge Nursery, Onalaska, Washington (www.burntridgenursery.com)
TyTy, TyTy, Georgia (www.tytyga.com)

Top 5 Edible-Landscaping Books

Gaia's Garden by Toby Hemenway (Chelsea Green Publishing)

Landscaping with Fruit & Weedless Gardening by Lee Reich (Storey Publishing)

Edible Forest Gardens Volumes I + II by Dave Jacke & Eric Toensmeier (Chelsea Green Publishing)

Maintaining Your Edible Landscape Naturally by Robert Kourik (Permanent Publications 2)

Paradise Lot by Eric Toensmeier & Jonathan Bates (Chelsea Green Publishing)

Top Online Resources & Organizations

Apios Institute's Edible Forest Garden Wiki (www.apiosinstitute.org)

Plants for a Future Database (www.pfaf.org)

North American Fruit Explorers (www.nafex.org)

California Rare Fruit Growers (www.crfg.org)

Northern Nut Growers (www.northernnutgrowers.org)

Ethan Roland Solaviev and Dyami Solaviev

Permaculture Designers

AppleSeed Permaculture LLC

Top: Multispecies understory planted beneath an old apple tree with Nanking cherry, anise hyssop, and bee balm. **Center:** Edible and medicinal foundation plantings include sweet cicely and American wild ginger. **Bottom:** Back-yard orchard polyculture to walk out the door to harvest fruit, herbs, and flowers.

FIND YOUR GARDEN STYLE

50

Contemporary/Modern

The setting. Minimalism is the mantra whether it's for the palette, materials, or design. Paving may be constructed from a stained or natural brushed concrete that is often scored in a simple grid pattern. Travertine, slate, natural hardwoods or large expanses of gravel or crushed granite is often used as the hardscape. Railings, retaining walls, planters, and accents are stainless steel, Corten steel, or brushed aluminum.

Plantings. The plant palette tends toward simplicity with grasses, non-invasive bamboo, weeping serpentine cedars, and a bonsai tree or two.

Furnishings. Less is always more and with little embellishment, whether furnishings, lighting, and accessories. Find a few pieces rather than multiples—one bench, one oversized pot, one great piece of art. Far Eastern pieces work well in this setting. Stainless-steel table and chairs, polished aluminum, glass and granite tops reflect clean lines and minimal ornamentation.

Opposite (clockwise from top left): Joe Eisner, AIA LEED AP, Eisner Design LLC in New York, designed a pool house as two separate cubicles, connected by a trellis canopy for shade; one cubicle is for storage; the other, a shower/changing room. The pool house designed by Joe Eisner can be seen through the living room's glazing; wood finishes and cabinetry elements coordinate with the pool house materials. Arterra Landscape Architects designed an art-inspired focal point for this garden: layered walls and materials combine to create a contemporary site sculpture. **Above:** The layering of planes, surfaces, and materials extends to the outdoor living room Arterra Landscape Architects designed; these link the garden with the clean lines and the progression of spaces.

Asian-Inspired

The setting. Whether classic or relaxed, symbolism is a very important principle in this style. The architecture uses stylized slate tile roofs or wood shingles, and all materials are natural, for example, slate, flagstone, redwood, cedar, Japanese black rock, and moss-covered boulders. Walkways and *engawas* (Japanese-style wooden deck or terrace) are usually staggered, offset, or tiered.

Plantings. Asian-inspired gardens create an idealized miniature landscape. A rock can represent a mountain; a tree can represent a forest. And a dry creek bed can suggest a river. The garden elements of an Asian-inspired space must always have water, but may also include rocks, sand, or bridges, and color is used sparingly. Monochromatic flowering plants are mixed with green and gray textures. The most common plants found in this style include azaleas, camellias, weeping cherry, ginkgoes, Japanese maples, bonsai pines, ornamental grasses, and bamboo.

Furnishings. This style is very simple; less design is more effective. Modern pieces work well as do classic Asian designs: black lacquered wood pieces, granite stone lanterns, Buddha heads, gongs and wind chimes, bamboo spouts and reflecting bowls, or stone or clay Asian-inspired sculptures.

Top: An antique Javanese gate that once led into a temple now leads into a California garden where landscape architect Jarrod R. Baumann of Zeterre Landscape Architecture designed the homeowners' garden with a circular stone patio, black bamboo and mondo grass. The house is French but the clients have a wide-ranging collection of art so Baumann wanted to mimic that in the eclectic garden. **Bottom:** In the same garden, entered from the Javanese gate, an Indian stone basin, once used for livestock, now serves as a water feature. **Opposite:** To offer sitting and cooking all in one in an Asian-inspired sheltered outdoor garden room, designer Troy Adams of Troy Adams Design in West Hollywood, California, designed his "tapanyaki grill table" with grill with infrared heat and down draft. Bamboo walls, overhead wood decking and lots of lush plantings provide an intimate setting.

FIND YOUR GARDEN STYLE 53

Maintaining Your Landscape

After you install a well-planned, sustainable landscape, you must remember that gardens are alive and are a work in progress. Even "no maintenance" landscapes require regular care. Some of this care includes the following important tips.

Softscape Elements

- **Landscape adaptation.** As your garden grows and matures, it may develop different microclimates. Areas that once were sunny where roses may have thrived, may become shady as trees grow up and outward. Conversely, as trees reach maturity and die, areas of shade where ferns and hostas may have been growing may become sunny and inhospitable to these plants. Additionally, even in the best-planned gardens, as plants grow they may crowd each other, requiring thinning or selective removal. Be flexible with plans to revise planting some areas according to these natural changes. (See also The Enchantment of Shade Gardens, page 74.)

- **Fertilizing.** Plants need to be fertilized regularly. For example, lawns need a fertilizer high in nitrogen every three months. Blooming plants should be fertilized lightly with 0-10-10 (no nitrogen, 10 parts phosphorus, 10 parts potassium) that stimulates root development and flowering.

- **Pruning.** Trees and shrubs need to be pruned once per year, at least. If they are deciduous, pruning should be done after the plants have lost their leaves. Pruning invigorates and shapes the plants. Flowering perennials need to be cut back and divided yearly.

- **Replanting.** Annuals need to be planted seasonally. Many bulbs need to be dug up, stored, and replanted annually. Plants in pots need to be replaced approximately every two to three years because they become root bound and overgrown.

- **Weeding and mulching.** Weeding is important to keep plants from being overtaken and choked by unwanted plants. Mulching needs to be done every year, and sometimes twice a year, to help with weed abatement and water retention.

Above: An English cottage garden designed by John Cowen features typical fencing, a curving brick path to the front door, and plantings of hydrangea, alchemilla, ferns, sedum, astilbe, and one that is not typical—rose of Sharon. All work as a welcoming entrance to a seaside cottage.

- **Irrigation.** All types of irrigation need to be checked for proper coverage because sprinkler heads can be disturbed and change orientation or become clogged or damaged. Drip systems in particular need extra attention because emitters can clog due to hard-water deposits, and animals can disturb or damage the plastic pipes. Additionally, as plants grow and change, so do the emitter orientation and efficiency. For example, adding or changing the location of a plant will require restructuring of the system. Irrigation systems in cold climates should be drained before the first freezing temperatures.

Hardscape Elements

- **Patios and walkways.** At least once a year, concrete and stone patios may need to be pressure washed. Some hardscape will need to be resealed every few years for protection from stains and fading. Colored concrete surfaces will need to be re-stained and sealed about every five years to maintain the freshness of the color. Tiled walkways, patios, and backsplashes may need the grout to be cleaned and sometimes replaced about every five years.
- **Wood structures.** Fences, overhead shade structures and trellises should be restained or sealed every three to five years to prevent weathering and to maintain the aesthetics of the stained wood.
- **Swimming pools.** Pools need to be skimmed of debris, filter traps cleaned, and pH managed at least weekly. Retiling and replastering are done every 10 to 15 years.
- **Decorative water features.** These water elements should be drained and cleaned at least twice a year. In places with hard water, descaling agents need to be added to the water on a weekly basis. Algae abatement usually requires weekly attention.
- **Ponds.** Ponds with fish and plants need to be backwashed monthly and require careful weekly attention to pH levels and filter function.

Final note: A landscape is only sustainable and looking its best if it is maintained. Without proper care and attention, the beauty of a newly installed landscape can become a garden fraught with problems and unplanned expenses.

Above: An enlarged view of the elaborate design Greg Schaumburg did for an estate property; here the terrace is for dining and is accented with pockets of plantings.

Chapter 5

DESIGN PRINCIPLES FOR A FUNCTIONAL AND AESTHETIC OUTDOOR ENVIRONMENT

Good design, much like anything else, starts with understanding the basics to fashion a balanced and beautiful landscape that helps you communicate your key theme. It's not unlike using the right ingredients and spices to create a sumptuous meal.

Michael Glassman has developed his own set of principles that he recommends to clients because they help compose a functional, aesthetically pleasing, and holistic, healthy landscape. (For more information, see also Design Ideas to Turn Your Back Yard into an Oasis, page 33.)

General Tips

Separate modes of transportation. Cars need driveways, and people need walkways. Main front walkways should be a minimum of 5 feet (1.5 meters) wide while minor paths should be a minimum of 3 feet (91.5 centimeters) wide. It is considered bad feng shui for pathways to the front door to be a straight line. Use more organic shapes such as staggered pads or curved lines, and break up long walks with a bench, tree, or grouping of plants. Mix and match materials for different walks judiciously; too many will look disconnected, like a badly composed painting.

Boulders should be buried. To give your landscape more interest and a natural appearance, boulders should be buried up to the soil line rather than simply placed on top of the soil. Use enough for accent, but not too many unless you want it to look like a lunarscape. When using rocks and boulders to accent your landscape, use those that are indigenous to your region. In northern California, for example, moss rock or fieldstone will enhance your landscape whereas red or black rock from Hawaii will look out of place and unnatural.

Mounds should be subtle. If you decide to mound soil for topographical interest, the slope of the mound should be gradual and not higher than 24 inches (61 centimeters) from the base so it doesn't look like a burial mound. A steeply sloped, high mound of soil is hard to irrigate and can cause drainage problems. The water simply rolls off the mound rather than being absorbed or causes erosion of the mound.

Hardscape materials should be uniform or share some similarities. Similar hardscape materials make small yards appear larger. Using mixed materials especially for patio surfaces, for example, a concrete dining area abutting an interlocking paver sitting area, will look like two small adjacent spaces done at different times rather than one large uniform space. You can use more than one material, but you need to have a theme with repetition. For example, if you have an all-brick house and choose a gray slate patio to complement the deep red brick, you can re-introduce the brick into the landscape as a trim on the patio or a seat wall surrounding the patio.

Opposite: Landscape designer Howard Roberts designed this wooded setting for a fundraiser on an old suburban New Jersey estate. "We wanted to create an illusion as if a Gothic-looking treehouse with a pond that had been neglected was resurrected and restored," he says. He built it from scratch using lots of water irises.

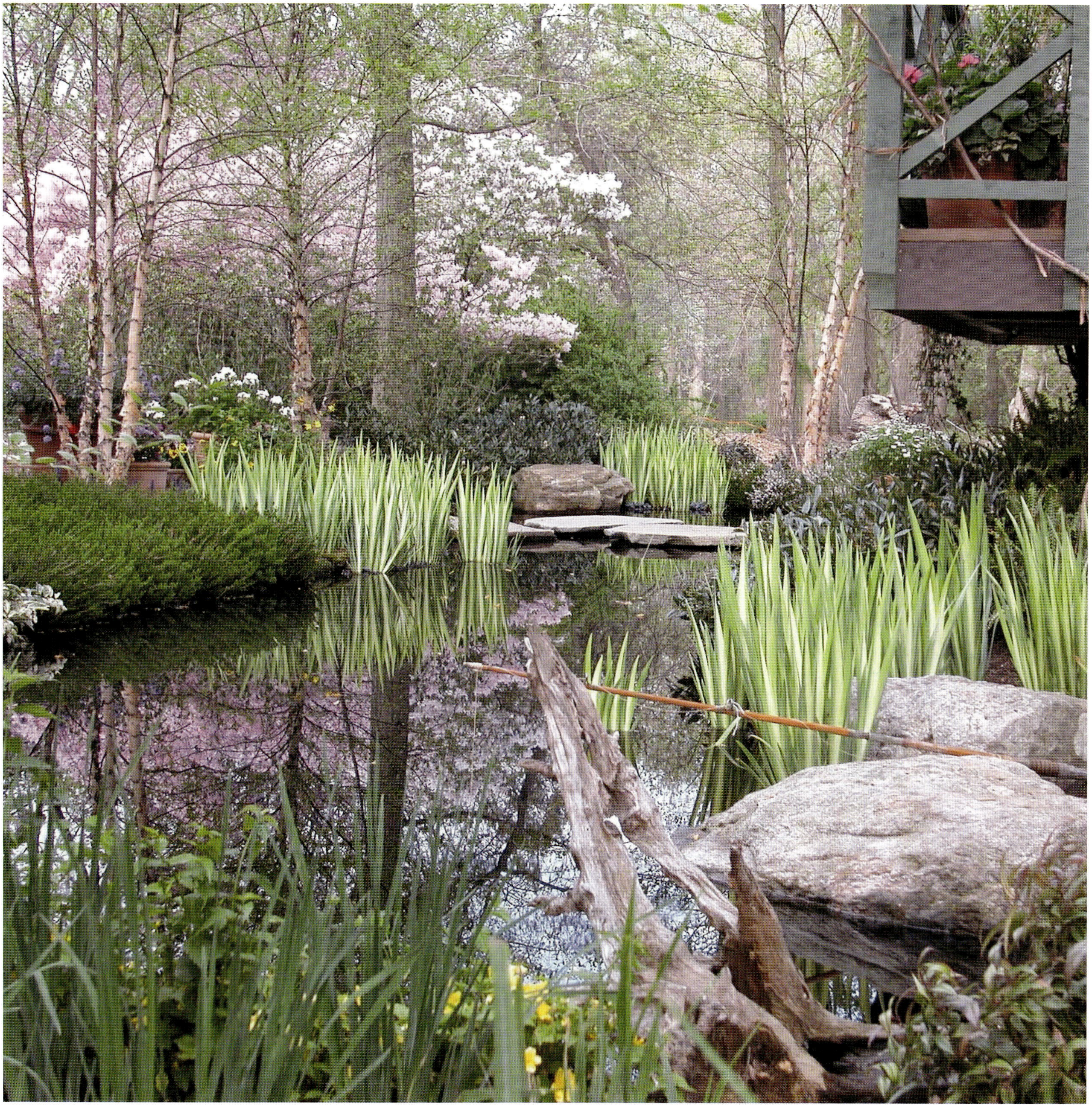

Design for your activities. Inside your home, you have rooms for dining, sleeping, and bathing. While developing your garden master plan, think about how you would like to use your outdoor space and then design areas in your garden for these activities in the same way as you have rooms in your house. For examples, you can design distinct areas for vegetable gardening, pool activities, dining, cooking, and lounging. When you plan this way, your landscape will flow and no space goes to waste. You will also have distinct areas to keep the pool floaties or basketballs away from the dining area, and smoke from a barbecue away from those lazying in the hammock underneath a giant oak tree.

Focal points are critical. Design something special for your landscape that will grab attention in your yard. Why do you have a painting on your living room wall? Why put a vase of flowers on a table? Having artistic pieces that become the center of attention is pleasing to the human eye and personalizes your space. Gardens are no different. Focal points can be sculptures, water fountains, unusual rocks, architectural plants, or specimen trees that change color throughout the year. Though some designers think having only one focal point is best, the number can depend on the size of the garden or number of rooms. The key is not to overdo it, but have eyes fixated on one, two, or three main objects.

Less is more. Many people have a tendency to collect rocks, pots, small sculptures, gnomes, and place them all over their garden. This is not good design as it becomes distracting and chaotic. It is far better to choose two or three large pots and/or one or two prominent sculptures, which then become strong focal points rather than eyesores.

Front Yard Success

Seven steps to help produce a memorable entry.

- **Consistency.** Too many types of materials will fight with one another. Use one or two types of hardscape, which complement the color of your home and its architectural style. Remember that less is more; a simple landscape can be more effective than a busy, cacophonous one.

- **Focal point.** Lead eyes to the front door by downplaying surrounding areas. Create impact through plant materials, color, texture, and height. Don't forget to make the front door attractive with color or detailing, even a great looking knocker or doorbell.

- **Camouflage.** Conceal unkempt neighboring homes and eyesores like an air-conditioning condenser with plantings or architectural elements. Plant trees, shrubs, and use garden ornaments to highlight what's most beautiful in your yard.

- **Accessorize.** Add a handsome mailbox, some smart outdoor furniture, or classy house numbers to complement your home's style. But again don't overdo it, err on the side of less is more.

- **Add color.** Whether in flowers, berries, or a brightly painted bench—color adds a punctuation mark; repeat the palette throughout the front yard and with shutters and the door for cohesiveness.

- **Minimize.** Use only minimal hardscape so it's not harsh unless you live in a drought-prone area. Use one or two materials and soften with plantings, especially a walkway and front steps.

- **Light.** Think about how the landscape and house will appear as the sun goes down. Pretty lanterns flanking the door add another focal point and make it safer as someone approaches; it will also help deter burglars. Don't forget to add small lamps at the base of important bushes and in trees; but again less is more. You want to see the light's effect, not the source of the light.

Opposite top: Landscape designer John Algozzini of K&D Landscape Management, Inc. re-did an entry with bluestone paving and limestone treads and selected large pots planted for seasonal interest. The boxwood hedging provides a strong horizontal line against the verticality of the plantings and house, located in suburban Chicago. **Opposite bottom:** Rather than creating the straight walk that his client suggested, landscape designer James Drzewiecki of Ginkgo Leaf Studio designed a simple S-curve instead. The sweeping path visually pulls visitors through the space between the garage and home to the inviting front door. **Top left:** When constructing a pool and spa, access from the house needs to be easy, especially for a spa to be used in winter, so homeowners don't have to walk a long distance from the back door. The pool should also be designed aesthetically so it draws visitors to explore the landscape. Design by Brian Hahn, Botanical Decorators, Inc. **Top right:** Nestled in the woods and away from the house for safety, this elegant modern stucco and cement fireplace becomes an all-season focal point. Because of the land's slope, landscape architect Brian Cossari of Hoffman Landscapes in Wilton, Connecticut, designed steps to access the fireplace's "platform patio." **Above:** A beautiful axial pool with bloodgood Japanese maple at the far end of the axis sits on one side of the property, which leaves lawn for games. The pool has a 24-inch-wide (61-centimeter-wide) bluestone coping; furniture by Janus et Cie; design by John D. Cowen Landscapes Associates Ltd.

DESIGN PRINCIPLES FOR A FUNCTIONAL AND AESTHETIC OUTDOOR ENVIRONMENT

Designing Your Outdoor Kitchen

You'll want to spend many hours enjoying cooking and entertaining outdoors, so it's worth taking the time to design your outdoor kitchen like you would plan for your indoor kitchen. (See also Outdoor Kitchen Staples, page 24.) Following are some key design pointers.

- **Space.** Make sure you have at least 4 to 5 feet (1.2 to 1.5 meters) of space in which to work.

- **Amenities.** Incorporate amenities that you will use such as a barbecue, sink, refrigerator, pizza oven, warming draw, dishwasher, and plenty of storage space. If you can locate the sewer line, you can include hot and cold running water for a sink and even a dishwasher. Provide dedicated electrical outlets with GFIC (Ground Fault Interruptor Circuit) for additional appliances, such as blenders and mixers.

- **Entertaining.** Design an area such as a bar counter where people can sit and talk to you while you cook, and lay out your workspace so that you can face your company.

- **Materials.** Use materials that are similar to those in your indoor kitchen so you will have design continuity. Be aware of different climate variations. Good countertop materials are granite slabs, poured and sealed concrete, porcelain, travertine, or frost-proof tile, and very costly sheets of copper or zinc. Beware of marble since it stains easily and any porous material may present problems in colder climates. The best material for drawers and doors is stainless steel, which withstands rusting and heavy-duty wear and tear.

- **Shade structures.** Provide shade in the form of an umbrella or an overhead structure. In your shade structure, provide 110 volts electrical for outdoor lighting and fans to control bugs and possible misters to control heat.

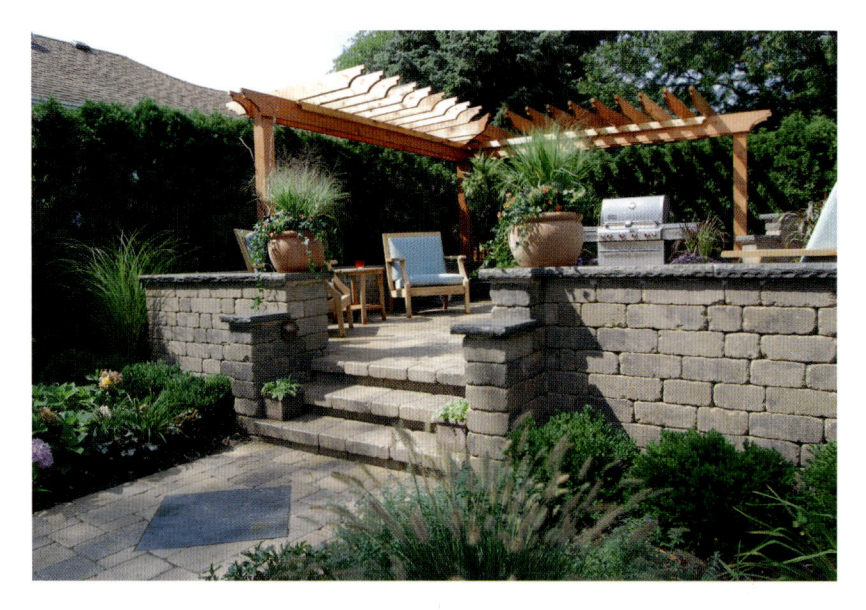

Levels can add interest. Hardscape for entertaining should be at one level. When you are entertaining groups of people, a large level space is more conducive to intermingling and conversation. Preparing and carrying food trays is also easier without having to climb stairs or steep walkways. However, changes in elevation to delineate spaces in a landscape add drama and separate outdoor activities. For example, raised planters can provide additional seating, create privacy, and add visual interest. Looking down on the pool at a lower level from the dining space can be a beautiful vista and offer a better vantage point for watching children swimming. Take advantage of natural changes in terrain, the way wineries terrace their hillsides for growing grapes.

Design is in the details. Small elements can have a profound effect on the cohesiveness, drama, and beauty of a landscape. Even the eclectic style, that meshes more than one style, still needs to have cohesiveness in the details. Placing Victorian backdoor light fixtures in a contemporary yard can be jarring. Even though a shock of color can be dramatic, it must be suitable with the rest of the design and palette.

Opposite far left: An outdoor kitchen designed by Richard Poynter includes a barbecue with adjacent honed limestone countertops, a material inspired by a nearby fire pit. Supports for the countertops were fabricated from the same material. **Opposite top:** Landscape designer Renee Mercer designed a multilevel terrace because of the home's construction. She built it from Unilock pavers because of the product's good value and mottled colorations. Bluestone diamonds were installed at each entrance and exit to provide continuity and a lively spark. A wood pergola adds height. **Opposite bottom:** Western Maryland ledge boulders were carefully chiseled to form a stairway down to a sunken garden by a rear pool terrace. To reinforce the area's naturalness, landscape architect Jeff Plusen planted native black-eyed Susans. **Top left:** To add drama and intrigue, Michael Glassman designed a custom fire and water feature at the center of a rectangular swimming pool. **Top right:** Landscape designer Michael Glassman designed this rustic pergola with Peeler core posts and rough-sawn beams planted with grapes to soften the patio and provide shade from the afternoon sun. **Left:** Landscape designer Howard Roberts added a green framed addition onto his home in suburban New Jersey with a pergola for architectural interest. This structure deflects sunlight from steaming into the interior. Clay brick, similar to the material on the main part of the home, was used as the paver.

DESIGN PRINCIPLES FOR A FUNCTIONAL AND AESTHETIC OUTDOOR ENVIRONMENT

Planting should be limited and organized. When you are at the nursery looking at many beautiful, colorful plants, it is easy to want to buy one of each kind. However, in landscape design, plants should always be used in repetition to be effective. Formal designs use even numbers of plants, called block planting, while natural designs use odd numbers of plants with random placement. Single plants should only be used when they act as a focal point for the yard or as living art and are large enough to command attention.

Good examples of focal point plants include Japanese black pine bonsai, weeping serpentine cedar, dwarf weeping Japanese maple, gnarled multitrunked olive, and a spiral juniper topiary. Do some research when selecting plants for your yard. Find out how tall and wide they will become at full maturity for proper balance and spacing. If you want foundation planting at the base of your house, it is better to choose a plant that grows 3 to 4 feet (91 centimeters to 1.2 meters) high rather than having to constantly prune a 10-foot (3-meter) plant to that height. When planting slow-growing plants, some landscape designers will suggest overplanting for a more immediate, lush effect, however homeowners should note that over time, they will need to remove some of the overcrowded plants.

Top left: Fountain grasses border a bluestone coping around a 40-foot-long (12-meter-long) pool with a large suburban yard on the North Shore of Chicago, designed by landscape designer Carol Heffernan of Herffernan Landscape Design. **Bottom left:** A focal point in a clients' front home by the Jersey shore consists of a big urn turned into a recirculating water feature; decorative gravel surrounds the urn with a bluestone pathway and lots of hydrangeas, designed by Howard Roberts. **Above right:** In his own yard, landscape designer Howard Roberts' pool—and pergola in the distance—align with the center of the home for symmetry and balance. Roberts carried the home's brick out to the walk and pool decking. **Opposite top left:** This Pacific Heights home in San Francisco features a rooftop wellness garden curated by a Michelin-starred restaurant specialist, designed by Troon Pacific Inc. and Shades of Green Landscape Architecture. The result: herbs and vegetables for daily cooking. **Opposite top right:** Kettelkamp & Kettelkamp Landscape Architecture designed the front yard of a home in Evanston, Illinois, to provide its owners with a new concrete front walk, which changes widths to slow down visitors and owners to enjoy the new garden setting. To minimize irrigation and mowing, the design pros chose drought-tolerant materials, sedum and creeping phlox. **Opposite bottom left:** Michael Glassman designed this beautiful drought tolerant landscape with colorful plants, drip irrigation and rock mulch. **Opposite bottom right:** Laurie Van Zandt removed a lawn to make room for locally quarried sandstone paths and bursts of color from drought-tolerant perennials and grasses.

Xeriscaping Guidelines

Because of the drought in California and other regions of the United States, as well as elsewhere in the world, concern is growing to choose plant materials and grasses that need little or no water. Here are more guidelines:

- **Go native.** Replace thirsty lawns with plants that require little irrigation such as dwarf manzanita, myoporium, wild lilac, and native grasses. Native species or species that have been introduced into a region for a long period have evolved to survive an area's climate, and withstand long dry spells without rotting out in heavy winter rains, for example.

- **Think grasses.** Ornamental grasses grow tall, make pleasant rustling sounds with breezes blowing, require little water, and produce an array of colorful flowers. Consider also faux grasses that look real.

- **Downsize water.** Instead of big water features that consume gallons such as ponds and pools (even if they recirculate), you can get enjoyment and hear the charming sound of trickling with a small bubbler in a fountain or urn.

- **Irrigate judiciously.** Though it's hard work, lugging around a hose gives you exercise and lets you use water only when vital and at the base of a plant. If you want to install an automated system, choose one that has drip spray or emitters that water the root system of the plant.

- **Use organic or natural mulches.** Doing so helps with weed abatement, water retention, and erosion.

DESIGN PRINCIPLES FOR A FUNCTIONAL AND AESTHETIC OUTDOOR ENVIRONMENT

Plant with colors and textures to create different moods. When choosing plants at the nursery, think of your color palette and style. Asian-inspired gardens use green and gray plants of different textures and this promotes a relaxing effect. Wildly colorful perennials and annuals are used in English cottage gardens or cutting garden areas of your landscape, and inspire excitement and joy. An all-white garden looks beautiful at night when the moon is out, hence its name: moon garden. Contemporary landscapes tend to use a single bright color like red or purple to invoke drama and passion; adding yellow flowers to a planting bed make other colors pop. See also Garden Colors: How Do Your Garden Colors Grow? (page 70).

Views from the indoors out are important. When you are designing your landscape and placing your focal points, consider the views of your garden from inside the house, too. Your garden should be a place that you love looking out toward, even when you cannot be outside but must remain indoors. This is particularly true in the winter months of cold or rainy climates.

Above: Landscape designer John Algozzini of K&D Landscape Management, Inc. designed this suburban Chicago garden to include a decomposed granite path, which leads throughout the site. The garden provides big volumes of color throughout summer with oversized beds packed with an assortment of shrubs, perennials and grasses. **Opposite top left:** A heavily shaded front yard in suburban Chicago needed plants that would grow with little sun and that would remain low so they would not overshadow the home's architecture, says its designer John Algozzini. **Opposite top right:** A transition space, once an asphalt parking lot and between the homeowners' house and at-home office on the right, now provides a gathering space for family and staff, thanks to designer John Algozzini's creativity. **Opposite bottom:** The clients had a large back yard with unused turf. They wanted a park-like feeling so they could walk and enjoy nature. Carrie Stanker of Garden Gate Design Studio designed meandering lawn paths through lush beds that convey a sense of exploration and surprise.

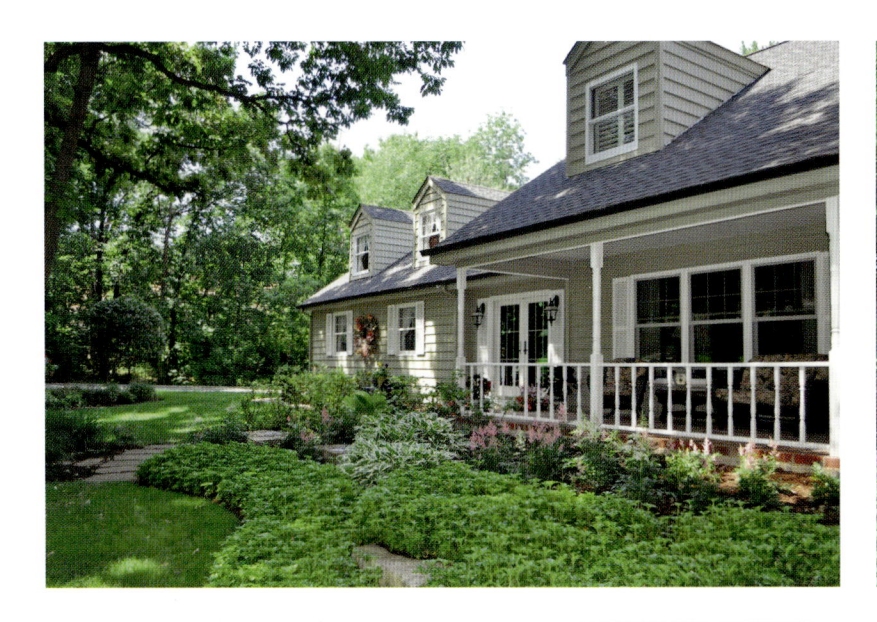

DESIGN PRINCIPLES FOR A FUNCTIONAL AND AESTHETIC OUTDOOR ENVIRONMENT 65

Remember to include storage. When the rain or snow comes, where are you going to put all the cushions, outdoor lights, sports equipment, and anything else that you use outdoors? A shed that is tastefully designed or skillfully concealed by a fence can be a good alternative to stuffing these items into the front of your garage or crowded basement. Some sheds can even resemble children's playhouses or be miniature versions of your house. Add shutters, plantings, and you've introduced more garden whimsy.

Plan borders for boundaries. When front yards lack sidewalks, boundaries can still be built to separate a home and front lawn from the street. Railroad ties, cobblestones, low boulders, or low stone walls, split rail, or picket fences planted with colorful vines, flowering rose hedge, or clipped boxwood hedge can provide a great way to create this separation.

Lighting Primer

Lighting not only helps you enjoy your outdoors more and for longer periods of day and night, but it will also let you enjoy the view from inside your home. Go with more energy-efficient LED choices that you also won't have to replace often; most choices today can be installed without hiring an electrician. Pick ones that you don't see or those that mimic garden creatures such as frogs or edibles like mushrooms so they blend into the landscape. Most are available in an array of sizes and materials. When it comes to different types of landscape illumination, there's a basic vocabulary to master:

- **Path lighting.** This is primarily a safety measure, but also can add drama; install lamps directly into the ground or in walls along walkways.
- **Downlighting.** Place a few lamps within more important trees, in bushes, or on pergola roofs to illuminate living or entertaining areas, the simply beautiful materials or architectural additions.
- **Moonlighting.** Lamps can also go into trees and simulate the effect of a full moon, as well as create foliage shadows on the ground.
- **Uplighting.** Dramatize your home's architecture and create stunning effects by placing lights on the ground to light up trees and plantings.

Opposite top: A redesigned 1960s ranch also gained a new elegant and simple landscape, by Howard Roberts. He paved the main rear terrace in bluestone with a brick border and lush plantings with a boxwood hedge as a frame. **Opposite far left:** Landscape architect Steve Chepurny, RLA, of Beechwood Landscape Architecture & Construction designed a wood shed using reclaimed wood to mimic a barn in its shape and architecture. **Opposite right:** Within the potting shed, Steve Chepurny designed custom cabinetry, applied wood on walls and beams, and had a stone floor laid. He added a copper sink, and heated the space to make it work for most of the year. **Top right:** A chic outdoor fireplace and landscape lighting designed by Cripiano Landscape Design complement this glass-tiled pool. The design was inspired by the homeowner's modern taste and a recent stay at a luxury hotel. **Above left:** A mass of plantings—purple summer beauty alium, black-eyed Susans and reed grasses—help conceal a fence surrounding a swimming pool in Cedarburg, Wisconsin; design by James Drzewiecki. **Above right:** A curved bed with a cottage garden feeling adds great curb appeal to a front lawn. "The owner wanted lots of blooming sequential color," says landscape designer James Drzewiecki.

DESIGN PRINCIPLES FOR A FUNCTIONAL AND AESTHETIC OUTDOOR ENVIRONMENT

Fire Features—Making the Best Choice

A fire pit or fireplace can add drama and a focal point to a landscape. It can also provide warmth and enjoyment well into the winter months in colder climates. In some locations, fire features have become so popular that builders construct them as part of the home or condominium package. Styles, sizes, shapes, heights, and materials vary; choice should be based on the space available, budget, and local ordinances. Fire features of any kind—small or large—demand serious attention to safety. Options to consider are as follows.

Fire pit versus fireplace. Permanence is a key difference between them with a pit sometimes built in, though many are lightweight and portable. A fireplace is also much larger and permanent, which makes it easier to make it the focal point in your yard.

Size. Generally, fire pits are small, about 4 to 6 feet (1.2 to 1.8 meters) in diameter and 18 to 30 inches (45.7 to 76.2 centimeters) high. The flame is what you want to see rather than the structure itself. Make it proportional to the size of your yard, and be sure you have room for seating and circulation all around, and possibly a nice path to it. Fireplaces can be wide or narrow; they can be wood-burning or gas with synthetic logs or fire glass. They can have chimneys or be rear-vented.

Price. So much depends on whether it's custom or prefabricated. A custom design generally matches materials in your garden or on your house, and may be designed and built by a landscape professional or contractor, who will suggest proper

Above: Landscape designer James Drzewiecki used his client's hardscape to showcase stone from the family business. Hardy reliable plants, including ornamental grasses and coneflowers, enclose the sitting area by a fire pit. **Opposite top left:** For a rustic design, James Drzewiecki paired boulders, ornamental grasses and a brick terrace, the latter for low maintenance. A portable fire pit sits atop, easily moved elsewhere. **Opposite top right:** Michael Glassman designed this outdoor fireplace as a focal point using the formal grounds of this large estate as an inspiring backdrop. **Opposite bottom left:** Landscape designer Laurie Van Zandt made a double-sided fireplace from locally quarried blond sandstone, and it divides the outdoor area into rooms. **Opposite bottom right:** To vary materials, landscape designer Richard Poynter went with a natural stone veneer for a fire pit and kitchen, and honed limestone for the countertops.

materials. Copper or stainless-steel fire pits are lighter and usually portable, but the metal needs to be rust resistant. Costs can be less if you can do the construction yourself. Sometimes, it can be as easy as digging a hole and surrounding it with large stones, or purchasing a simple unit at a big-box store or online resource. On the other hand, they can also cost up to several thousand dollars when seating, stone walls, and more expensive materials are used. Still, they're less costly than a fireplace, which can run upwards of U.S. $10,000, depending on the construction, height, width, materials, accessories, and labor. Favorite materials for fireplaces include concrete masonry unit blocks faced in natural stone or ledgestone, firebrick to keep them insulated, granite, or decorative tile to give them more visual interest and drama.

Wood or gas. For either a fire pit or fireplace—you have a choice. Those who favor a true outdoor smell usually prefer burning real logs. Some communities have outlawed the use of wood-burning fire features. An alternative is to use gas or propane for an instant fire.

What to set it on. It's best to place a fire feature on top of a natural surface, such as concrete, stone, gravel, brick, slate, or a fire-resistant composite. Putting it on a wood deck can be dangerous.

How far from your house. Many communities require a 10-foot (3-meter) distance from a house and neighbors' yards. Most pits don't require a building permit, while fireplaces usually do.

Seating. Go with chairs that can be portable, or a low stone wall that's at least 18 inches (45 centimeters) wide.

DESIGN PRINCIPLES FOR A FUNCTIONAL AND AESTHETIC OUTDOOR ENVIRONMENT

Garden Colors: How Do Your Garden Colors Grow?

There are few places many of us love as much as a beautiful garden. The reason often is because of rich magical displays of color. They can reflect simple rows of flowers in an orderly or loosely arranged design in one color or many, or a combination that blooms sequentially throughout the season. Here are some ideas to consider before you start.

Tie your home and garden together. Choose colors that complement your building palette. For example, if your home has some warmer colors such as beiges, yellows and reds, add warmer golds and yellows to your garden, such as daffodils, black-eyed Susans, and forsythia. If your home is painted in cooler grays or blues, plant colors in the cool color family, such as irises, dusty miller, or even beautiful blue hydrangeas. Adding colors that are "complementary" colors on the opposite side of the color wheel brings in more contrast, accentuating the brilliant colors of your garden. For the blue house, that would be yellow flowers, for the green house, red flowers. Don't worry about being too precise; colors don't have to match exactly but reflect the same family.

Make your garden a work of art. Here's a different approach. Think of your choices as a way to make your garden a work of art. If this appeals, decide if you want to focus on brighter colors, more subtle hues, or those flowers with more than one tone. Whatever you choose, have the style consistent throughout your garden or at least in different sections or "rooms." The more consistent you plant, the more balanced your design will appear, allowing your focus to be on the colors themselves rather than any cacophony.

Think green. Yet, another design possibility for your garden is to adhere to the concept of working strictly with plants whose beauty is in the green-family foliage. Gardens can be made up of a variety of greens: hosta, for example, come in a wide variety of options from elephant ear, which is a touch more blue-green, to the smaller traditional variegated leaf of green and white hosta. Ornamental grasses are also predominantly green with spots of lighter yellow greens, or they can have variegated shades and wheat-like blooms. Any trees in the pine family can bring in blue-greens from the spruce family to the darkest of greens for a rich saturated backdrop. This option has the benefit of consistency from early spring to later in the season and tends to be a lower maintenance choice. Though the range of colors is narrower in staying with greens, you can insert drama through different heights and textures and other colorful accents in furnishings.

Have your garden rock. Rock gardens offer a distinct opportunity to fashion order in a hilly, rocky terrain and keep soil in place when rain washes over it. Opt for plants in between that don't require as much soil, and be sure to insert new rocks of all sizes, shapes, and hues. In a warm climate, think about using succulents and cacti.

Go year-round bloom. What can be beautiful, but often is most challenging, is to design a colorful garden that stays appealing throughout your garden season and even year-round. This requires research to know when each choice will bloom, and another will pop out when the last stars are past their peak. For cold climates, good choices are those that have colorful bark and berries to take over when flowers are gone; consider hews with a rich dark green foliage or pines such as blue spruce with a needle that is almost more blue than green. What also contrasts against the traditional green foliage is the birch tree: its white bark with hints of gray has remarkable luminance against the dark green foliage in the warmer months and shines against any winter backdrop.

Amy Wax
Color Consultant
Your Color Source Studios, Inc.
www.amywax.com

Opposite far left: Color expert Amy Wax loves the brilliant red of these daylilies against the weathered wood for a border. **Center:** For a vacation garden bordering Lake Michigan, the homeowners worked closely with landscape designer Leslie Rohrer of The Carter Rohrer Company in Canton, Georgia, to have colors that would absorb sunset hues and look good with the lake. **Below:** A pergola provides partial shade by a pool for the couple with a house that borders Lake Michigan. Designer Leslie Rohrer tried to offer enough patio space but also planted perennials and ornamental grasses for summer interest. The perimeter comes alive with a honey locust tree, which is hardy as the winters are cold.

DESIGN PRINCIPLES FOR A FUNCTIONAL AND AESTHETIC OUTDOOR ENVIRONMENT

Chapter 6

RECOGNIZE PROBLEMS BEFORE YOU START

Every site has certain indigenous challenges and problems that you need to consider. If you do not address these issues, you may end up wasting time and money, have a non-functional outdoor space, and want to redo work you've already done.

After many years of experience, Michael has seen almost every possible challenge and mitigated clients' problems through the years due to different kinds of topography, climates, wishes, and budgets. He has also been exposed to other challenges in his travels and reading about gardens. Here are some of the most common problems to consider (and discuss with your landscape professional) as you embark on your garden project.

Most Common Problems

Lack of privacy. You're trying to enjoy your back yard and decide to take a swim in your pool or enjoy dinner on your gorgeous new patio. Oops, you forgot to leave room for plant screens or trees to block the views of your neighbors' two-story houses on either side. Guess what? They can peer into your yard. Now you feel like you live in a fish bowl.

Drainage. Your patio slopes back towards the house causing water to collect under the foundation. You plant a lawn without considering proper drainage for irrigation; it is now a muddy swamp. Your raised planters do not drain properly and most of your plants are dying from crown rot.

Soil. You have forgotten to research the type of soil indigenous to your site, whether clay, loam, or sand. You dig a hole to plant a tree, you then fill the hole with water, and discover that the water does not drain. A day later the water is still sitting there. Trouble lies ahead. You have hardpan, a non-permeable layer of compacted soil that sits below the uppermost topsoil layer and it can be several inches or as much as 20 feet to 30 feet (6 meters to 9 meters) thick. Planting in this kind of soil is like planting in a pot with no drain.

Noise. Your home is less than a mile from a freeway or backs up to a well-traveled street. Your neighbors have frequent loud social gatherings and dogs that bark at all hours of the day—and night. When you sit in your beautiful garden, you do not find it peaceful. In fact, you can't wait to run back indoors.

Mixed materials. Your back yard is a hodgepodge of materials, colors, and textures. You have too many levels to traverse, and there is no harmony, continuity, or relationship to the interior of your residence.

Improper layout of hardscape. You shortchanged yourself by building your deck or patio without measuring the patio furniture. Now it does not fit or must be crowded together. There's no room to walk around it and circulate. You do not have enough room to entertain the number of guests you usually invite for dinner. There is no place to sit around the pool.

Improper layout of walkways. Your sidewalks are too narrow, forcing your friends to walk single-file to your doorstep. Driveways are for cars, and walkways are for people, however, you do not have separate modes of transportation so your guests must squeeze by your cars to find your front door.

Slopes and erosion. Your yard is on a bare slope, but you want a swimming pool, patio, and a vegetable garden. Without proper retaining walls and plantings with fibrous root systems to hold the soil, you find mud on your new hardscape after each rain. Even more precarious, your landscape drains onto your neighbor's property. You live by the ocean and have a beach, which unfortunately is eroding over time and the plants you continue to install keep dying due to the salt and sea coastal environment.

Top left: Example of erosion and drainage problems. In the rainy season, water and soil runoff collect on the homeowner's driveway. **Top right:** Trees with shallow, invasive roots are not well suited for front yards. In this garden, the root system of the central tree has destroyed the front sidewalk. The soil is too root bound to allow plants to grow. **Center left:** This backyard suffers from the use of mixed materials. There's a lack of cohesion that gives the yard a cluttered, small, and unattractive appearance. **Center right:** Due to lack of proper grading, water flows back towards the house and under the foundation, creating huge problems for the homeowners. **Bottom left:** This backyard shows what happens when builders do not plan sufficient entertainment and living space on their patios or decks. This raised patio is too narrow for a typical dining table with four or more chairs, not to mention sufficient room for children's play. **Bottom right:** This home has no separate front walkway for pedestrians. The owners and visitors must skirt around parked cars to reach the front door.

The Enchantment of Shade Gardens

Even when there's no or minimal sun, numerous materials can flourish in your garden. They also will provide the additional benefit of a cool respite during your summer's greatest heat. Many provide foliage, texture, and varied colors, as well as flowers that bloom and thrive without much sun.

Why shade. Several factors cause shade. An area's climate can limit the amount of sunlight year-round, but on-site conditions are the more typical contributions. Structures, including the house itself and large elements like a pergola, will cast strong consistent shadows, especially on spaces on the northern side of a building. Trees are the most common contributor. Large-leaved densely foliaged deciduous trees cast a shadow as heavy as a structure; tall conifers produce the same effect year-round.

What to plant. Know just how much sunlight an area in which you consider planting will receive before you make plant choices, so you don't waste your time or money with wrong selections. Study the area over the course of a few days, or, better yet, over the entire cycle of a growing season. Photographing the area that you are considering planting at various times of the year will help you remember how it looks.

Three variations. Shade gardens can be broken down into three distinct categories. A space is considered heavy shade if found on the north side of a building or in an area with tall trees, especially those with a heavy canopy. There will be little to no direct sunlight that reaches the ground. Light shade occurs in areas typically receiving about four to six hours of sunlight per day, or where there is dappled light that can penetrate more open tree canopies. Finally, medium shade falls in varying degrees somewhere between the other two more extreme categories.

What to do. In extreme shade, where there's not enough light to grow plants, cover the ground with non-plant materials such as mulch, gravel, boulders, recycled grass, and pine needles. They will keep the area looking tidy, and you can go a step further and add seating that offers a respite from the sun's harshest heat. Voilà! You no longer have dead space. Base your selections also on whether you want to draw attention visually to the area or let it fade away. With light to medium shade, some foliage plants that will thrive and attract attention include vinca minor (also known as dwarf periwinkle) and hosta; both flower but their leaves also last long-term. Others to consider are carex (commonly known as sedge) and rodgersia. To let the shade area fade away, plant it with baby tears, ajuga, campanula (commonly known as bellflower), or mondo grass.

Planting beneath a large tree such as a maple is challenging since you have to contend with dense surface roots. Since tree roots compete for water and nutrients, a good suggestion is to plant large 36-inch by 36-inch (91-centimeter by 91-centimeter) pots in these shade areas. You will not have to deal with surface tree roots, the pots can be drip irrigated, and you can layer the planting in the pots with assorted and colorful shade plants.

John Cowen
Landscape Designer
John Cowen Landscape Associates

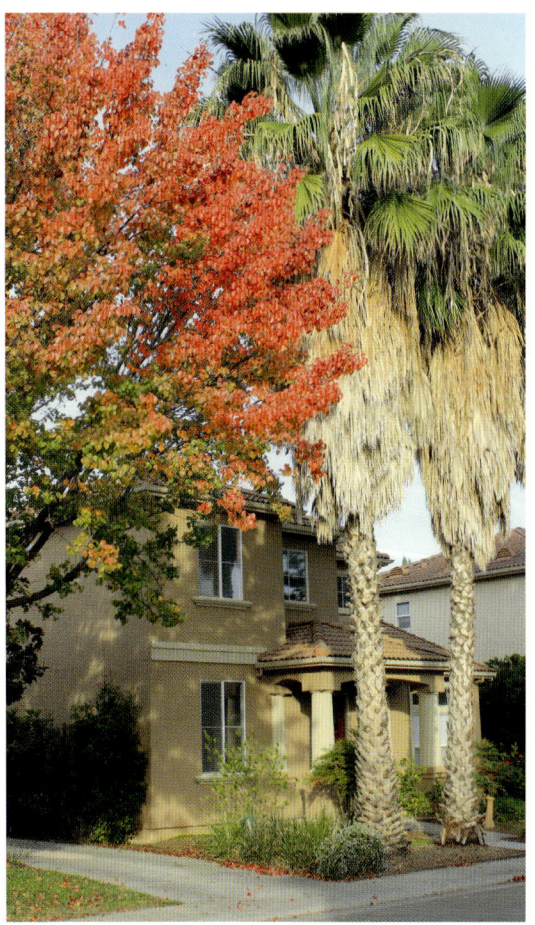

Wind. You plan an outdoor breakfast nook to overlook your ocean view, but do not consider that your site has strong north winds. Eating or having a cup of coffee there is almost impossible on most mornings. And the idea of reading a book or the newspaper leisurely will never happen with pages flapping all about.

Too much sun or too much shade. You plan a patio with no shade and in mid-summer the patio is searingly hot in the afternoons. An umbrella helps but not sufficiently. You outfit a great kitchen, but it's also too hard for the chef to barbecue except at night when it's dark and cold. You have too many shade trees in your back yard that make your home dark, your garden is dingy, and the leaves are always landing in your pool.

Wrong plants in the wrong place. You plant a weeping willow too close to the house, and the invasive roots get into your sewer system and crack your patio. You plant shade plants next to sun plants or plants that need less water next to plants that need a lot of water. You end up with dead plants.

Covenants, codes, and regulations (CC&Rs), easements, building permits, and improper setbacks. There are building codes and restrictions of which you are not aware or ignore. You get fined for putting up a shade structure in the wrong place, and the county or city informs you that you must remove it—now!

Drought risk/dry climate. You have planted a lawn and the city has restricted your water use due to a drought. Your lawn turns brown and dies. You planted palm trees too close to the house and have not cleaned up the dead fronds. Now your palms and home are at risk of being destroyed by fire.

Opposite left: This front yard demonstrates what happens when the wrong plants are planted in the wrong place. Here the shade-loving ferns are burning from exposure to hot afternoon sun. **Opposite right:** This front yard has no separate pedestrian walkway to the front door; no curb appeal or plant interest because the large tree overwhelms the small yard; and the tree drops organic material year-round for a poor entryway function. **Above top left:** These homeowners eventually will have to deal with sewer and foundation problems since they have planted a weeping willow in their small front yard. The roots of this tree are invasive and destroy pipes and concrete in their search for water. **Above top right:** This flat, dry landscape gets very hot in the summer, has rocky clay soil that makes growing plant material difficult, and has no planned drainage. **Above bottom left:** This backyard looks haphazard. Mixed materials (concrete patio, wooden deck, painted solid overhead next to stained wooden shade structure) were used to create multiple levels that make moving around the yard difficult. The patio is too small for barbecues, a post for the solid overhead was placed right in front of the back door, and the homeowners frequently trip when navigating the step up to the deck while carrying food. **Above bottom right:** In this front yard, the homeowners planted palm trees too close to their home, and they have created a significant fire hazard by not keeping them trimmed of dead fronds. The size of these palms is also out of scale with the home.

RECOGNIZE PROBLEMS BEFORE YOU START

76

Safe Play

Some tips when landscaping children's outdoor play areas:

- Install children's play equipment in a shaded rather than full-sun area.
- Build a "floor" for kids to land on that's made of a soft material such as mulch, grass mats, artificial grass or turf, rubber tiles, recycled shredded rubber, or heavy-duty rubber mats.

Cold/freezing climate. You live in a climate that has lots of cold, snow, ice, sleet, and maybe hail. As winter begins, the roses you planted during the spring and summer defoliate and turn black. Your beautiful mortared rock wall is developing cracks and falling over because of expansion and contraction, and your irrigation pipes are shattering because you forgot to drain them.

All-seasonal challenges. Your enthusiastic spring buying spree at the nursery made your spring garden a place of wonder, but now that winter is here you stare out at your bare sticks of dormant plants. You did not consider planting for four-season interest. During the spring and summer, you planted some young shade trees, but forgot to properly stake them and the autumn winds blew them over. You look forward to fall but forgot to include plants with berries or leaves that offer color and interesting branch shapes. (Four-season variations aren't always possible due to where you live, but you should always inquire.)

Wildlife. Deer are eating your roses faster than you can grow them. Voles are digging up your vegetable garden, and squirrels are feasting on your strawberries and cherries. Raccoons are rolling up your newly laid sod lawn looking for grubs. Worse yet—snakes are climbing onto your patio to sun themselves. Need even more examples of how you didn't play attention to the creatures that were there before you?

Pets. You have two dogs that urinate on your newly laid sod lawn and dig up your ground-level plantings. Your cats use your outdoors as a kitty litter box and chew on your poisonous plants.

Human health issues. You plant scotch broom for their beautiful yellow flowers, and your guests are sneezing and coughing from pollen allergies. Your kids find playing in the garden painful because you planted sago palms with sharp fronds too close to their sand box. You build a raised vegetable garden to last a lifetime from pressure-treated wood or railroad ties only to learn later that the wood preservatives may cause cancer.

Too little support. You've installed a new deck or terrace. Perhaps it's just for furnishings and people … or maybe also for a hot tub. You find that it can't support the weight since your professional didn't plan properly, or you didn't share how you were going to use the deck or terrace.

Do-it-yourself gone wrong. You construct a raised deck for entertaining, but in building it you never considered researching the proper support board span. Now the top decking boards sag, split, and break under the weight of your furniture. You replace your falling-down 6-foot-high (1.8-meter-high) property fence with a decorative 7-foot (2.1-meter) one to block your neighbor's windows without researching the codes for your city or community. When neighbors complain, the city may not approve your job. You build a raised planter against the property line fence and use the fence as the back of the planter to save money. Two years later, your fence falls apart because the posts have rotted.

Summary

In the following chapters, we showcase different landscapes as case studies of these problems and how landscape designers and architects resolved them. We also provide a range of solutions for different budgets. The key here is to do your research in advance with a professional to understand your problems and the many possible solutions. There's never just one!

Opposite top left: Deer will eat many of the plants. **Opposite top right:** Natural lawn is not compatible with owning dogs that have free access to urinate in the back yard, as this dying lawn demonstrates. **Opposite center left:** This front walkway is not inviting with sharp-pointed plants and cactus that can cause bodily harm to pedestrians approaching the front door. **Opposite center right:** These acacia trees flanking the entryway to this beautiful home are highly allergenic and not welcoming to guests with allergies. They also drop organic material, making planting the understory difficult. **Opposite bottom left:** This is a finished do-it-yourself front yard. The homeowners were hoping to create a natural waterfall, with various elevation interest using different features and elements. However, without a focal point, with mixed materials that are not cohesive, such as a stylized water fountain next to a natural stone waterfall, the effect looks more like a work in progress or a dumping ground for landscape material. **Opposite bottom right:** This do-it-yourself walkway is hazardous. It is too narrow for comfortable walking, and the small elevation rises are too shallow and uneven to be steps; instead they will become tripping or ankle-twisting hazards. The walkway was constructed without a proper sand or concrete base and thus the bricks lying directly on dirt will become more uneven and unstable over a short period of time. The brick also does not relate to the surrounding rock borders or gray concrete, making it a disjointed, unattractive welcome to these homeowners' front door.

Chapter 7

GREAT GARDENS TO INSPIRE

In redesigning your garden, there are always choices, more than one path to consider for your major and minor landscape challenges and constraints based on your wish list, property value, neighborhood, timetable, climate, and budget.

This chapter presents real case studies of how landscape professionals working in different climates and with different homeowner parameters solve problems. Objectives, challenges, and solutions are outlined, followed by specific examples and "before" and "after" photos.

Our goal is for you to read about sites and landscape challenges that you may relate to, borrow ideas to resolve your own dilemmas, and satisfy your wish list within your price range.

This garden designed by Michael Glassman showcases how a cohesive plant palette with different colors, textures, and plant heights creates a natural and beautiful landscape.

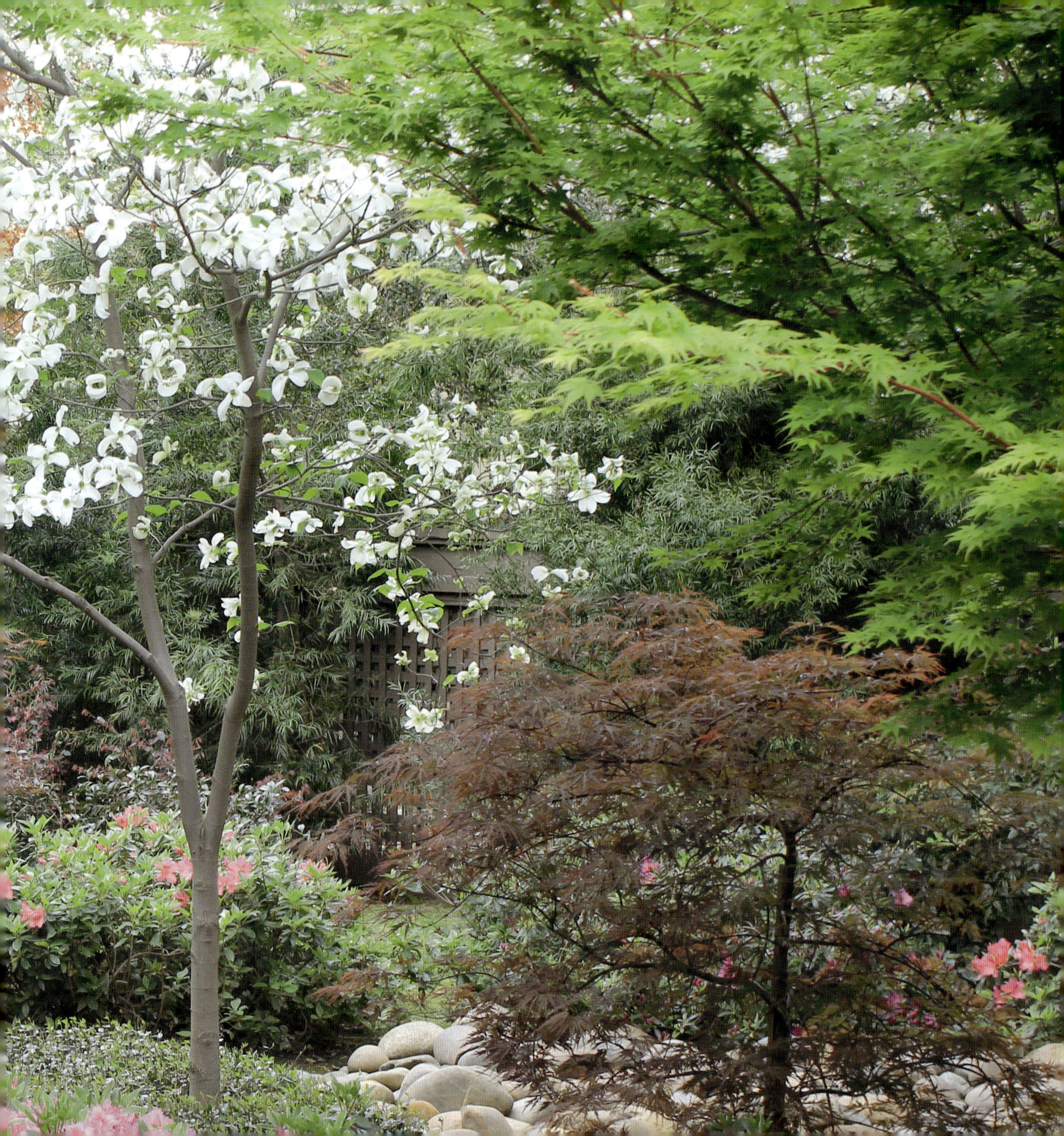

80

ZEN GARDEN

"Our yard was boring. When we remodeled our house, we also discovered major drainage problems: water flowing back and standing at the foundation," says Carrie Schore, whose house, shared with husband Neil, is located in Davis, California.

Site Problems

- Privacy
- Drainage
- Noise
- Improper hardscape layout

The Schores rarely used their yard and did not have a clue how to begin redesigning the space so it would look different, and address their drainage issues. They also didn't know who to hire or trust to develop a solution.

Finding a Professional

Through a referral from friends, the Schores found their way to Michael Glassman, who was familiar with the couple's concerns. At Michael's initial consultation with the Schores, he analyzed the problems, both in the front and back yards, and suggested several solutions and names of landscape contractors who could perform the work. The Schores interviewed three contractors that Michael knew, and hired Matt Haseltine, whose finished workmanship they studied at another location, and whose quote for the project compared favorably to other bids.

FRONT YARD

Project Challenges

- No curb appeal
- No separate front walkway; pedestrians had to walk up the driveway, navigating parked cars to get to the front door
- No plants in the planter along the front of the house because it lacked drainage so it leaked and separated from the home's foundation
- Poor grading, which led to areas of standing water
- Numerous weeds because the homeowners did not have time to keep up with mowing the grass and removing the weeds

Wish List

- Repair and plant the front planter
- Design a separate front walkway
- Install no-mow grass
- Create an overall effect of simplicity and tranquility

Problem-solving solutions

Based on Michael's master plan, Matt rebuilt the raised planter and made it a self-contained unit, independent of the house structure to prevent water from the planter getting under the home's foundation. He sealed and waterproofed the inside of the planter and installed new drain lines. Michael planted chain ferns (Woodwardia) and Cordyline "Red Star", and sago palms (Cycas revoluta) that would thrive in morning sun and afternoon shade.

To install a separate front walkway, Michael designed new quartzite-faced stepping pads, so that guests can walk up to the home entry without using the driveway. Matt regraded the yard to slope away from the house, and installed a low-maintenance, no-mow medium fescue lawn, accented with large boulders for drama. Two specimens of European white birch trees (Betula pendula) introduce curb appeal. Michael's design includes low-voltage, energy-efficient LED accent lighting on the birch trees by the large boulders and along the walkway for additional nighttime accents, curb appeal, and safety.

Cost-saving alternatives

Instead of pouring concrete and facing it with expensive quartzite tile that would be highly labor intensive, a more economical option would be to use oversized flagstone pieces as stepping stones, and to set them in sand or on a mortar base. This solution is work that homeowners can tackle themselves.

Opposite top left: Before: The front yard had a poorly designed front planter, no front walkway, and no curb appeal. *Opposite top right:* After: The redesigned front yard now has a separate front walkway set among meadow grass plantings and multistem birch trees that are in scale to the other garden elements. *Opposite bottom:* After: The rebuilt front planter was planted with lush shade-loving plants, and a private, secondary walkway with stepping stones separated by baby tears creates textural interest.

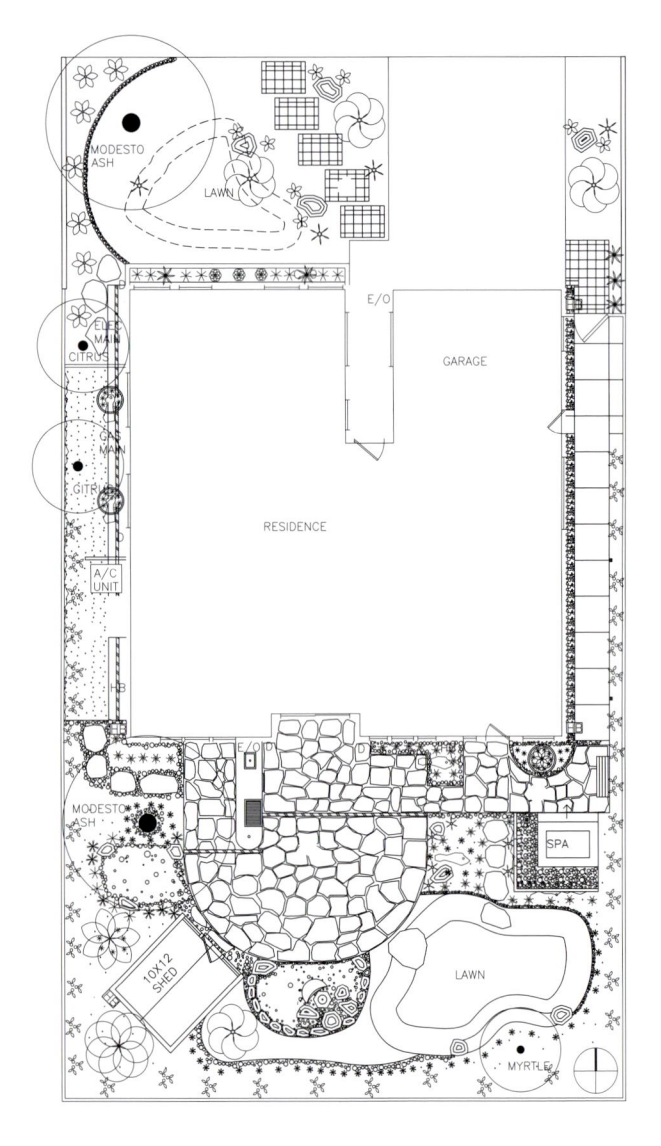

Top left: Before: The non-functional space off the master bathroom stepped out onto lawn that was dying from the deep shade. **Top center:** After: The space off the master bathroom was converted to a private spa retreat separated from the main back yard by a custom bamboo and iron screen. **Top right:** After: As a focal point of the back yard, Michael designed a natural pond and monolith water feature, which blends well with the homeowners' Buddha face sculpture. **Center right:** After: The curved quartzite flagstone patio is large enough for barbequing, dining, and lounging. **Bottom right:** After: The storage shed blends seamlessly with the architecture of the house and unifies the landscape. **Above left:** The master plan for the front and back yards.

82

BACK YARD

Project Challenges

- No usable patio space, a dying lawn, decaying old shed, and dilapidated perimeter fence
- Improper grading, so water flowed back to the home's foundation
- Little privacy, with adjacent houses looking directly into their property
- Too much noise since the Schores could hear sounds from their neighbors when outdoors, as well as surrounding street traffic

Wish List

- A storage shed to house furniture, cushions, and garden tools
- A style that matched the architecture of the Schores' contemporary home
- A private retreat with spa directly off their master bedroom
- Low maintenance and easy care, as they both traveled often and were away from their home

Problem-solving solutions

Michael suggested an Asian, Zen-style garden to complement the house's modern lines. Matt re-graded the back yard, so water flowed away from the home. He also connected downspouts to solid drain lines to get water away from the foundation and out to the street. A new natural dry creek bed now runs along the edge of the patio to help remove additional drainage problems.

A large patio (20 feet by 35 feet [6.1 meters by 10.6 meters]) that's paved in random-sized quartzite pavers serves many functions: room to eat at a large table, lounge in chairs, and cook at an outdoor kitchen. The barbecue and countertop are in the same granite the Schores used in their indoor kitchen, which ties together the two spaces.

A custom redwood-sided shed matches the style of the house to make it appear as a small guest house. To shield the homeowners' new spa, a screen of iron, copper, and wood offers privacy.

A dramatic treatment and focal point of the yard now is a meandering pond with a large original stone Buddha mask and flowing monolith stones. The sound of running water from the monoliths helps mask neighborhood noises, but it recirculates to conserve water, critical in this dry region of California. A new perimeter fence stained the color of the house maintains architectural integrity.

Michael planted two types of clumping non-invasive bamboo (Bambusa oldhamii and Bambusa multiplex "Alphonse Karr"), offering additional screening and some dramatic height. Because the homeowners liked the concept of Asian-inspired simple greens, grays, and textures, rather than a more colorful palette, Michael also introduced a Bonsai Japanese black pine (Pinus thunbergii), serpentine cedar (Cedrus atlantica "Pendula"), several decorative sedge grasses (Carex Spp), blue fescue grass (Festuca glauca), and lace leaf Japanese maples (Acer palmatum "Dissectum Viridis"). The low-maintenance no-mow fescue lawn gives the illusion of a meadow and unifies the back and front yards.

Cost-saving alternatives

Instead of a custom pond, a pre-fabricated fountain or pot fountain would reduce the landscape budget. Rather than a custom iron screen, a cost-saving option would be to install pre-made iron screens with vines. A French drain with decorative rocks could be used to accomplish the same purpose of siphoning away water instead of the more costly dry creek bed.

Budget

The Schores were willing to spend 15 percent of their home's value. The project went over budget because the couple added amenities to their wish list during the construction process.

Challenges Along the Way

The City of Davis has very strict building codes that required multiple inspections and slowed the project's progress; it took six months instead of the anticipated three or four.

Key Design Details

- Decorative iron, copper and wood privacy screen that surrounds the spa
- Pond with the one-of-a-kind Buddha mask that the Schores found at a local festival
- Custom storage shed

The New Garden—An Epilogue

The landscape has a calming, peaceful effect. The Schores spend most evenings and weekend days relaxing and entertaining in their new large outdoor room. The garden styles of both the front and back yards fit into the neighborhood aesthetic of older homes. The new landscape provides the much desired curb appeal without looking out of place. "Whether we are inside looking out, or outside in our yard, our landscape creates a private space of beauty and serenity," says Carrie. The couple's primary maintenance requirements are minimal and affordable: pruning, sweeping the patio, and some weeding.

PROJECT AND TEAM CREDITS: Client Carrie and Neil Schore **Location** Davis, California **Landscape designer** Michael Glassman, Michael Glassman & Associates, Sacramento, California, www.michaelglassman.com **Contractor** Matt Haseltine, R C Haseltine Construction, 530-574-3016 **Project duration** Six months **Completion** 2013

84

THE ECLECTIC OUTDOOR ROOM

"When I bought my house, the back yard was a do-it-yourselfer's nightmare. I also didn't realize how hot a south-facing back yard could be, nor that I would have no privacy once the trees that screened my neighbor's two-story house lost their leaves. Basically, I had no usable outdoor space, and I love to be outdoors," says homeowner Elaine Waetjen, a physician, who moved into her house in Davis, California, knowing the back yard had major problems. But she intended to rectify them once she saved sufficient funds.

Site Problems

- Privacy, when deciduous screening trees were bare
- Drainage; the patio sloped back toward the concrete pad off the back door
- Noise, with the home less than a mile (1.6 kilometers) from a busy freeway
- Too much sun
- Mixed materials and uneven pavers
- Do-it-yourself yard gone wrong

Wish List

- Outdoor room for relaxing, dining and unwinding after a busy day at work
- Place to feature two of her Shona stone sculptures from Zimbabwe
- Shade to sit outside most of the day, but without losing winter light for rooms at the back of the house
- Water feature that would block freeway noise
- Lush planting all around but with low water needs and low maintenance
- Eclectic style using natural materials
- Eliminate ugly air-conditioning unit

Finding a Professional

Looking for help to fix her landscape, Elaine asked at her equestrian community and learned that landscape designer Michael Glassman boarded a horse at the same barn. After chatting with him about her many landscape problems and finding him insightful and agreeable, she hired him for a one-hour consultation. Michael recognized that the previous owners had done many things wrong in the tiny yard, which measured just 25 feet by 30 feet (7.6 meters by 9.1 meters).

Problem-Solving Solutions

To create a privacy screen, contractor Matt Haseltine, whose work Elaine knew, added raised planters with evergreen, non-invasive, clumping timber bamboo (Bambusa oldhamii) that grows to 35 feet (10.6 meters) tall. He also regraded the yard so water would flow away from the home, and added new channel drains in the patio (with removable grates) in the planting beds and under the downspouts to drain water. To mitigate noise, Michael designed a custom 6-foot-tall (1.8-meter-tall) water wall faced in honey-gold ledgestone that flowed into a raised basin. A new large shade structure with stained timbers covered with shade cloth blocks enough sun without reducing light. A fan offers another cooling element.

Because of the uneven patio, Michael designed a new concrete slab, which was overlaid with 16-inch by 16-inch (40.6-centimeter by 40.6-centimeter) desert-rose slate tiles. The choice of a single material for a small space yields the illusion of a much larger area. Dirt that had piled up against the home's stucco walls was also removed to correct the do-it-yourself gone wrong, along with the uneven interlocking pavers.

The result is new shade-loving plantings that can thrive in the area's soil, which is alkaline (due to the boron in the water). Plant selections include sago palm (Cycas revoluta), variegated lily turf (Liriope), pony-tail asparagus ferns (Asparagus meyeri), big leaf philodendron (Philodendron selloum), creeping fig (Ficus repens), and Alphonse Karr bamboo (Bambusa multiplex Alphonse Karr). For summer and fall color, coleus and impatiens grow well in this Californian climate. While red blooming Yuletide camellias (Camellia sasanqua, Yuletide)—picked for its winter bloom—prefer acid soil, Michael put these in self-contained pots with a specialized soil mix. With the shaded environment and thick mulch, this garden's water requirements are modest.

Opposite top: After: The ultimate outdoor dining room. **Opposite bottom left:** Before: The southern exposure, poor drainage, uneven brick patio, and the two-story house that looked into the back yard made this an unusable outdoor space. **Opposite bottom right:** Before: The air-conditioning unit was a prominent feature for the sparse planting. The rose arch blocked light into the master bedroom.

Top left: The custom water feature creates a relaxing sound that blocks the freeway noise and gives a lovely backdrop to "Asleep In Stone," one of the homeowner's Shona sculptures. **Bottom left:** The custom-made decorative screen hides the air-conditioning unit. Every year, the homeowner plants a variety of shade-loving coleus that provides glorious annual color from spring through fall. **Above right:** The large beam overhead structure covered with shade cloth makes the outdoor room usable, even in the middle of a hot summer day. Michael designed a special pedestal for "The Rainmaker," another of the homeowner's Shona sculptures. **Opposite:** The master plan of the back yard.

Cost-Saving Alternatives

To cut the cost of the project in half, Elaine could have chosen a pre-fabricated fountain instead of the water wall; large umbrellas instead of the overhead shade structure; plain wood lattice screening around the air-conditioning unit instead of the custom screen; and a colored, stamped concrete patio instead of the natural slate.

Budget

Elaine originally had planned to spend 5 percent of the cost of her home on her back-yard project, but after considering the equity she had in her home, the long length of time she planned to live there, the additional living space her outdoor room would provide for her small house, and the amount of time she would use her outdoor area, she decided that a budget of 10 percent of her home's current appraisal was worth the additional investment.

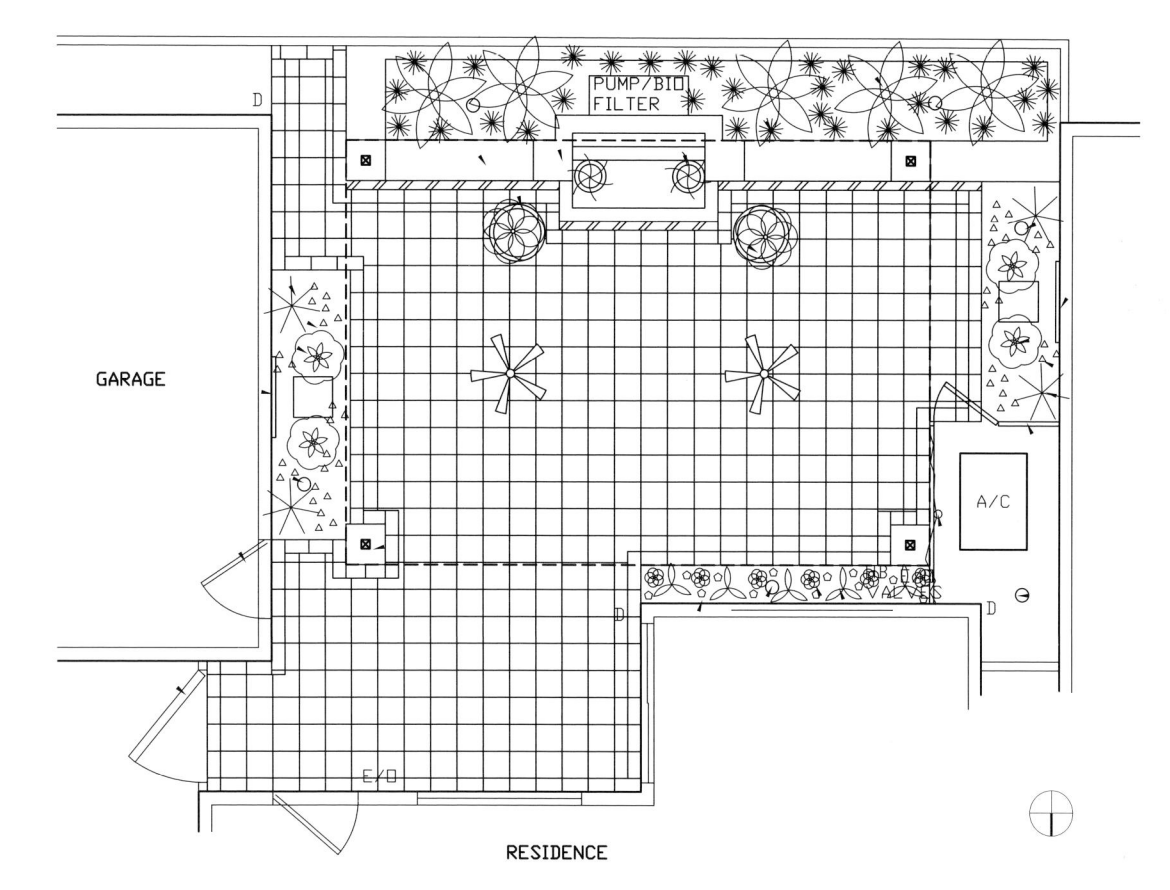

Challenges Along the Way

Building codes for the city of Davis presented a challenge since they allow for garage setbacks to be 3 feet (91 centimeters) from a property line but other structures must be 5 feet (1.5 meters). As a result, Michael recalculated and redesigned the size of the patio. In addition, he replaced a back property fence that turned out to be rotted from the dirt the previous owners had piled against it.

Key Design Details

- Matt built two pedestals, which are faced and capped in polished rainbow limestone to showcase Elaine's sculptures. These are strategically placed one so that they can be seen through the back door as well as in the garden, and the other inside the fountain.

- He also designed a one-of-a-kind water wall that acts as a backdrop for one sculpture and camouflages the air-conditioning unit with a decorative screen.

The New Garden—An Epilogue

Over the course of designing and building this project, Elaine and Michael fell in love and married seven years after they met. Almost every evening during the spring, summer and fall, they eat dinner in their now-shared back yard. They love entertaining their families and friends for breakfasts, brunches, and barbecues. When they bring work home, they find inspiration while sitting outside, and listening to the sound of water while they write or design.

PROJECT AND TEAM CREDITS: Client Elaine Waetjen **Location** Davis, California **Landscape designer** Michael Glassman, Michael Glassman & Associates, Sacramento, California, www.michaelglassman.com **Contractor** Matt Haseltine, R C Haseltine Construction, 530-574-3016 **Project duration** Six months **Completion** 2012

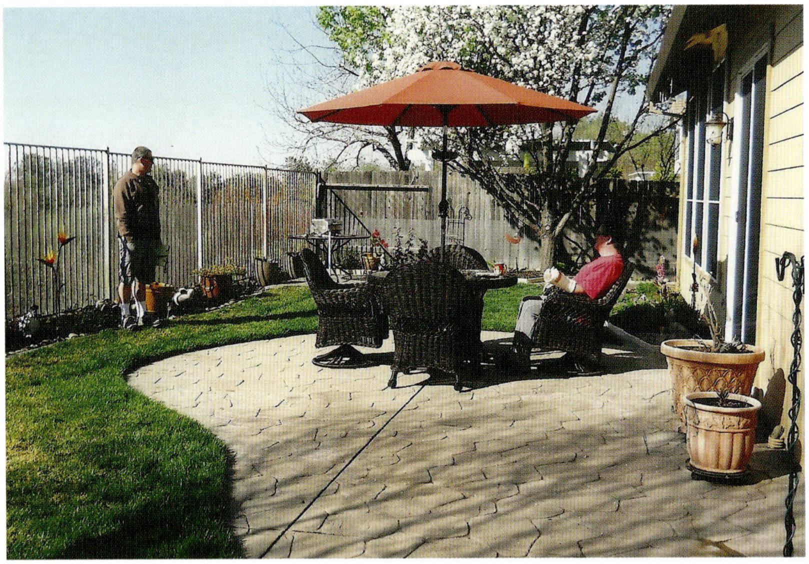

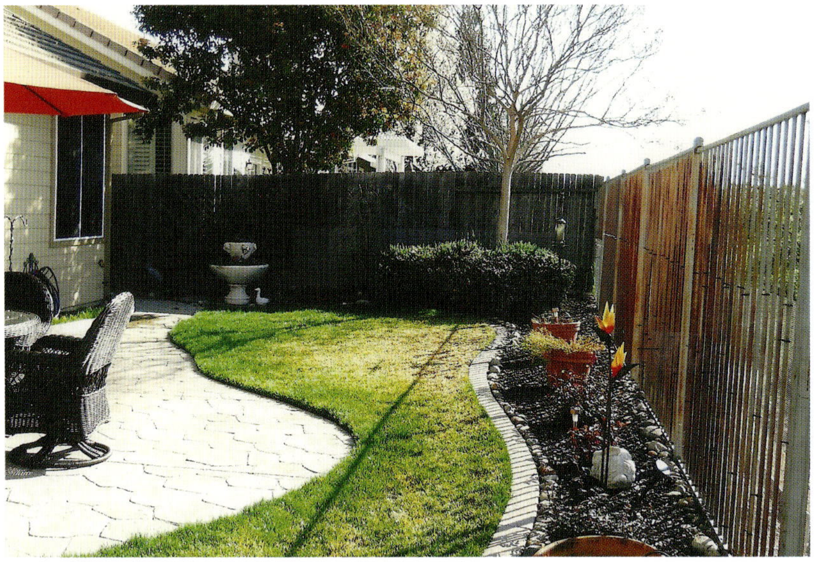

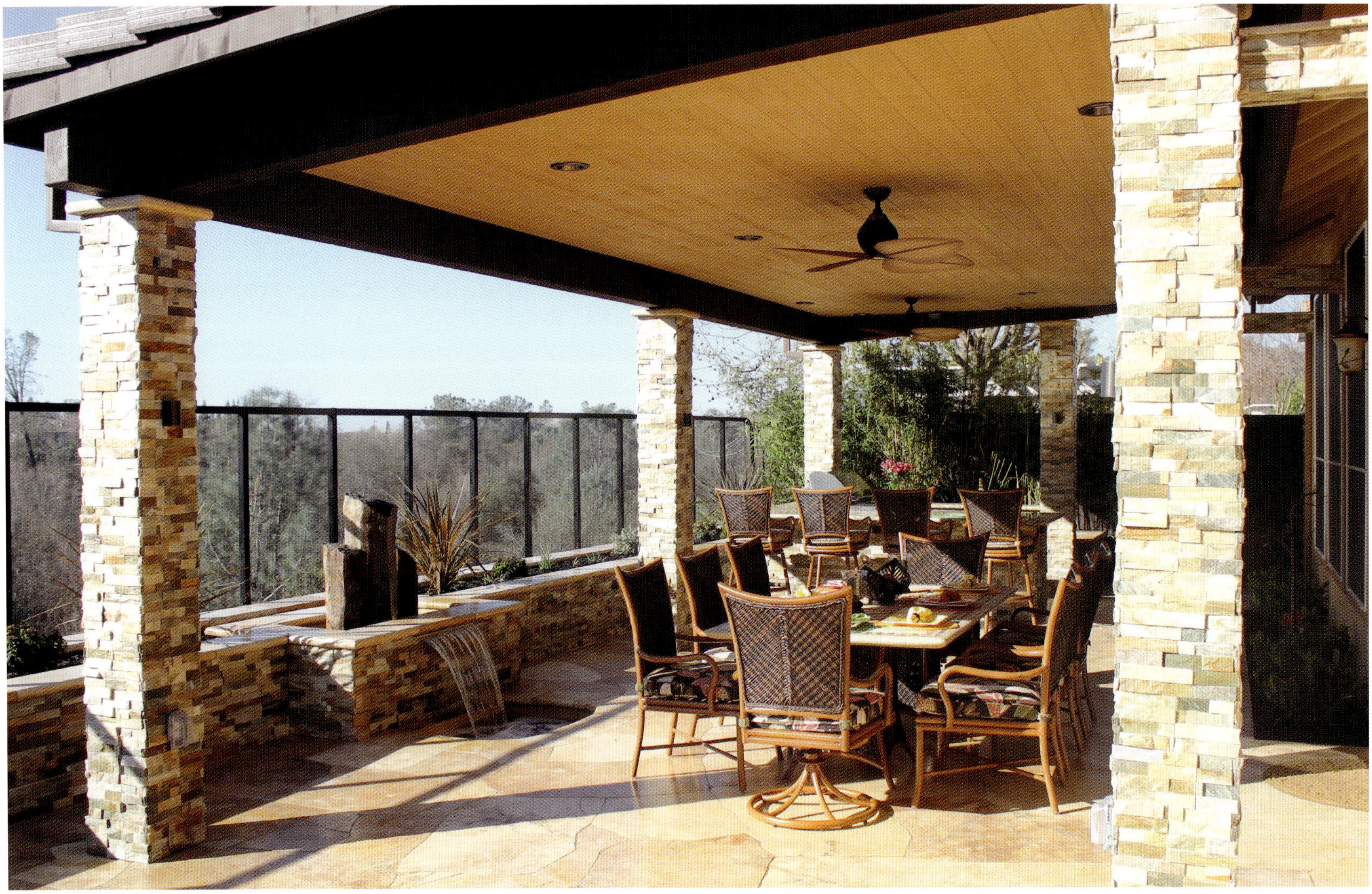

ADIOS SNAKES

Paul and Bernie's 20-foot by 60-foot (6-meter by 18.2-meter) back yard had a beautiful view overlooking an open nature preserve in Folsom, California. They had lived in their home for 13 years and had hoped to update their landscape when finances allowed. "Having my wife nearly bitten in the face by a rattlesnake was a defining moment," says Paul.

Site Problems

- Snakes
- Drainage and erosion
- Noise
- Privacy
- Improper layout of hardscape
- Too much sun
- Drought risk/dry climate

The location by a nature preserve sounded idyllic and it was, yet it presented challenges. Rattlesnakes would routinely come up from the preserve to sun themselves on the couple's small patio. Bernie had almost been bitten six times while she gardened in the yard. While the drainage sloped away from the house properly, it went toward the steep bank at the back edge, causing concern for erosion during heavy rains. Although the preserve would seem to be quiet, a path along the bottom of the steep bank behind the house for hikers and cyclists meant their voices were carried into the yard. The sides of the property also lacked privacy from neighbors, the west-facing portion offered no shade, and the patio reflected an all-too-common problem—it was too small to fit comfortable furnishings. An existing iron fence obscured views into the preserve. Due to the state's worsening drought, city leaders in their town considered establishing a moratorium on irrigation.

Wish List

- A fully equipped kitchen with serving bar and outdoor TV to entertain on favorite occasions, such as Super Bowl Sunday
- A custom fountain to screen noise
- A cover to protect the kitchen and dining areas from hot sun and rain
- A fireplace to enable use of the outdoor area in the colder months
- No lawn to maximize entertaining and lounging space
- A look and ambience that would convey a vacation resort

Finding a Professional

Paul and Bernie had seen Michael's work in *Sunset Magazine*, read articles about him in a local newspaper, and followed up by studying his website. After an initial consultation, they felt good hiring him and interviewed three contractors he recommended, selecting the one who promised to work only on their project and be on the project daily, alongside staff.

Problem-Solving Solutions

To address the snake challenge, Michael designed a 6-foot-high (1.82-meter-high) iron and wire-mesh snake fence, with mesh installed to an underground depth of 2 feet (60 centimeters) around the entire yard so that snakes could not dig underneath. The mesh offered an additional advantage—a clear view into the nature preserve from the couple's yard.

To improve drainage and avoid erosion, the new concrete patio slopes away from the house, and it's overlaid with large pieces of gauged travertine flagstone. An 18-inch-high (45.7-centimeter-high) raised planter of concrete masonry unit blocks along the yard's back is faced in elegant honey gold ledgestone. A 3-inch (7.6-centimeter) channel drain with a removable grate helps keep water off the patio along the front edge of the planter. The channel drain and planter drains connect to solid lines that direct water runoff to the street at the site's front rather than down the hill.

A new custom fountain works as the low focal point of an 18-inch-wide (45.7-centimeter-wide) seat wall to dampen sounds of hiker and cyclist traffic. Water flows down three monolithic stone spires into a raised basin and cascades out into a patio-level foot-soaking pool. To mitigate views of neighbors, Michael planted a favorite, Buddha's Belly (Bambusa

Opposite top left: Before: The small back yard had only a small patio with no shade, a perfect environment for snakes to sun themselves.
Opposite top right: Before: The homeowners had only a narrow strip of dying lawn and few plants. They kept their garden barren to discourage snakes from hiding. **Opposite bottom:** After: The back yard is now a spacious, shaded, and functional outdoor room surrounded by a snake-proof fence that doesn't obstruct the view into the nature preserve.

ventricosa) bamboo, along each side of the yard. This clumping bamboo variety becomes very dense and grows to 20 feet (6 meters) tall.

To gain a larger entertaining space, Michael ripped up the small patch of lawn and designed a 16-foot by 40-foot (4.8-meter by 12-meter) patio as a replacement, which is big enough to accommodate a dining table with eight chairs, sitting area with four large lounge chairs, fireplace, and small outdoor kitchen with four barstools. And because strong sun was a challenge during the summer, a solid overhead structure, complete with fans, shades and cools diners, making the area work not only then but also during rainy winter months. It also protects the lights for nighttime use and the TV that Paul wanted for sporting events.

By removing the lawn, the couple cut down on their water usage. A new drip irrigation system sufficiently waters materials in the raised planters and prevents water runoff and evaporation. Plantings are all low-maintenance, drought-tolerant perennials in vivid colors: bougainvillea, Cordyline "Electric Star", Carolina jessimine vine (Gelsemium sempervirens), gardenia, and Japanese maples.

Cost-Saving Alternatives

Instead of facing planters with ledgestone, plastering or painting the block with the house color would have been less expensive. The patio could have been constructed with stamped, colored concrete. For the overhead structure, the homeowners might have used 6-inch by 6-inch (15-centimeter by 15-centimeter) wood posts instead of facing block columns in ledgestone, or they could have chosen a wood-slatted ready-made pergola. They also could have chosen prefabricated fountains, and a fire pit or fire table instead of a pricier fireplace.

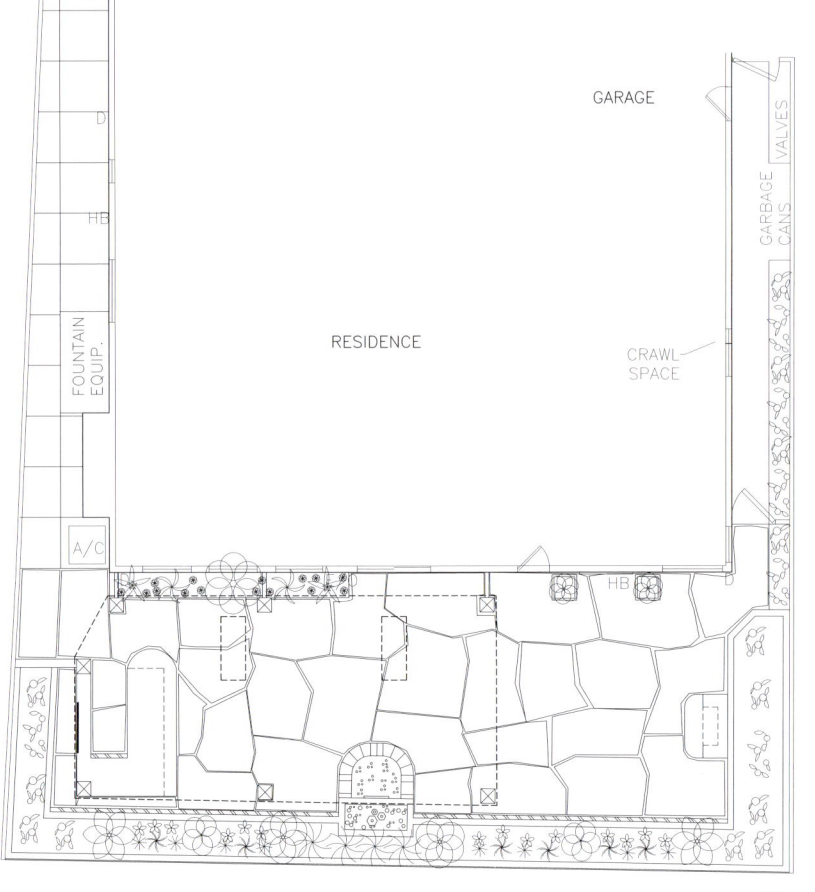

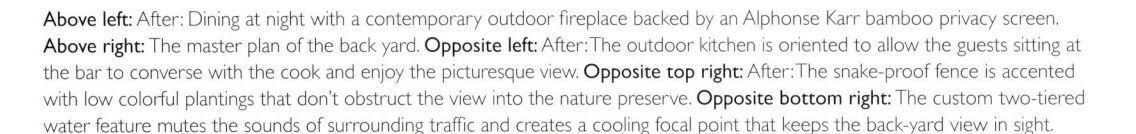

Above left: After: Dining at night with a contemporary outdoor fireplace backed by an Alphonse Karr bamboo privacy screen. **Above right:** The master plan of the back yard. **Opposite left:** After: The outdoor kitchen is oriented to allow the guests sitting at the bar to converse with the cook and enjoy the picturesque view. **Opposite top right:** After: The snake-proof fence is accented with low colorful plantings that don't obstruct the view into the nature preserve. **Opposite bottom right:** The custom two-tiered water feature mutes the sounds of surrounding traffic and creates a cooling focal point that keeps the back-yard view in sight.

Budget

The couple spent 20 percent of the cost of their home on their landscaping because they wanted to use high-end materials since they spend so much time in their yard. They rationalized that they were doubling the size of their small home with the equivalent of an outdoor room.

Challenges Along the Way

Michael incorporated building requirements and HOA restrictions into the working drawings, but needed to revise the plans several times due to zoning and the city of Folsom's strict regulations. To prevent snakes from coming into the yard, he had first designed a 6-foot-high (1.82-meter-high) glass fence, but that wasn't approved. It took months to get the planning department to approve a mesh design. He also had to redesign the overhead shade structure from a freestanding to attached design, also because of city regulations. The revisions were included in the couple's design fee because the changes were due to HOA requirements rather than homeowner preferences.

Key Design Details

- Michael designed the custom fountain as a focal point that would not obstruct views into the nature preserve.
- The custom mesh fence is almost invisible (to permit good views), yet prevents snakes from digging underneath.

The New Garden—An Epilogue

Before their renovation, Bernie and Paul rarely used their back-yard space. They had to maintain it, but mainly to prevent it from becoming overgrown and to deter snakes. Since the renovation, they relax outdoors, thinking they're on vacation, and now do not worry about snakes or maintenance. They also entertain more frequently. And after seeing photos of beautiful yards in magazines for years, Bernie finds it hard to believe her yard now reflects that same beauty she always admired. "Every time I walk outdoors, I'm continually amazed," she says.

PROJECT AND TEAM CREDITS: Client Paul and Bernie Bratovich **Location** Folsom, California **Landscape designer** Michael Glassman, Michael Glassman & Associates, Sacramento, California, www.michaelglassman.com **Contractor** South Canyon Construction Inc., Victor Zakernichnyy, Sacramento, California, 530-902-7894 **Project duration** Eight months **Completion** 2014

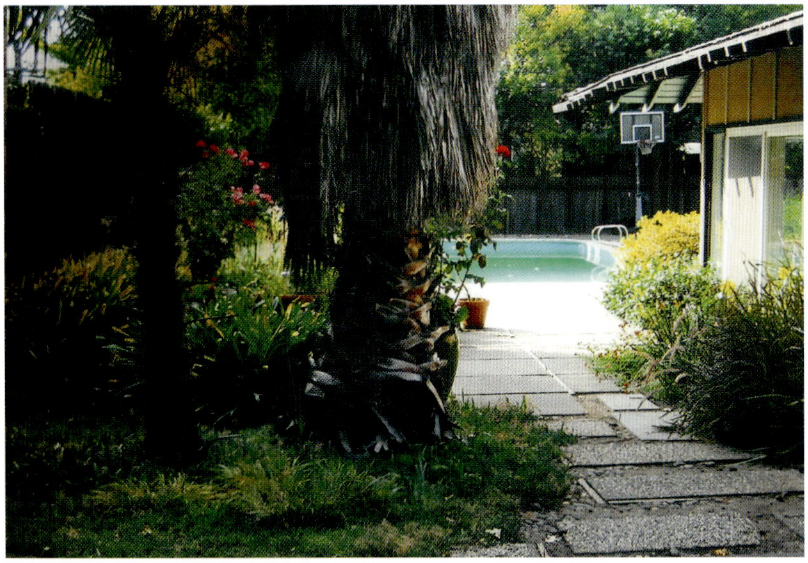

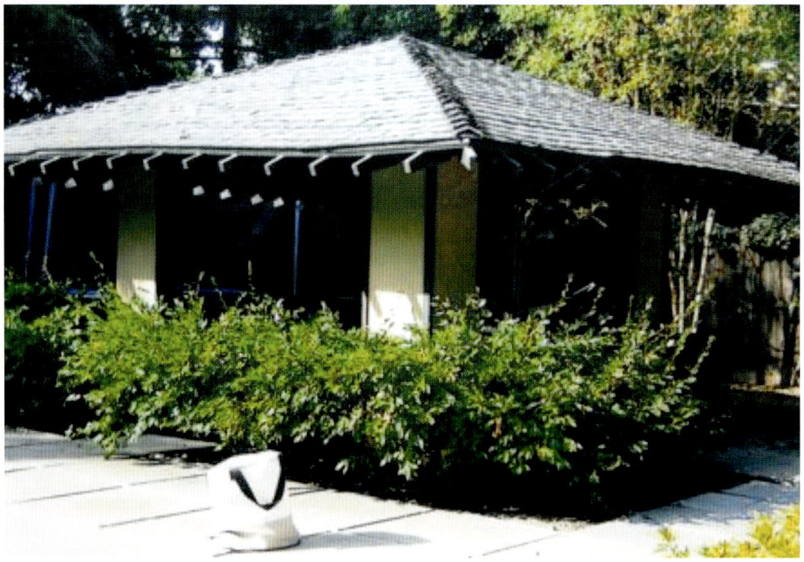

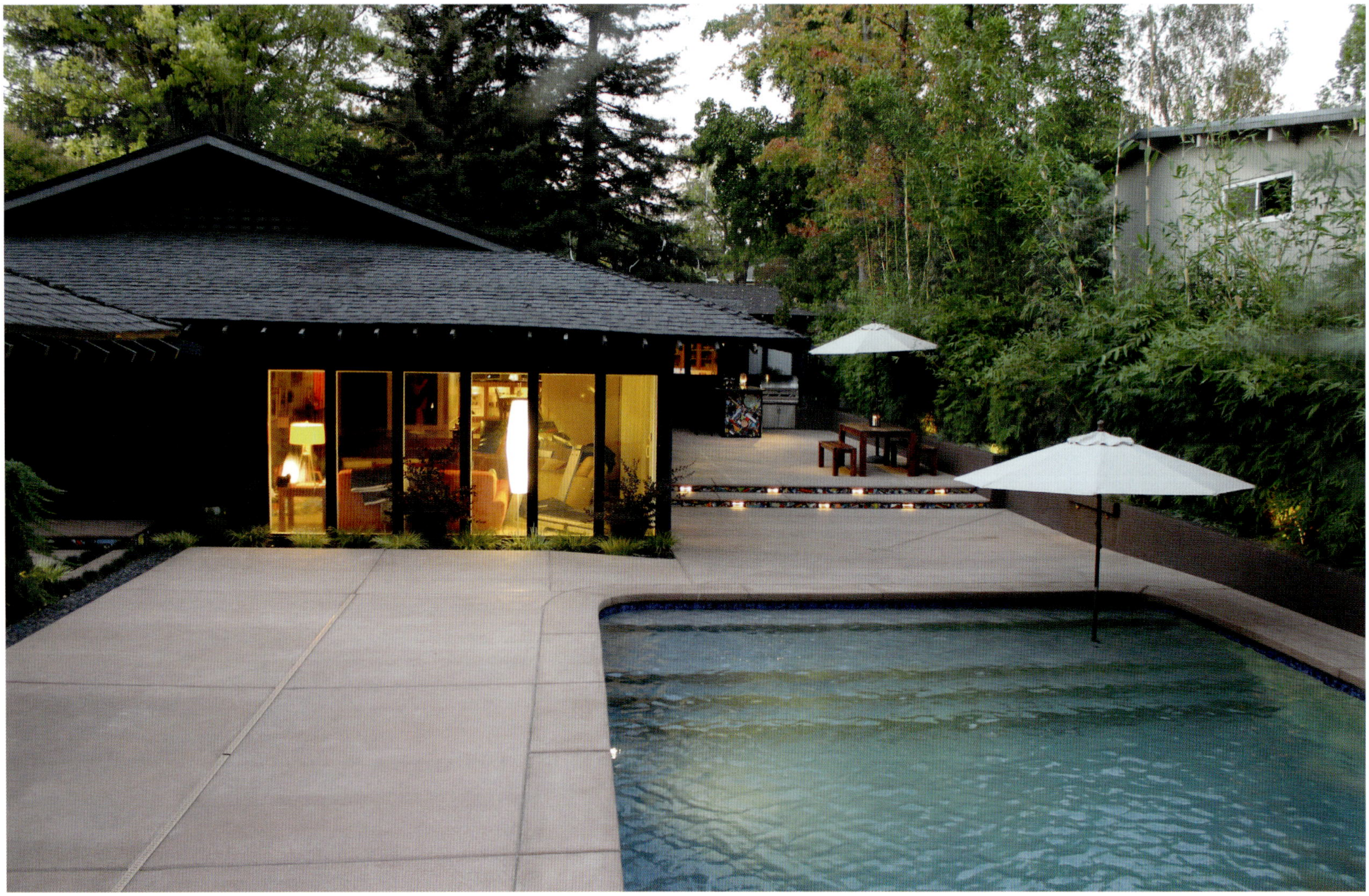

ARTIST'S RETREAT

Homeowners Lindsay and Scott Filby had fallen in love with their home because the architectural style was unusual—a Japanese farmhouse built in Sacramento, California, in 1962. But they described their back yard as a "disastrous, horror of a behemoth mess" that made them embarrassed to entertain. It lacked design cohesiveness, with a rotting deck, cracking concrete patio, falling-down freestanding teahouse, and bad drainage problems that flooded the yard. In addition, their pool leaked. For 16 years they lived with the landscape, thinking they could fix it themselves. They never did.

Site Problems

- Bad drainage
- Improper layout of hardscape and cracked concrete
- No privacy
- Too many different materials
- Wrong plants in the wrong places with many dying

This couple loved their home but not its yard, and felt overwhelmed. Because the living room was located at a lower elevation than the yard, it frequently flooded during winter rains. An old pool compounded the problem as it leaked and the water ran toward the living room. Although the pool could be used to swim laps, it did not work for socializing with only one entrance, and the surrounding deck sagged and was not safe to use. Furthermore it consisted of cracked concrete in multiple finishes, plus aggregate pavers and wood decking. Privacy was a concern: the neighbor's house on one side provided a perch from their second level that overlooked the couple's yard, while their own yard looked down a slope into the same neighbor's yard. To top off myriad challenges, the former owners had planted materials without considering their location and how they related to the home and site.

A large palm tree stood in the middle of the back yard, cutting off the flow of space, which was mostly of dying lawn. Roses, a sun-loving choice, had no light, and ferns grew in the sun—which they did not need as they are shade-loving.

Wish List

- Outdoor kitchen with place to dine
- Place for Lindsay to showcase her mosaic artwork
- Family- and child-friendly pool
- Covered outdoor sitting area
- More privacy from neighbors
- Open feeling of yard
- Remove or salvage the teahouse

Finding a Professional

The couple hired a landscape designer, who left the profession to become a fine artist. He recommended Michael Glassman as his replacement. During an initial consultation, Michael noticed some of Lindsay's contemporary mosaic art inside the home and suggested she incorporate several pieces in the landscape. The match of designer to homeowners proved perfect.

Problem-Solving Solutions

A new colored concrete patio with a 1-percent slope away from the house and pool with large catch basins, French drain, and drywell filled with drain rock and recycled broken concrete, and back-up sump pump all siphon water to the street and keep it from damaging the house and pool. A major remodeling of the pool involved replastering, retiling, new equipment, shallower depth for easier children's play and for adults to lounge on chairs in the water, as well as new steps for entry and exit. In place of the rotted deck, there is a large colored concrete patio off the kitchen with equipment and a granite counter for cooking, and enough space for a picnic table to seat up to 10. Instead of removing the rarely used teahouse, Michael renovated it and installed lights for nighttime use.

Giant timber bamboo (Bambusa oldhamii) in new raised planters block views of a neighbor's house along the side yard; the neighbor's home at the back is concealed now with a new 10-foot by 10-foot (3-meter by 3-meter) dramatic water feature, with Lindsay's colorful mosaics against it appearing as a big piece of modern art; hand-troweled walls are painted a vivid coral, and ledges for sitting are made from precast bull-nosed concrete capstone. New serpentine cedar (Cedris atlantica "Pendula") and bonsai black pine (Pinus thunbergii) add living art.

Opposite top left: Before: The yard had no entertainment space, broken concrete, poor drainage and the wrong plants in the wrong place. Example: a palm tree was planted too close to the house and did not fit the style of the home. **Opposite top right:** Before: The Japanese teahouse was collapsing and non-functional. **Opposite bottom:** After: The new concrete patio was poured to eliminate drainage problems, creating a seamless hardscape that makes the yard look bigger.

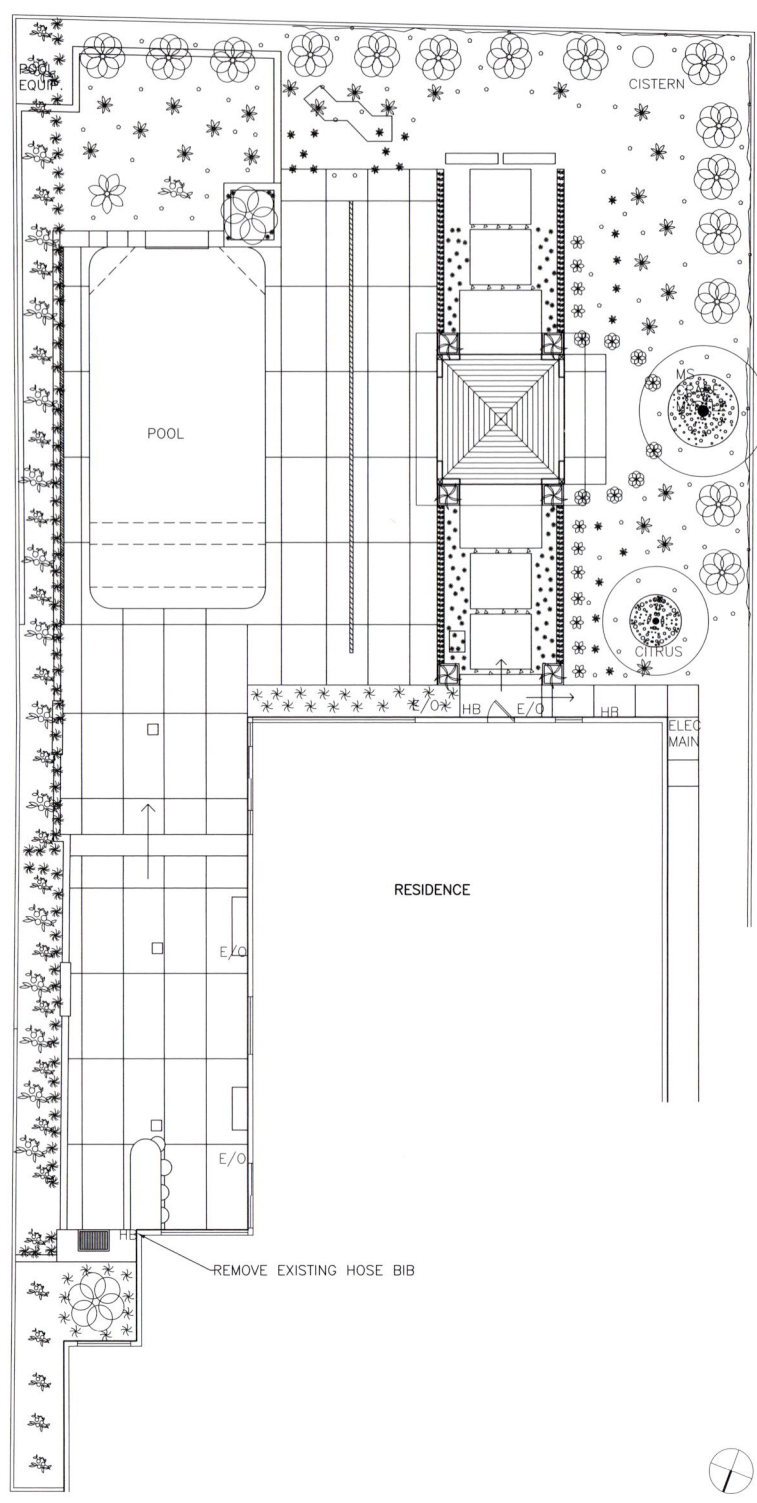

Top left: The new dining space off the kitchen has a grand view of the renovated pool and dramatic fountain focal point. **Center left:** The outdoor kitchen was customized to showcase the homeowner's mosaic artwork. **Bottom left:** The renovated Japanese teahouse provides a pool-side retreat. **Above right:** The master plan showcases the architectural layout of the back yard. **Opposite top:** Laser-cut red panels give the teahouse a contemporary look that complements the mosaic art of the homeowner. The structure now functions as a shaded pool-side area for relaxation. **Opposite bottom:** The homeowner's dramatic art is showcased in this sheer descent fountain.

94

To give the yard a cohesive look, all patio surfaces have the same colored concrete and brushed finishes, which makes the area appear larger. To help plants thrive, Michael removed the palm tree, transplanted roses to a sunnier corner near the teahouse, along with sea-green junipers in the form of topiaries, and relocated the ferns to a shaded patch.

Cost-Saving Alternatives

There's no shortcut to fixing problems; those always should be attended to for a long-term solution, says Michael. But rather than remodel the teahouse or install a custom water feature, prefabricated designs in the form of a gazebo and fountain would cut costs.

Budget

The couple spent 20 percent of the value of their house on yard improvements, but a large proportion was allotted to fixing drainage and pool problems.

Challenges Along the Way

None.

Key Design Details

- Sheer-descent mosaic water wall with homeowner's artworks

The New Garden—An Epilogue

The homeowners feel that hiring a landscape designer was money worthwhile since they gained a master plan that has saved them from having to continue fixing problem areas. They would never have been able to resolve many of the new garden's design ideas themselves, such as salvaging the teahouse, and installing Lindsay's artwork in the garden as a focal point. They now entertain frequently as a family and also with friends, and Lindsay has gone on to show and sell her works at local art galleries.

PROJECT AND TEAM CREDITS: Client Lindsay and Scott Filby **Location** Sacramento, California **Landscape designer** Michael Glassman, Michael Glassman & Associates, Sacramento, California, www.michaelglassman.com **Contractor** Josh Martin, Charis Pools & Landscape Inc., www.charislandscape.com **Project duration** Four months (a large portion of that involved regrading and installing drainage and underground utilities) **Completion** 2011

96

SAVORING A VIEW

After landscape designer Richard Poynter and wife Peggy, a writer, and avid horticulturalist, constructed their dream home on 3 acres (1.2 hectares) in Wildwood, Missouri, a St. Louis suburb, they began work on the garden and amenities. And as Richard does with clients of his Poynter Landscape & Architecture firm in Ballwin, Missouri, he developed a master plan to make the best use of the site and meet the couple's needs. The aims: to salvage a small historic building and convert it into his office (the building had been constructed when railroad lines took city residents to the country to enjoy the Meramec River); develop a space between the office and house for a courtyard for entertaining under a covered pergola with fireplace at one end; and at the other end—the icing on the cake—an elegant pool for lap swimming that would also take advantage of the gorgeous, steep ridge site and distant views.

Site Problems

- Layered limestone rock throughout the property
- Steep grade at the back along the ridge where the pool would be

Wish List

- Small hardscape-paved courtyard between house and detached office
- A 17-foot-tall (5-meter-tall) brick fireplace with stone accents
- Gunite pool on opposite side of courtyard from fireplace, by the ridge for vanishing effect, and large enough for lap swimming

Finding a Professional

Because of his expertise and that of landscape architects on his staff, Richard didn't have to look far for help. "We collaborate on most projects to end up with the best options," he says. He served as general contractor for construction of the landscape and features.

Project Challenges

- Budget, keeping work to a "reasonable" amount and balancing it with best material and plant choices
- Vanishing pool by the ridge with its steep slope, with minimal access for equipment
- Designing all to look like a good fit with the rustic cedar shake house with lodge-pole columns

Problem-Solving Solutions

Because Richard doesn't like to add too much hardscape to any outdoor setting, he made the paved courtyard as small as he could at 19 feet by 35 feet (5.8 meters by 10.7 meters), but still large enough to suit the outdoor entertaining he and his wife prefer. He paved it in big squares of travertine (16 inches by 16 inches [40.6 centimeters by 40.6 centimeters]) laid on a diagonal for an elegant look, and repeated lodge-pole columns that are part of the home's design. The area can comfortably fit as many as 25 people. To make the fireplace more visually interesting, he accented its brickwork with stone detailing. Because the pool's prime purpose is for lap swimming, Richard knew a classic rectangular shape close to 40 feet (12 meters) long would be best, and constructed it by the ridge to let the ground fall away for the dramatic, modern vanishing effect. The water "falls" over the slope to a basin at the bottom and is recycled back to the top. The hard part in doing this look is equipment access, which in this case was minimal, but Richard solved this by bringing in a back hoe with huge rock breaker, which allowed him to break out the rock where necessary without causing too much vibration that could hurt the house.

To avoid deer destroying hosta and other newly planted materials, Richard located a number of coyote decoys about the yard and also poured coyote urine crystals. "You need to use multiple deer avoidant disciplines to keep animals away from your desirable plants by keeping them moving, so when they see the coyote decoys they just keep moving," he explains.

Opposite top: After: Sitting under the pergola looking toward the new infinity-edged pool with the fireplace behind the dining patio. **Opposite bottom far left:** Before: In winter. **Opposite center (top and bottom):** Before: looking down from the second floor of the house during the pool's construction. **Opposite bottom right:** After: the pool was designed with a minimal amount of travertine decking to show off the elegance of the vanishing-edge pool and its clean straight lines.

Top left: The brick and stone fireplace was constructed on an axis directly opposite the pool. **Top right:** The dining table has a direct view of the newly constructed pool. The columns help frame the eye toward the pool, and are softened by colorful plantings at the base of the columns. **Above left:** The homeowners' "sugar shack," tucked away for shelter, is a place where they can go and sit, even when it's raining, and enjoy their landscape and pool. **Above right:** A copper sculpture was installed as a focal point on the lawn. **Opposite:** The cedar pergola with its beautiful travertine floor provides shade for the client to dine under. Another material, local limestone, was used to construct the seat wall, bordered with plantings.

Cost-Saving Alternatives

The courtyard's hardscape size could have been pared or a less costly material than travertine used—possibly, concrete, which then could be scored for a more high-end style. A fire pit could have been selected instead of a fireplace, though it then wouldn't be as much of a focal point in the yard. The vanishing edge could have been eliminated, though that cost was compensated for by the pool's rectangular shape, which is much less expensive than a free-form design (the travertine banding around the pool is minimal and is laid in a traditional grid pattern here rather than on a diagonal).

Budget

The project allowed for 30 percent of the home's value.

Challenges Along the Way

Local county guidelines require sufficient fencing, but Richard doesn't like the look of fencing or how it would hinder functionality behind the vanishing edge in this case. Instead, he fenced all the way to the property lines, which kept the space looking larger, rather than have it be cut off by the fence and, thus appear smaller. By lowering the vanishing edge water reservoir, he negated the need for fencing only behind the edge. The fence now terminates on either side of the edge and leads the eye toward more distant views. Because Richard found leaf debris accumulated over time in the basin at the bottom (which stopped water from being recycled back up to the pool) he retrofitted it with an Astroturf material with perforated vinyl that effectively blocks leaves and other unwanted materials.

Key Design Details

- People notice the vanishing edge right away.
- The couple likes to garden in urns and containers, which allows them to easily change out materials, preferably annuals for color, for different seasons, sometimes five times a year.
- They replaced the two banana trees they planted by the pool for a tropical effect with narrow blue spruces in stunning copper containers that they think look better throughout the year.
- They planted copper window boxes with annuals for additional pops of color.
- For good perennial cover throughout the garden, Richard installed rudbeckia, liriope, and hosta, and dwarf wisteria along the pergola posts.
- He used Japanese red maple, magnolias, Serbian spruce, boxwoods, and hydrangea for flower color, fall color, and lots of green in winter.
- To fasten a beam in place between the office and house, Richard commissioned a blacksmith to make brackets that are both decorative and functional.

The New Garden—An Epilogue

The owners have enjoyed seeing their landscape mature and evolve: "A good hardscape looks good from day one, but it takes softscape time to grow. And now after six to seven years since we finished, everything looks so much better." The pool and courtyard have inspired the Poynters to entertain much more in good weather, though they're able to use the outdoors right up until Thanksgiving because of the fireplace.

PROJECT AND TEAM CREDITS: Client Richard and Peggy Poynter **Location** St. Louis, Missouri **Landscape designer** Richard Poynter & Bob Wilhelm ASLA Poynter Landscape Architecture & Construction, Ballwin, Missouri, www.poynterlandscape.com **Project duration** Five to six months **Completion** House: 2002; fireplace, pergola, pool, and landscape: 2006

100

RECLAIMED HAVEN

How difficult is it to be your own client? Not at all according to husband-and-wife landscape designers Greg and Janie Schaumburg. They loved the process of transforming the tiny yard of their small Buffalo Grove, Illinois, home (originally just 875 square feet [81.3 square meters]), in part because they tackled the project on their own and could show their two young children how a garden literally grows. But the do-it-yourselfers proceeded slowly—doing work mostly in the evenings and on weekends over the course of 11 years. Because their property had almost nothing on it—except for a crabapple tree and one coreopsis, both of which they kept, and a green ash they lost to the emerald ash borer—they had the advantage of starting from scratch to achieve the garden they had long-imagined. Their prime challenge was the desire to maintain a tight budget, which inspired them to cleverly recycle hard- and softscape materials, many of which Greg found in his job as a designer at Bertog Landscape Co.

Site Problems

- No privacy with close proximity to nine different neighboring yards
- Severe drainage issues

Wish List

- Privacy from so many nearby homes
- Entertaining space suitable for bare feet
- Improve front yard for neighborhood curb appeal
- Place for their young children to dig and explore
- Fire pit
- Edible plantings
- Detached garage and workshop

Finding a Professional

Between Greg and Janie, they handled all tasks, from the design development to the actual work, and many design evolutions as new materials became available. And although Greg urges clients to develop and start with a master plan, he and Janie preferred to personalize their garden, leaving their process in flux as the spaces evolved over time.

Project Challenges

- Working slowly in stages, which required patience and planning
- Deciding to construct the project by hand, with minimal use of machines for deliveries only
- Keeping an eye open for hard- and softscape materials suitable for reuse

Problem-Solving Solutions

Both Greg and Janie had grown up in much more bucolic wooded areas with far greater separation among homes, so privacy from the many surrounding neighbors was crucial. To start, Greg planted arborvitae at the back and side yards that were originally headed for a landfill; these became a good screen and backdrop.

"One reason we kept my pickup truck for many years was to haul materials easily to our house," Greg says. For their desired entertaining space, he reclaimed 700 square feet (65 square meters) of 30-year-old aged bluestone that was also being discarded, and which Greg knew most clients wouldn't want since it was too thin for most masons to install without breaking. By carefully

Opposite top left: Granite and fossil-marked limestone boulders make up a "campfire-style" fire pit, a nod to Greg and Janie's long history of family camping trips. The irregular bluestone sitting area is surrounded by techny arborvitae to provide privacy from neighboring homes. **Opposite top right:** A low bluestone retaining wall forms a circular lawn border central to the rear yard, connecting the fire pit, vegetable garden, garage, and dining terrace. Mixed planting beds of perennials and hydrangea, and bordered by boxwood, provide continuous blooms, textures, and seasonal interest. **Opposite bottom:** Greg's design for the family's detached garage recreates a coach house–style architecture, which becomes a backdrop to the reclaimed bluestone terrace. The crabapple tree to the left of the terrace was original to the yard, and serves as a canopy over the dining area, herb garden, and lawn panel.

handling the large sheets of stone, he was able to work the stone and yield huge cost savings. "It would have cost around U.S. $40 a square foot (90 square centimeters) for someone else to install new stone for us, so in the end it was a tremendous savings," he says. He installed the large pieces as a giant puzzle, sweeping the joints with crushed bluestone and planning both herb and perennial "cutouts" within the patio. Greg also hand-selected and recycled limestone and granite boulders to use for a secluded fire pit that he built for a Mother's Day surprise for Janie. "The rocks had wonderful fossils within them, which I knew our kids would like," he says.

An "edibles garden" became a project for his wife and son. They planted several serviceberries, which the family harvests for fruit to incorporate into pies, jams, and scones. They also carved out room within the bluestone patio for an herb/kitchen garden, highlighted by a small birdbath. A larger produce garden, initially located by the side of the driveway, was relocated during construction of their garage. Their garden produce changes seasonally—one year it may be tomatillos, squash, and cucumbers, and another year veggies to make fresh salsa.

To improve drainage, the couple incorporated a rain garden for several years, demonstrating to their kids how rainwater could be enjoyed safely from a distance as an ephemeral pond feature. With the garage addition, they phased out half of their rain gardens, and regraded the site so water would spill away from the house and feed into their municipal drainage easement. To connect different areas of their small site, there are now paths of reclaimed bluestone steppers and crushed limestone gravel.

Above left: A rustic birdbath and whimsical cast limestone frog, gifts from friends Daniel and Charlotte Ward at Longshadow Planters, serve as focal points along the edge of a rain garden, which Greg and Janie engineered as drainage to carry water away from the home's foundation. The couple integrated many differently sized stones within the border. **Above center:** Decorating for special occasions doesn't just happen indoors. This tall copper planter contains a colorful blue hydrangea for a neighborhood Fourth of July party, dressing up a quiet corner of the yard. **Above right:** After nearly 12 years, the "everyday view" for the Schaumburgs went from a blank slate to a private garden. The backdrop of arborvitae provides screening for the family and friends as they gather around the fire pit, entertain on the terrace, or share a meal together. The small home has doubled in size with the outdoor living spaces. **Opposite:** The plan for the yard shows how plantings were interspersed throughout, around the house, and by the garage for maximizing the land.

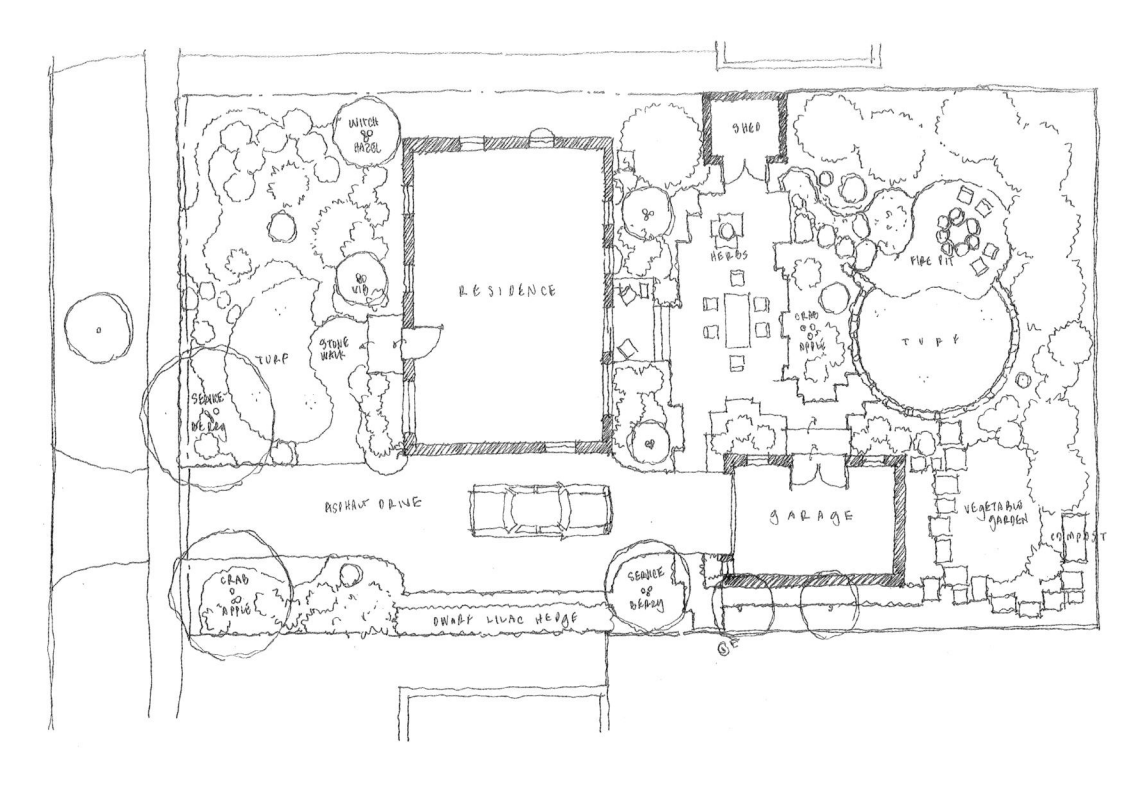

Key Design Details

- Amount of bed space; quality of materials, from bluestone to granite and limestone boulders; a cedar deck; mix of perennials, including vinca (periwinkle) and liriope groundcovers, evergreens, boxwood, and several types of hydrangeas.

- "Some criticize our yard for not having enough color, but that was an intentional choice to use many green shades, whites, and foliage plants. It's not an offensive blast of color, but more a muted blend from early spring bulbs to pockets, textures, and fall colors," Greg says. While he is generally opposed to annuals due to the continual need to replant and replace, Janie and their daughter surprised him recently with a beautiful showing of alyssum and nasturtium grown from seed. "They're always full of surprises, and always find some new way to make it better."

The New Garden—An Epilogue

This project became a family undertaking and laboratory for the couple's young children to explore and learn about the outdoors, including how much sun certain plants need, how long it takes to grow flowers from seed, how to handle rainwater, and the optimal time to prune, train, and care for their plants. The couple's handiwork became a decade-long hobby, improving their site in the process, and providing a welcoming entertaining space for neighborhood social gatherings for young and old alike.

Cost-Saving Alternatives

The entire yard reflects smart economics and being green, from the creative use of once-overlooked recycled materials and plants, many of which had to be slowly nursed back to health, to personalized projects like the fire pit and edible gardens.

Budget

Greg estimates the cost of work and materials at a fair market value of roughly U.S. $120,000, but his actual cost was less than U.S. $15,000 in materials. "It was worth every penny of the market value to spend time constructing our gardens together," he says of his time working side by side with Janie and their kids.

Challenges Along the Way

"Impatience at times on our part," says Greg. "Toward the final phases of work, we'd look back and say, 'I can't believe what this used to look like, and boy am I ready to be finished!' But I wouldn't trade a bit of it for the end result, and teaching our children the joy and balance of working toward a long-term goal with them in the process. We never realized we weren't 'finished' until we looked around and realized we were done."

PROJECT AND TEAM CREDITS: Client Greg and Janie Schaumburg **Location** Buffalo Grove, Illinois **Landscape designer** Greg Schaumburg, Bertog Landscape Co., Wheeling, Illinois, www.bertoglandscape.com **Project duration** 11 years **Completion** 2002–2013

104

DESIGN IS IN THE DETAILS

Mary Jo and Doug Marjama downsized and bought a home that she had shown as a real estate saleswoman and liked for its 100-year-old oak tree in the front yard. She also liked that the property's prime outdoor entertainment was at the front in a private courtyard. But what it lacked was any Japanese influence to become a suitable place for Mary Jo's Asian art collection, inspired by a childhood spent in Okinawa, Japan.

Site Problems

- Mixed materials
- Difficult site for pets to navigate safely
- Privacy for a master bathroom
- Existing pool needed new coping and tile

The hardscape was chopped up with different materials, including cracking concrete, rotting wood expansion joints, and Trex (composite) decking. A raised wood bench and decking surrounded the large oak tree, which dropped substantially below the ground level, which was fine for adults but not for small pets as they could easily fall into the pit. Furthermore, the owners felt the decking and bench did not give the tree adequate prominence. The master bathroom's sliding glass doors were located too close to the home's entry, which eliminated any sense of privacy.

Wish List

- More open space
- Privacy for the master bathroom
- Revamped setting to reflect a love of the Asian-inspired style
- Turn the existing majestic oak tree into a focal point

Finding a Professional

Landscape designer Michael Glassman had designed two other homes for the couple, so they were familiar with his work and he understood their style and how they liked to work.

Problem-Solving Solutions

Michael redesigned a new terrace. The contractor removed the old, cracking concrete and repoured the new space and covered it with a dark travertine flagstone. This unified the yard and gave the couple a much more expansive surface, which they liked. He painted the garage wall a dark gray to pick up the gray accent color in the travertine, and placed a Buddha sculpture fountain with decorative lights nearby to help establish a serene mood and also offer pleasant trickling water sounds.

To make the tree more of a focal point, he removed the decking and bench and installed a raised metal platform (called pan decking) that he overlaid with concrete and then covered in the same travertine as the courtyard. He covered the ground underneath the tree in various-sized river cobble- and monolithic stones. Cable railing all around the tree prevents the couple's dog and visiting pets from falling into the tree pit, yet allows full views of the oak's enormous trunk.

To provide bathroom privacy, Michael and Mary Jo designed laser-cut metal panels with a bamboo motif to suggest a small courtyard, and placed the couple's Japanese sculpture in front of the bathroom to further block views. The existing block wall that separates the sliding bathroom door from the front door became a water wall with a fire pit, another focal point.

Cost-Saving Solutions

Instead of a travertine-covered concrete, the clients could have chosen stamped concrete; bamboo screening also could have replaced the pricier laser-cut metal panels.

Budget

The couple spent 15 percent of the cost of their home, which was more than they had expected, but certain design elements they wanted added to the expense. "The project grew and took on a life of its own," says Glassman.

Opposite top: After: Kello travertine flagstone and the night lighting focused on the living architecture make the pool area glow.
Opposite bottom left: Before: Drab brushed concrete paving, square boxwood hedges, and a dirty cream-painted gate did not match the homeowners' Asian-inspired style. **Opposite bottom right:** After: New paving, sculptured planting, and a laser-cut bamboo gate transform the area into an Asian-inspired paradise.

Top left: Before: The large oak tree was surrounded by a wooden bench and deck. **Top center:** After: The open cable railing and the flat surface of the pan decking highlight the architectural form of the tree from its base. **Top right:** After: Laser-cut rusted metal panels provide privacy for the master bathroom. **Above:** After: The water and fire wall feature showcases the home's entry. The individual elements of this landscape illustrate how design is in the details. **Opposite left:** The master plan of the front courtyard. **Opposite top right:** Postscript after: With the tree removed and the hole filled, the yard has lost its main drama, though the new plantings provide a different kind of Asian-inspired architecture. **Opposite bottom right:** Postscript after: Until the Ginkgo trees grow to create shade, there is a new, open beauty.

Challenges Along the Way

When the contractor removed the coping around the existing pool, tiles fell off, so the pool had to be retiled, an unexpected extra cost, but which gave the homeowners the chance to make it more their own. Glassman helped pick a mottled gray ceramic tile. In addition, the salesman who sold them the travertine tile ran out of the stone, which delayed the project six weeks as it had been produced and shipped from Peru.

Key Design Details

- The pan decking that Michael designed highlights the tree's architectural features.
- The water and fire wall give the front entrance both drama and instant warmth.
- Michael and Mary Jo together designed the privacy screen, which a local artist cut and finished.

The New Garden—An Epilogue

The clients were excited to have a yard that became an extension of their home. The outside now flows into the inside seamlessly. They are also relieved to be able to allow their dog out to play without supervision for fear of its safety.

Postscript

Unfortunately, two weeks after the garden was completed, the main oak tree in the front courtyard collapsed due to age and weather, rotting from the inside out. Everyone involved was terribly upset. New work proceeded. The tree was removed, the hole was filled in with 80 yards (73 meters) of soil, and three specimen Ginkgo trees were planted to become the focal point of the yard, very different from the former result but equally beautiful and dramatic. When the tree fell, it damaged part of the garage as well, pointing up the value of the homeowner's insurance, which covered part of the replacement costs.

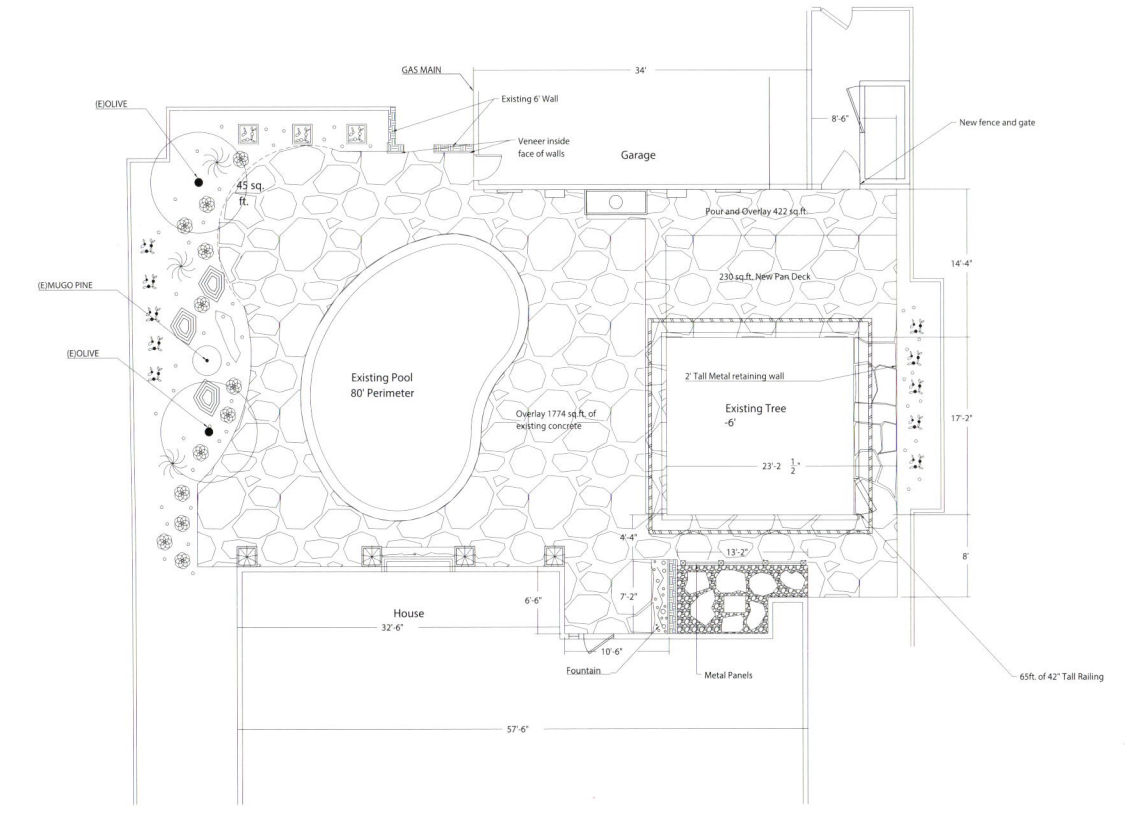

PROJECT AND TEAM CREDITS: Client Mary Jo and Doug Marjama **Location** Sacramento County, California **Landscape designer** Michael Glassman, Michael Glassman & Associates, Sacramento, California, www.michaelglassman.com **Contractor** Josh Martin, Charis Pools & Landscape Inc., www.charislandscape.com **Metal artist** Allen Polinsky, 209-3339-9494 **Project duration** Five months **Completion** 2013

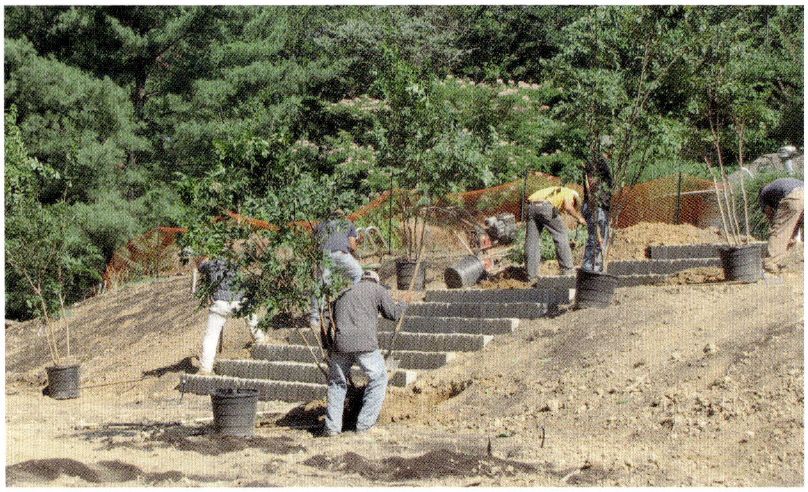

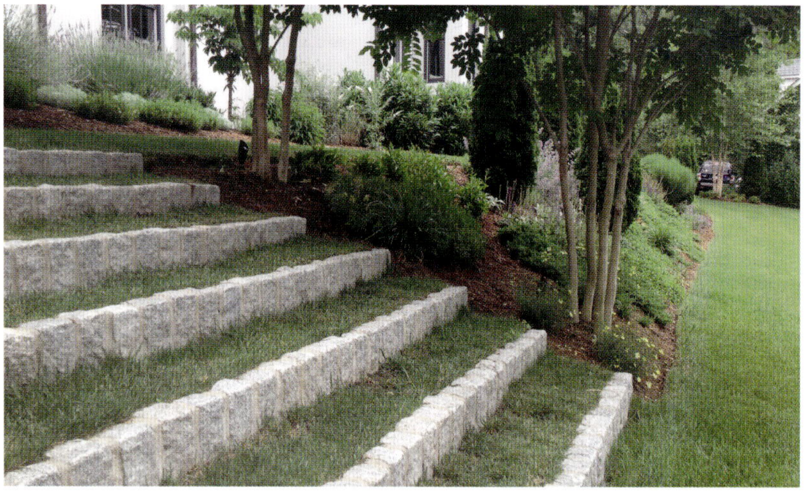

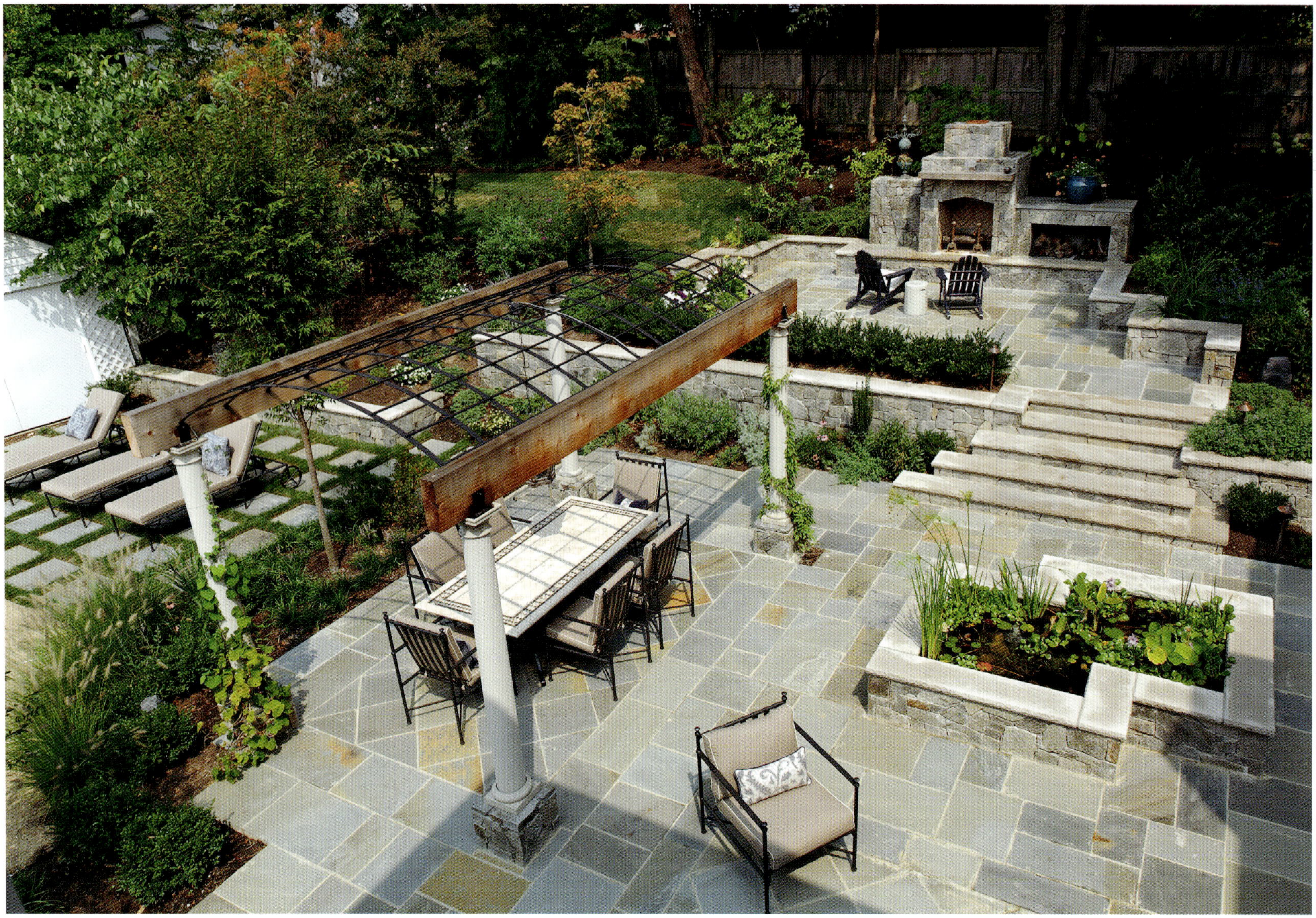

BUCOLIC FARM REDO

During the renovation of their small historic farmhouse on a two-acre (0.8-hectare) site that included a pool and tennis court, Alex and Caulley Deringer were ready to tackle the exterior and its many challenges. They hired Fyffe Landscape Architecture in Arlington, Virginia, to help integrate the existing outdoor features into a beautiful living space. A prime goal was to unify the interior and exterior "rooms" with amenities for a seamless environment where they could entertain family and friends but also enjoy everyday living. Landscape architect Susanne Fyffe developed a plan that incorporate all the clients' desired functions—places for children to play, everyone to dine, entertain on a small and large scale, cook, and circulate.

Site Problems

- Steep grade change of 20 feet (6 meters) over the 70-foot-wide (21.3-meter-wide) property with potential for erosion
- Need to direct water onto other parts of the site rather than have it flow onto neighbors' properties

Wish List

- Identifiable circulation throughout the site
- Entertainment areas for different activities, including cooking, dining, swimming, and tennis
- A custom, signature stone fireplace
- Play spaces for the children to include a soccer field, sledding hill, and trampoline
- Expanded lounging areas at the pool side
- Upgrade of the tennis court and pool infrastructure
- Renovate the front driveway and create a signature entrance
- Install low-maintenance and four-season plantings

Finding a Professional

The Deringers found Susanne through a friend who had also hired her firm. "We've been around for 25-plus years and find most of our work through referrals. We are not a design build firm, but have long-standing relationships with a variety of tradespeople, including masons, landscapers, carpenters, welders, plumbers, electricians, irrigation contractors and others. We tap these resources to provide the necessary constructed elements for each project," Susanne says.

Planning the Budget

"We typically provide a schematic master plan and develop a rough order of costs for various elements that comprise the plan. Once the scope is refined in collaboration with the owner, we secure more detailed estimates based on drawings and conversations with trade contractors and develop the final budget. Construction then begins. During the process, the build-out becomes more visible, and the small details become important. As with any design and construction process, changes and needed refinements crop up once things are visible in 3-D. In the case of this project, having a savvy designer as a client helped make this a truly collaborative process, which also remained mindful of the overall budget."

Problem-Solving Solutions

Susanne took the massive cross-slope grade change on this site and turned it into an asset. She eliminated the change and erosion issues by designing a multitiered gardenscape that steps down the slope—a custom fireplace and wood storage area at the top act as a retaining and seat wall. Local Foggy Bottom fieldstone walls and step risers capped with Indiana limestone lead down to the main entertainment level. This is where a built-in grill/bar, fish pond/seat wall, and sitting area come together. These elements are anchored by a wrought-iron-topped antique timber pergola that surrounds the main dining table, which, in turn, is highlighted by a hanging lantern overhead.

A Chinese fringe tree is on an axis and visible through the side entrance pergola. All the living and dining room French doors open to the Pennsylvania

Opposite top left: Before: Terracing the slope of the property with granite cobbles and lawn steps created two levels.
Opposite top right: After: This graceful set of steps is flanked by sweeping perennials cascading down the slopes, accented with upright evergreens and an allée of white crepe myrtles. **Opposite bottom:** After: A view from the master bedroom balcony; a fish pond, dining terrace and, in the distance, a fireplace for gathering.

flagstone terrace with its diamond-patterned "rug" forming an intimate space for the outdoor seating area. Boulder-lined grass steps lead down to the 5-foot-wide (1.5-meter-wide) lawn and walkway parallel to the residence that connects to the drive and serves as an entrance for larger events. Another graceful slope leads down to the soccer field with the trampoline slipped into the grade to allow at grade entry.

Dry-stream boulder swales in the lower grade changes act as catch basins to collect all the house and site's runoff. But water then flows on into a slight grade dip that meanders and is lined with boulders, rocks and water-loving plants to slow the flow of water and direct it away from neighboring properties.

In the front, Susanne designed a grand stone pier with limestone house numbers inset, a wide cobble apron for a better looking and more functional vehicle turnaround, a gracious flagstone-paved main entry, and a pedestrian transition circle further identifying the side entrance connection to the rear terrace and mud room.

Cost-Saving Alternatives

The most important aspect of the project is its easy circulation, and how spaces and activities are organized logically. Cost did not affect these choices, but materials did make a difference. The stone wall and pillars that were used are more expensive than if a timber wall and pillars were used, even with plants layered over the timbers to conceal them to save money. Instead of cobblestones and exposed aggregate driveway with a fieldstone banding at the front, asphalt was installed and accented at the front apron.

Budget

The budget was about 20 percent of the value of the house.

Top: The dining terrace and fish pond with the pool in the distance. The pergola was made from precast concrete columns, antique wooden beams, and handcrafted wrought iron. **Above left:** Guests can converse with the cook over a drink. **Above right:** Nepta, salvia and hydrangeas border the walkway to the rear terrace. **Opposite:** Creating an overall master plan allowed the project to be built in phases. The landscape architect incorporated the existing pool and tennis court and created the circular driveway, the outdoor room, and the soccer field.

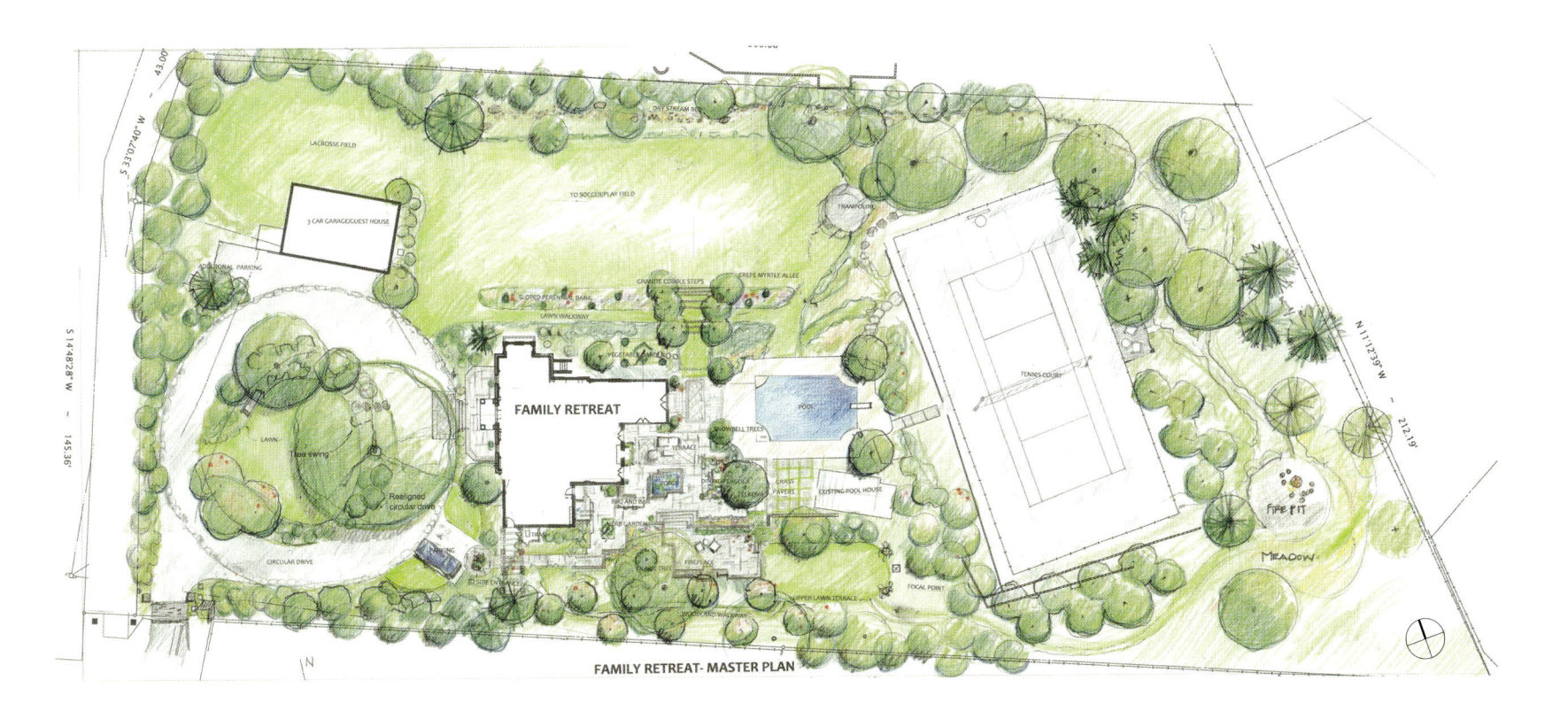

Challenges Along the Way

Weather and rushing a project are major issues in all projects. Timing and scheduling become very important aspects to ensure steady progress. Sometimes owners change their minds on some or several design details, and even decide to hold off on certain decisions. The key to overall success in such cases is having a master plan from the start so all can be done in phases, if desired. In this particular project, finalizing the contract and lining up the start date caused a delay in beginning construction. Once construction was underway, we hurried along to stay on track, says Susanne. Scheduling different contractors sometimes turned into overlaps and required juggling multiple deadlines. The weather and fine-tuning design details and a tight budget also became challenges.

The overall master plan helped keep everything on track and will continue to be important to finish the development of the property in phases down the road.

Key Design Details

- The side entry looks like part of the house, provides easy access, and screens the rear garden at the same time.
- The custom-designed stone fireplace and wrought-iron pergola with historic timbers each serve as a major focal point.

The New Garden—An Epilogue

They love their new property and feel that they are living at a resort every day. For Susanne, the project reaffirmed the importance of great details and making all choices in the beginning to secure the best pricing.

PROJECT AND TEAM CREDITS: Client Alex and Caulley Deringer **Location** Alexandria, Virginia **Landscape architect** Susanne Fyffe, Fyffe Landscape Architecture, Arlington, Virginia, www.fyffela.com **Landscape and mason contractor** Cesar Monroy, Monroy Construction, 4705 Sellman Road, Beltsville, Maryland **Lighting and irrigation** Reed Libby, Affordable Lighting and Irrigation, 133 Patrick Street SE, Vienna, Virginia **Project duration** Four to six months (for most of the work) **Completion** 2010–2011

Top: After: The view from a second-floor window showcases the two-tiered waterfalls and patio spaces surrounded by verdant gardens.
Above left: Before: The job site proved to be a difficult topography since the company was building into the side of a hill. The new construction was like working with a blank slate, offering the freedom to be as creative as possible without any structures hindering goals. **Above right:** After: A view from above the pool shows the paving of irregular crab orchard stone at the pool area.

WATERFALL FANTASY

"Sometimes, a significant challenge can yield the most imaginative results," says New Jersey landscape designer Chris Cipriano. The severe slope of a barren site where a new neoclassical brick house would be built consisted of a drop of about 26 feet (7.9 meters) from the rear property line to where the back door would be constructed. By terracing the land, the homeowners got the pool and hot tub they wanted, along with two dramatic waterfalls, big stone boulders, stone steps, and terraces for sitting and entertaining. Their front yard was also landscaped and improved.

Site Problems
- Severe slope throughout the site, but especially in rear

Wish List
- Swimming pool with hot tub, waterfalls, colored LED lights
- Entertaining terraces
- Four-season plantings
- Stylish driveway and front walk

Finding a Professional
The homeowners' builder had worked with Chris in the past and highly recommended the firm to the owners.

Project Challenges
- A 26-foot (7.9-meter) slope in back from a rear fence to the back door
- Need to carefully calculate total amount of impervious coverage for walks, terraces, and the driveway, since the suburban community where the house is located (and most of New Jersey) has stringent limitations. Some offer a credit for impervious coverage; others don't.
- Need for good water collection, which since the project was finished, dictates even more piping and more infrastructure to avoid water running off into the street, overflowing sewers, streams, and neighboring homes. "Nowadays, you need 1 gallon (3.7 liters) per every square foot," Chris says.
- Whether to go formal or informal posed a design and cost challenge, so Cipriano worked out two designs for his clients to consider.

Problem-Solving Solutions
The suburban community's strict limits on what percentage of a site can be paved meant that Chris first focused on developing plateaus in the hilly site that would work for entertaining and siting the pool, hot tub, and steps. These plateaus were kept as small as possible to stay within the prescribed limits. Because of the site, he designed the salt-water pool as two units—an upper level for cooling off and swimming, and a lower basin for catching water and recycling it back; each basin has its own waterfall and custom mosaic-tile rims, and the falls are visible from every vantage point in the rear. Chris also placed the eight-person hot tub on the upper level, along with a small sitting area fashioned from Tennessee gray crab orchard stone that was laid in irregular shapes for a more casual, contemporary look. Similar stone was fashioned into dramatic steps down to the bigger entertaining space, which can fit up to 80 people, and was constructed from regular, more formal-looking slabs of Pennsylvania bluestone, which Chris does not use by water because it becomes too hot for bare feet.

All about there are large boulders placed vertically to mimic natural outcroppings and pinned together with steel rods that help hold one another in place, as well as retain soil and plantings. He brought in more than 1,000 tons of boulders, some from Pennsylvania and some from local construction sites that were blasting and eager to recycle rather than see materials go to landfill.

To screen the site from neighbors, Chris planted a combination of Douglas fir, Norway blue spruce, and white pines. In front of these, he layered a mix of hardy deciduous viburnum, rhododendron, evergreens, spiraea, and lots of ornamental grasses, such as miscanthus, which look good in all seasons and also work well to hold soil in place.

He planted roses in sunny spots, and throughout introduced perennials, such as coreopsis, sedum "Autumn Joy," Black-eyed Susans, Stella Dora day lilies, and initially some annuals until the perennials matured and spread, and the annuals would not be needed. He made all choices to gain four-season color and texture. The spruces, junipers, and holly offer wonderful winter interest.

To make the yard work for entertaining, Chris placed an outdoor fireplace, full-service kitchen and bar, koi pond, and lots of seating. In the front yard, he paved steps in the same bluestone in a random pattern but used less costly Unilock pavers on the driveway. In the front, guests are greeted with stylish twin walkways that wind around an entry fountain with precast balustrades and brick walls.

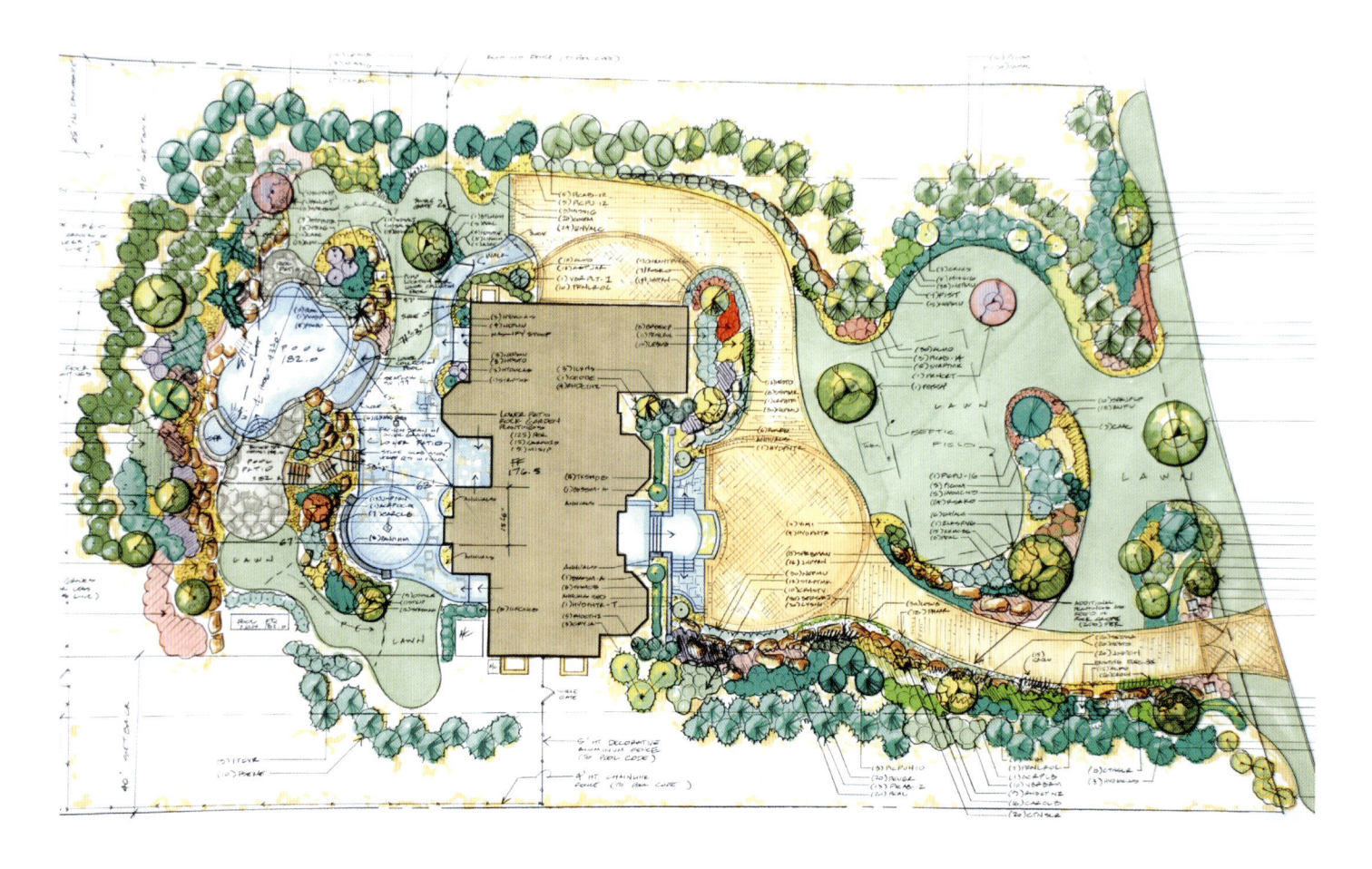

Top: The plan shows all the details of the property, including the pool, spa, hardscaping, and landscaping. Design by designer William Moore. **Above left:** Perennials and ornamental grasses were installed within the boulder rock outcroppings for stabilization and aesthetics. **Above right:** The view from the raised spa is of several dramatic multicascading waterfalls, inspired by the basalt mountain formations of the northwest United States. **Opposite left:** Regrading, terracing, as well as using multiple stone patterns, the company created "rooms" without building any walls. **Opposite right:** Viewed from the pools waterfalls, lush plantings were installed to soften the large amount of rock walls needed to retain the sloping property. Different colors in the landscape and the cascading water add drama, as well as beauty.

Cost-Saving Alternatives

Initially, the homeowners debated between a formal and informal design and opted for the latter, which is less expensive—about U.S. $100,000 or so because of less brickwork. But to cut costs further for other homeowners, Chris recommends precast pavers rather than stone set in concrete, and instead of large waterfalls use precast retaining walls. To save on flowers, shrubs and trees, Chris recommends massing flowers, particularly a huge field of ornamental grasses. "They look spectacular in all seasons and are good for slope retention," he says.

Budget

The budget was about 15 percent of the home's initial value.

Challenges Along the Way

To set the stones vertically, the project required extra equipment to be brought in to pin the largest stones to one another so that they stayed put and retained the soil.

Key Design Details

- Two dramatic, steep waterfalls
- Vanishing-edge pool with diving rock
- Terraces at different levels
- Colorful plantings interspersed between stones and lawn
- Great variety of stones used in terms of size, shape, and color

The New Garden—An Epilogue

Chris gained a greater appreciation for intricate stone-masonry, piping needed to recycle water, and how stones can be pinned in place with steel rods on a steep slope. For Chris the job was also a delight. "Between the challenges of the municipality, difficulties of the site, and a client who had faith in our creative direction even when he didn't understand what we were trying to build, the project was a fun and rewarding experience," he says. The verdict from the clients is that they now "never want to leave their back yard," says Chris, "which is always the biggest compliment I can receive. They love to entertain family and friends in their yard." Shrubs, trees, and flowers have grown and filled out over the last few years with greater color and textures, which also provide more privacy from the neighbors.

PROJECT AND TEAM CREDITS: Location Saddle River, New Jersey **Landscape designer** Chris Cipriano, Cipriano Landscape Design, Mahwah, New Jersey, www.njcustomswimmingpools.com **Project duration** Six months **Completion** 2007

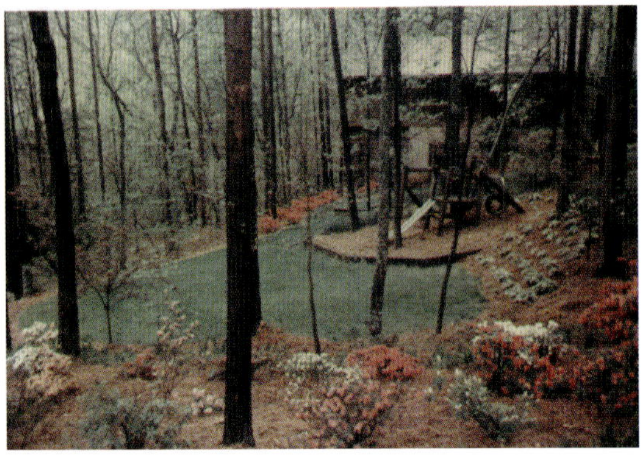
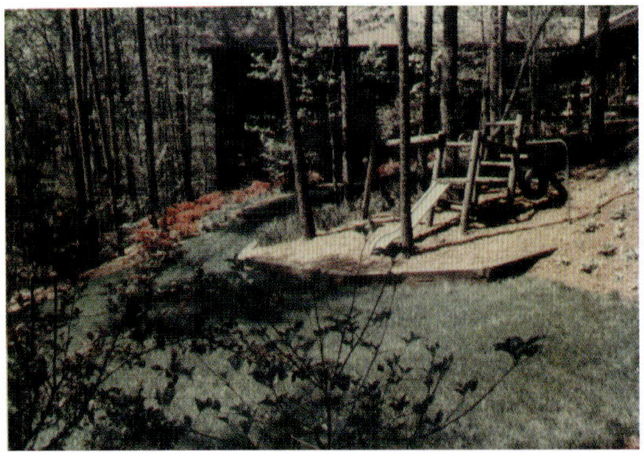
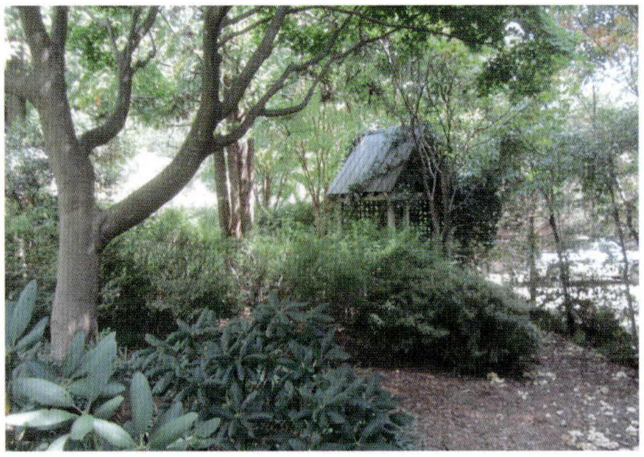
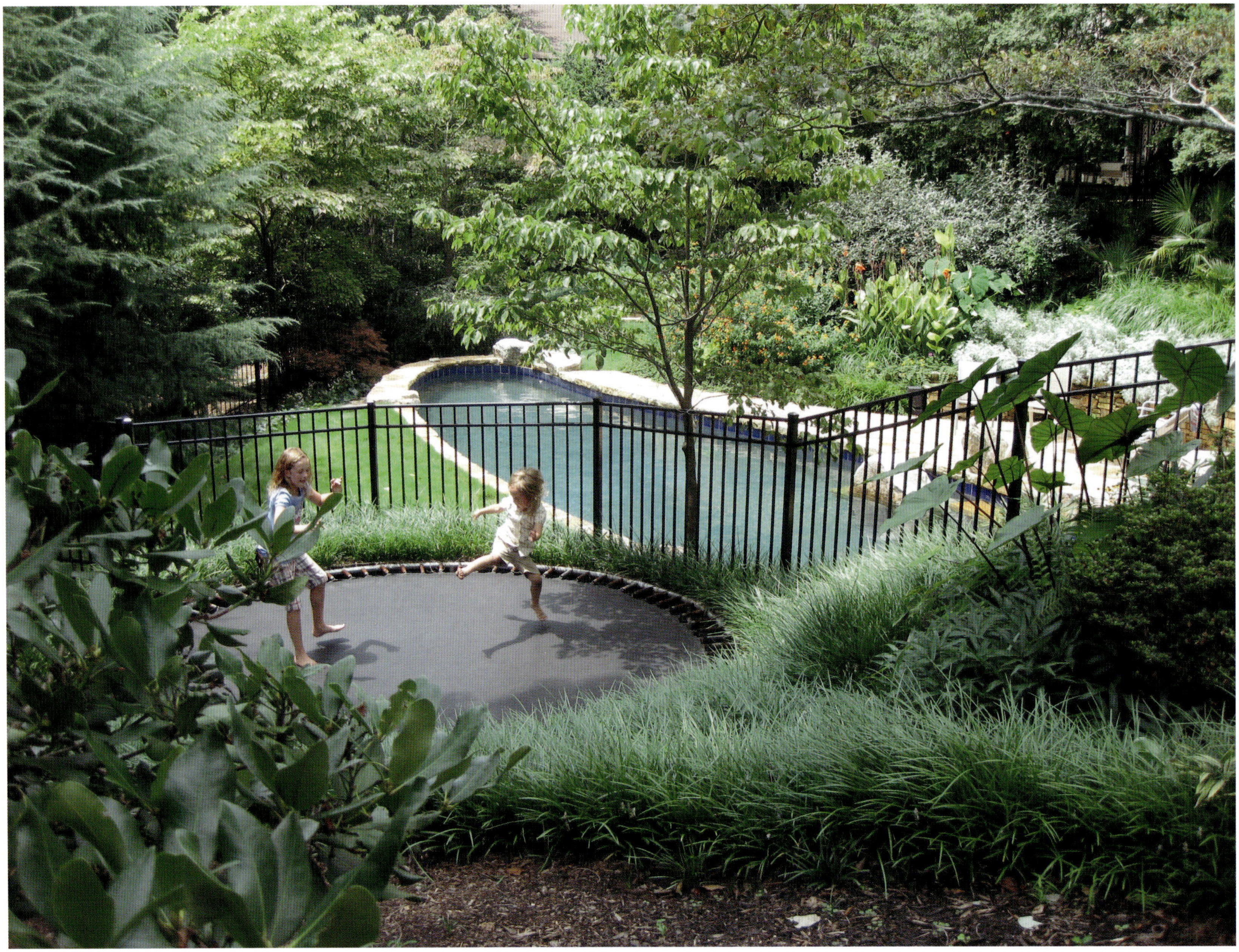

EXPERIMENTAL LAB

There's no better place to learn firsthand the wrath of Mother Nature, as well as the beauty she can bestow, which is what landscape architect Bill Renninger and his wife Beth found after they constructed their house in 1975. It was to be a home for their growing family of three daughters, the location for his home office, and an experimental garden for his gardening work for himself and clients. Yet, another goal was to add numerous water features for family pleasure and find the right plant materials for shaded and sunny areas, and to attract appropriate birds and wildlife.

Site Problems

- Steeply sloping site in Greenville, South Carolina, comprising 1.5 acres (0.6 hectares) with 20 percent to 40 percent of steep slopes

Wish List

- Add water features, including a swimming pool, koi pond, and natural creek
- Find the right spots for sun- and shade-loving plants
- Include materials that would attract hummingbirds and butterflies

Finding a Professional

This site is the personal home and experimental garden project of the landscape architect Bill Renninger.

Project Challenges

- Proper siting of features, such as a pool, waterfall, koi pond, sunken trampoline, and office
- Desire for experimental botanical garden on a steeply sloping site
- Blending a trampoline into the landscape

Problem-Solving Solutions

Nothing can be done about changing climate conditions, Bill has learned firsthand. Last year due to a freeze, the coldest in 15 years, he lost plants, such as rosemary, confederate jasmine, zoysia sod, certain bamboo, and some hydrangea blooms. "All of this can seem frustrating," he says, yet he turned the proverbial lemons into lemonade and gained an educational experience. "What I have learned more from this one project has sometimes come the hard way. I may walk outside during the day looking for sun in the winter or shade in the summer, and there will be delightful surprises, such as all the hummingbirds and butterflies at the lantana," he says.

To improve the aesthetics of the pool, built in 2006 in a long kidney shape and suitable for lap swimming, Bill added a boulder waterfall and small upper pool, the latter designed with future grandchildren in mind. To screen a fence, he planted various types of bamboo, palms, loropetulum, and cleyera. To cope with sun and shade, he pruned and removed some trees to allow in more light for areas of zoysia. Despite popular perceptions, daffodils, Encore Azaleas, certain hydrangeas and some impatiens also thrive there. For the shady areas, he planted autumn fern, Aspidistra, Aucuba, Florida leucothoe, azaleas, Lenten roses, and sedges.

Because the homeowners also wanted to attract birds and butterflies, he planted Miss Huff Lantana in sunny areas, and plants of a complementary color, such as Bog Sage, black and blue Salvia, and "Indigo Spires" Salvia next to the lantana. "On a sunny day, we may have dozens of butterflies and bumblebees, but on a cloudy day, they don't come," Bill says. To keep away herons from the koi pond, he inserts black netting over the pond for six months of the year. "Whether coincidence or not, herons only bother us in winter; fish are much slower moving in the cold weather then," he explains.

Cost-Saving Alternatives

Bill started with small specimen trees in many cases—a bare-root Japanese maple seedling, for example, has grown to 30 feet (9 meters) in 30 years. His experiences have taught him a lot about horticulture.

Budget

This has been calculated at 50 percent of the value of the house. "We'll never recover that when we sell, but it's been worth it," Bill explains.

Opposite top, left to right: Before: The house during the 1980s with pine trees. This was before ice storms, including the "storm of the century," destroyed all 100 of the pine trees. *Opposite bottom:* After: Twenty years later, a trampoline and the newly constructed pool are separated by a metal fence, which imitates wrought iron.

Top left: Looking down on the pool and its handsome Tennessee fieldstone decking and coping, a material similar to flagstone. **Top center:** The goldfish pond, between the pool and house and off the kitchen deck. **Top right:** A pergola shades a swing, built in the mid-1990s for the homeowners' pleasure. **Bottom:** The garden plan includes different areas, such as an experimental garden, literally for the owner to experiment and see what would do well and what wouldn't. It sits near an arched arbor with climbing vines and roses. **Opposite:** Variegated dwarf bamboo in the foreground with a glimpse of steps leading down to the pool; large boulders were used, which also came from Tennessee.

Challenges Along the Way

- Climate conditions, which can bring ice storms and an element of unpredictability regarding what will survive, or turn shaded areas into sunny ones

- Some plants thriving too well and becoming invasive, including certain bamboo, five-leaf akebia, Lousiana flag iris, and horsetail

- Some wildlife coming where they're not wanted, such as herons to the koi pond for "lunch"

Key Design Details

- The goal was to create inviting outdoor areas that lead seamlessly from one area to the next; the "experimental garden" was designed to be inviting, but be a bit shrouded and mysterious.

- Guests to the property are always pleased and even surprised as they walk through the gate and under the shaded arched arbor with each of the 12 posts having a different vine.

- The sunny pond is full of water iris, umbrella palm, cat tails, and a couple of friendly, croaking frogs.

The New Garden—An Epilogue

As trees have grown and sun has disappeared in certain spots over the past 40 years, Bill has found that keeping small areas of zoysia sod and certain bulbs alive, and herons away from fish in the koi pond, continue to prove a challenge. Planning and executing the garden additions became a delightful and educational experience for the family, including the daughters who are now grown. It also proved a professional success and the garden won a Merit Award in 1997 from the South Carolina chapter of the American Society of Landscape Architects.

PROJECT AND TEAM CREDITS: Client Bill and Beth Renninger **Location** Greenville, South Carolina **Landscape architect** William Renninger, William Renninger Associates, Greenville, South Carolina, www.williamrenningerassociates.com **Project duration** 30 years—but Bill says the garden never will be done. "We're always wanting to learn more about plants and materials. In my garden, I have the luxury that I can say that mistakes turn out to be an invaluable learning experience."

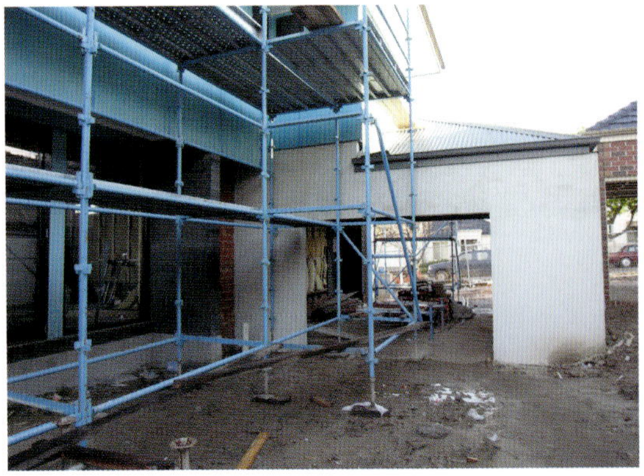

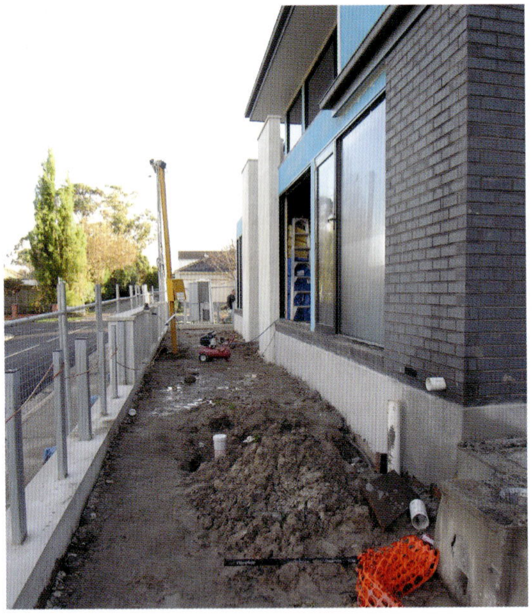

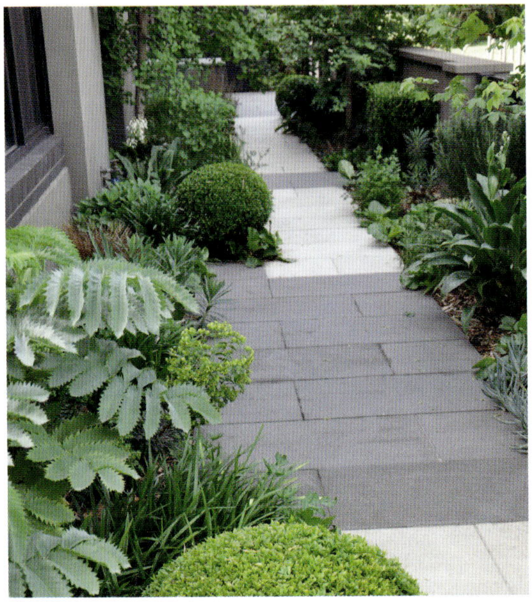

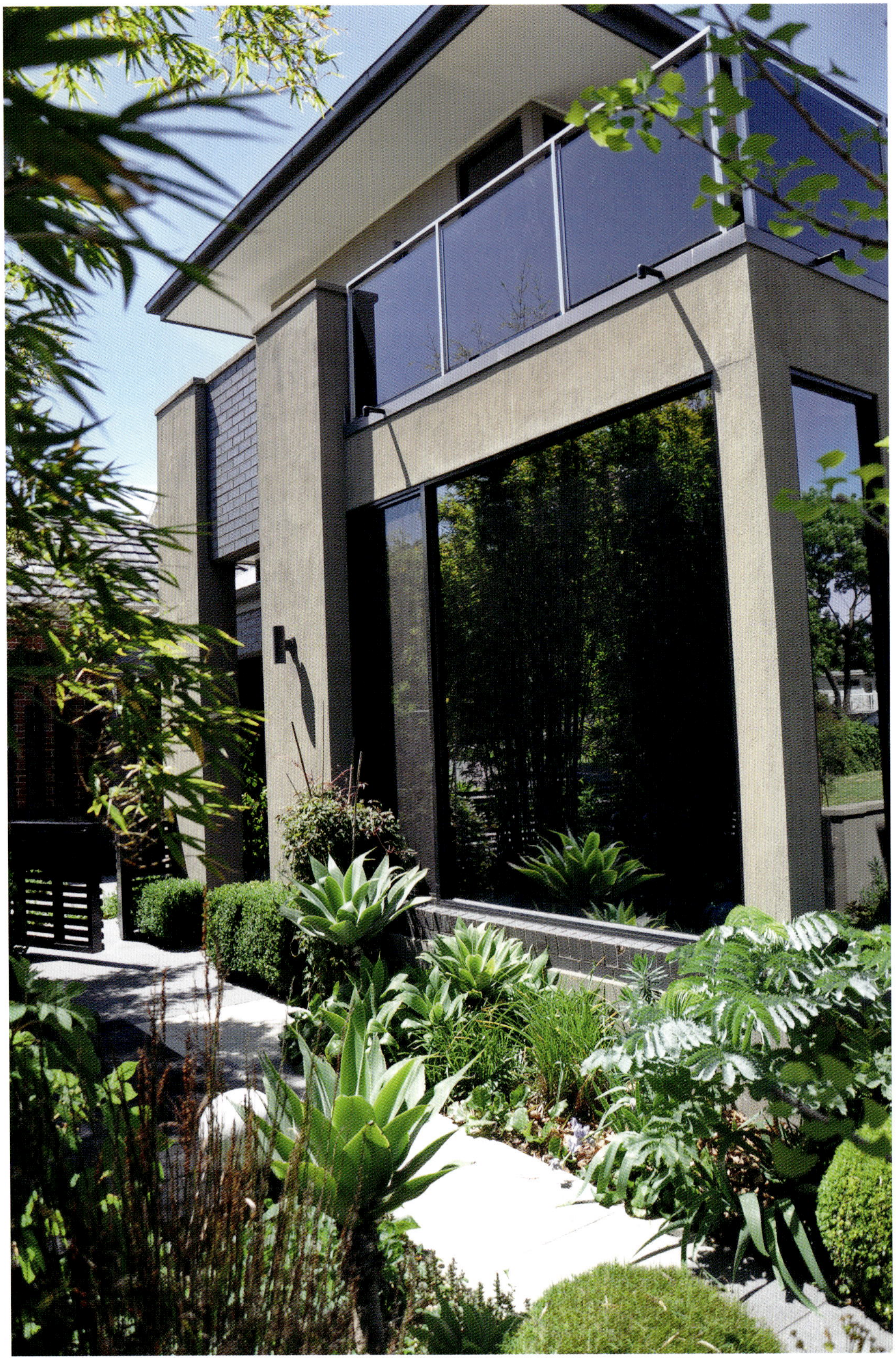

LOOK: NO LAWN

Almost nine years ago, Australian landscape designer Jim Fogarty and his wife Victoria moved into a brand new house, which gave him a clean palette to work with from the start. Yet, he needed to take into account a neighbor's two-story house that would look down on his pool courtyard once finished, and a major community restriction that limits non-penetrable surfaces. "That meant that at least 35 percent of the space had to remain as garden beds, mulched areas, but no lawn," says Jim, whose eponymous firm is based in Malvern, Australia.

Site Problems

- Small site needed a clever use of space
- Water restrictions meant no lawn since there could be no watering of it
- Allowing for a minimum site coverage of 35 percent penetrable surface, such as garden beds
- Needed to position a 2,642-gallon (10,000-liter) rainwater tank underground
- Needed to be smart about how the pool's safety barrier was incorporated into the small space

Wish List

- Pool
- Informal outdoor entertainment
- A nice, attractive front garden that also helped to provide shade from the hot afternoon sun
- Outdoor bar
- Front deck area that was more modern in appearance

Finding a Professional

The project was the landscape architect's own home and site.

Project Challenges

- The garden was designed during Melbourne's tough drought, which added another concern—how would new plantings be watered with stricter rules in place?

Problem-Solving Solutions

Because of the drought and the community's ban on watering, Jim designed the site without any lawn. He made rainwater a priority to conserve and recycle by installing a 2,642-gallon (10,000-liter) rainwater tank, hiding it under a front deck. To design a green garden that would appear abundant even during a drought, Jim used hardscape materials, including reconstituted concrete pavers and split-faced bluestone cobblestones, all in an interesting pattern whether viewed at ground level or from the second story of his home. In the pool courtyard, the cobblestones soften and break up the small space and make it visually enchanting, almost like a three-dimensional work of art. In fact, he inserted a wall sculpture by artist Valissa Butterworth, which was inspired by wet sand at low tide. To maximize outdoor space, Jim "borrowed" his garage as an extra entertainment space. He changed the garage's white lights to a more hip, novel red, and at night the garage looks like a submarine with PVC and copper pipes.

To keep the garage and courtyard separate, Jim designed a bar that doubles as a safety wall for the pool, cladding it in double-chiseled lava stone. On another wall, clad in the same material, water cascades down into the pool, creating a shimmering effect at night under blue LED lights. A bamboo pool fence works as a second line of defense, important as a backup since the clients have children. If desired, it can be taken down in seconds as it's built in three interlocking panels. Even better is that it was built using bamboo that grows in his and his wife's yard, is a good source of mulch, and can be a climbing surface for other plants in the garden. At night when the couple often entertains, they can turn on lighting, designed by Light on Landscape, a company in Melbourne: blue lights illuminating the lava stone under the bar; red shining down on an outdoor shower. In the front garden, Jim designed a large bed with interesting green foliage and a black-stained floating timber deck with benches by Dwell by Jo.

Who needs a lawn? Not these folk. But they did want additional plantings, which would include ones to screen the neighbors' house. This was a tough decision because Jim wanted something that would grow tall but not wide, have foliage at ground level so he and his wife wouldn't have to look just at tree trunks or have precarious limbs

Opposite top left: The pool courtyard before construction began. *Opposite center left:* The side garden before landscaping began.
Opposite bottom left: The side garden after landscaping (looking from the other end). Lots of green shapes provide the planting focus.
Opposite right: The front garden five years after planting. A small deck sits among lush green planting that reflects a variety of leaf shapes. Bambusa gracilis, a type of clumping bamboo, provides shade.

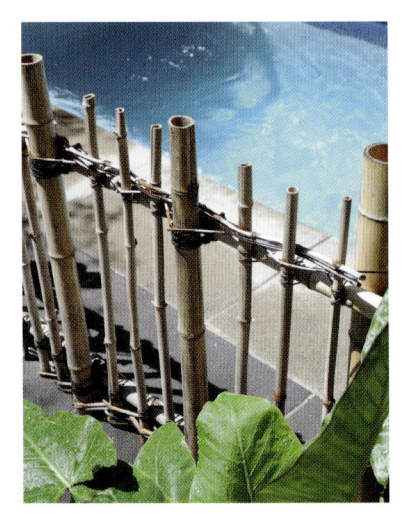

Top left: A bamboo pool fence provides extra safety to the already secure pool-safe perimeter; this is important with young children. The fence verticals are made from home-grown bamboo. **Top center:** Hand-split bluestone cobbles provide paving texture and lead the eye to the wall sculpture by Valissa Butterworth that hangs above the pool. **Top right:** Garden lighting can transform small garden spaces at night and create wonderful ambience. **Above:** The front garden with the black-stained timber deck hides an underground rainwater tank. Contrasting shapes share a focus on green to provide a lush cool-looking garden in the heat of summer. **Opposite:** The plan of the garden, especially the paving layout, color and texture, was planned so that it also looks good from balconies above. The aim was also to fashion different garden areas despite the small square footage.

overshadowing their courtyard and stealing sun, and also not create mess for their pool. He decided on black bamboo, planted with root control barriers, along with some liriope, ligularia, bergenia, and ajuga as groundcover to help keep the leaf drop from blowing into the pool.

To make the front garden interesting with lots of foliage plants and cope with not having any lawn, Jim designed a black-stained floating timber deck to sit amid the dense greenery. He used clumping bamboo for height but chose one that doesn't spread, and underneath it he planted Solomon's seal, hellebores, hosta, and more liriope. Lights placed under the bamboo create a great show at night from the dining room.

Instead of using color, Jim inserted lots of textures and shapes. He used clipped lineal hedging that contrasts well with clipped balls of Luma apiculate, Viburnum odoratissimum, and Buxus microphylla. He found Bamboo Bambini (Pogonatherum paniceum) to work since it's drought-tough, can be clipped into rough shaggy balls for definition, and has the most lush lime-green grass—like foliage that helps fill difficult parts of garden beds. He also planted herbs, such as rosemary, catmint, chives, tarragon, parsley, and sage for cooking.

Cost-Saving Alternatives

The use of gravel paths for the side garden would have reduced costs, as would the use of more pavers for an exposed aggregate surface instead of flagstone cobblestones.

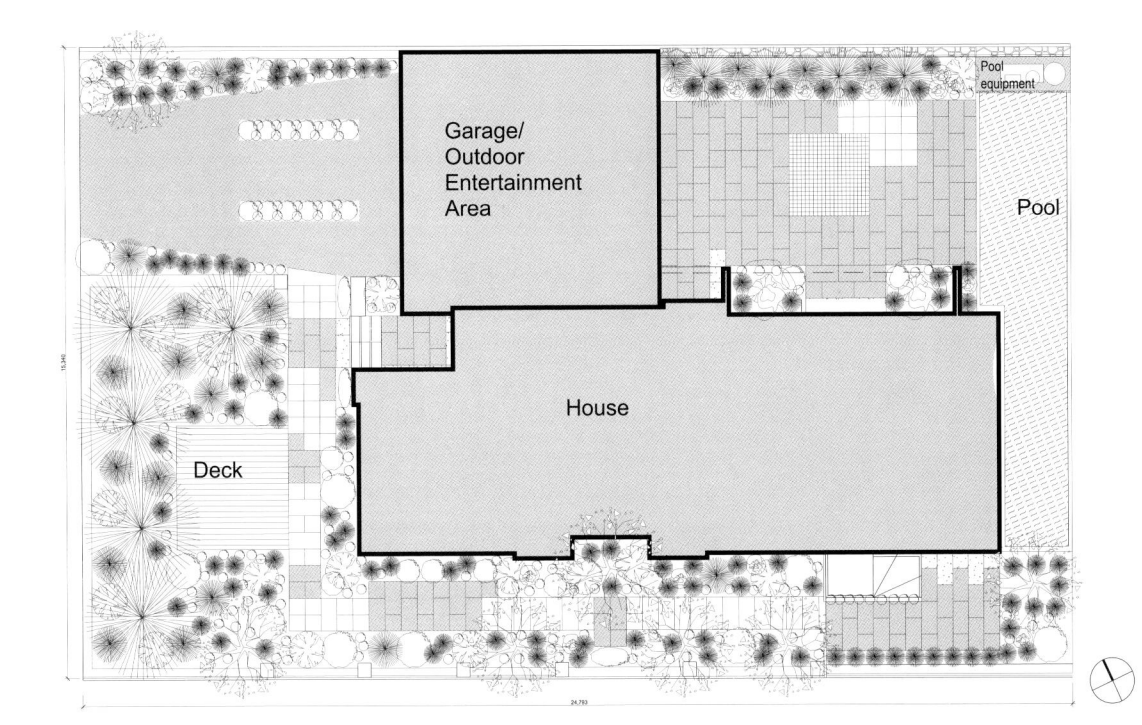

Budget

The budget was about 15 percent of property's value at the time, plus a design fee for others.

Challenges Along the Way

The yard is near a creek, and groundwater from the creek was seeping down the hill and rising to the surface. When the garden was planted, Jim used some plants that could tolerate having their root zone moist until the plants reached enough of a critical mass so they could use up excess water.

Key Design Details

- Wall feature by Valissa Butterworth that sits overlooking the pool
- Water feature that trickles down the chiseled lava stone into the pool below

The New Garden—An Epilogue

Not only does Jim enjoy the garden, but he and his wife also love the buzz from seeing so many neighbors and strangers look over their front fence as they walk past. The clever use of space has added to their lifestyle. "What I love about the bar is the ability to entertain in a very casual manner in reflection of my wife's time spent living in Dubai. We lay out platters of *mezze* (Middle Eastern–style dips and breads) and have casual drinks and conversation. This garden is not made for outdoor tables and chairs due to lack of space. The bar is very space-friendly, and a blue LED light under the bar lip creates a very attractive mood in which to entertain at night," he says. The deck in the front garden has saved the couple the expense of a mower and is now a great place to relax and soak up the late afternoon sun. "We wave and chat with our neighbors, many of whom comment as they stroll by on how lush and green our garden looks," he says.

PROJECT AND TEAM CREDITS: Client Jim and Victoria Fogarty **Location** Ashburton, Melbourne, Australia **Landscape architect** Jim Fogarty, Jim Fogarty Design, Malvern East, Victoria, Australia, www.jimfogartydesign.com.au **Contractor** Ashlar Landscapes **Wall sculpture** The Mod Collective, www.modcollective.com.au **Lighting** Light on Landscape, www.lightonlandscape.com.au **Project duration** Five months **Completion** 2005

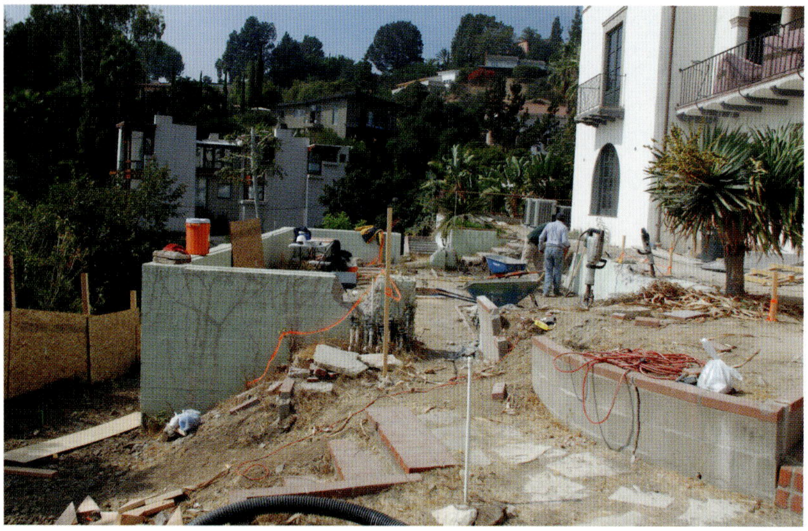

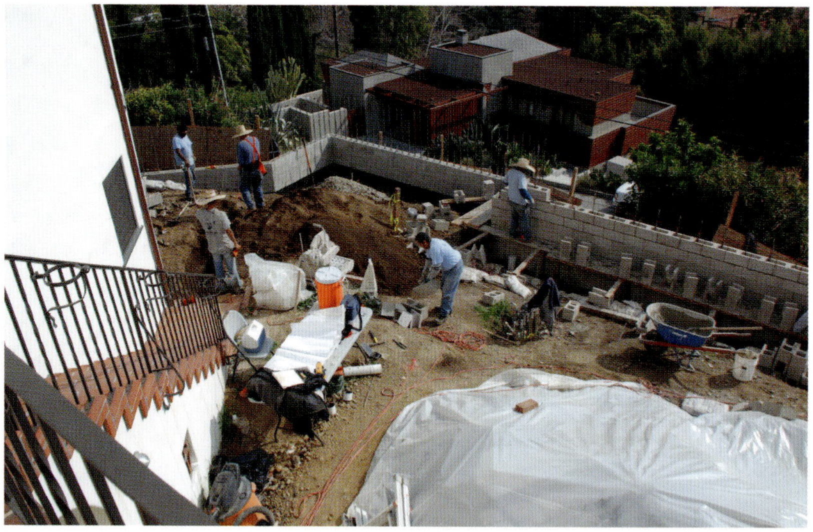

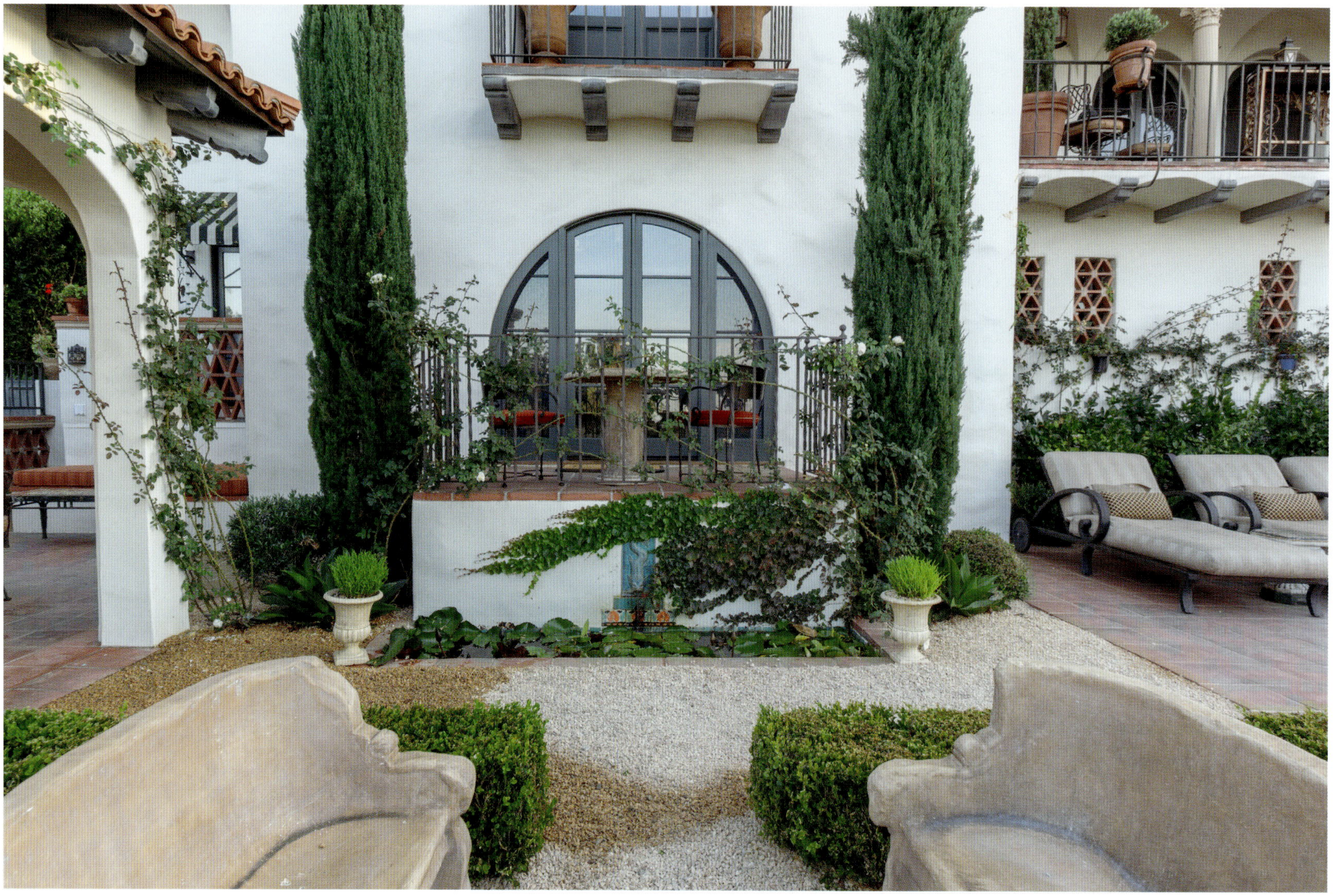

SPANISH COLONIAL REVIVAL MUSE

Homeowners Bruce Hatton and Tom Young wanted a garden to complement the extensive restoration they did of their 6,500-square-foot (604-square-meter) home. Originally designed by prominent architect Paul Williams in a classic Spanish Colonial Revival style in 1928 in the Hollywood Hills area of Los Angeles, the home was envisioned as a place where the men could frequently entertain large groups outdoors in a series of "rooms" for dining, swimming, relaxing, and getting away for private moments. They also wanted a garden with great architectural detail that would echo the home's style. For landscape designer Anthony Exter, the good part was that the home offered so much inspiration with a traditional hipped roof with red clay tiles, multipaned windows, smooth stucco façade, Corinthian columns, arched entrance door, and courtyard. And throughout the interior, there was additional inspiration with period fireplaces, box-beamed, coffered, stenciled ceilings, and wrought-iron detailing. But best of all, the property was almost a blank slate that would allow Tony to work his garden magic, though he needed to take into account a very steep slope with few flat spaces.

Site Problems

- Very steep slope
- Not enough flat space for the homeowners' long wish list of amenities

Wish List

- Swimming pool and spa
- Mediterranean-style garden
- Outdoor kitchen and covered dining area
- Fire pit and lounging areas
- Private garden areas
- Vintage fountains and objects
- Inviting motor court at front
- Cohesiveness of design

Finding a Professional

The couple admired a hillside garden that landscape designer Tony had completed, and which had been featured in a garden design magazine.

Project Challenges

- Lack of usable flat space
- Strict city permit rules—the home had received Historical-Cultural-Monument designation, which dictated limitations in the garden's amount of hardscape and aesthetic options
- Complex engineering to construct a pool into the hillside, with huge retaining walls and subterranean support columns necessary
- Green space left in areas, despite all the new hardscape plans
- Continue the visual connection between the house and the garden so the two appear as if completed at the same time and by the same hand

Problem-Solving Solutions

The clients cited an extensive program of features for entertaining large groups, while at the same time wanting a series of smaller private garden spaces just for them or a few people. Since there was so much hillside slope, Tony first built a series of engineered walls to create flat usable sites to accommodate the wish list. The pool measures 42 feet by 14 feet (12.8 meters by 4.2 meters) and its adjacent spa is approximately 6 feet by 6 feet (1.82 meters by 1.82 meters), and both have completely tiled interiors in keeping with the Spanish design. Because architect Paul Williams had used red clay tiles on exterior stairs and terraces, Tony repeated those throughout the garden, especially in the pool, kitchen, and lounging areas, finding similar tiles called Terra Bella pavers at Mission Tile West in South Pasadena, California. To repeat Williams' use of the tiles in a decorative chimney design, which Tony liked, he found a place at the base of the pool pergola where it would work. He planted the pergola's beams with vanilla-scented trumpet vine (Disiticis laxiflora), and repeated that choice in an "X" pattern on the exterior railing. Using similar materials and plant materials helped unify the various spaces and link the garden to the house.

Opposite top left: Before: The existing retaining wall was demolished and a new one added to support the swimming pool.
Opposite top right: Before: Stairs leading down to the pool deck and where the new wall is being built. **Opposite bottom:** After: The back of the house; two benches from the Italian Terracotta Company date from the 1920s; the area is a lounging/seating area close to a dining area; the terrace also has a table and chairs.

Top left: A memorial garden to the homeowners' pets with blue pots sitting on top of small pedestals. **Top right:** An arbor repeats architectural elements from the house; the columns were copied from those on a house terrace, a trumpet vine shades a pool and spa; three jets spray into the pool. **Above:** This garden was dubbed the "office garden" because it's adjacent to the office just inside. The wall has a criss-cross pattern to repeat a detail from a window in the front of the house. "We try to do that a lot." The fountain also is a 1920s item from the Italian Terracotta Company. **Opposite top left:** A detailed view of another lounging area with an olive tree that was craned in because of its size. **Opposite center:** A detail showing a difficult corner because of its sheer drop-off, which leads from the office garden toward the front of the house. A structural wall was constructed. **Opposite top right:** A gate leading to the rear of the property. **Opposite bottom:** The plan shows how Tony worked to maximize the space that could be used by the city's permit law. "We lined the pool up with a terrace at the rear of the house," he says.

Cost-Saving Alternatives

Gravel or decomposed granite would have been less costly than terra cotta tiles; a simple open pergola or large umbrellas could have been used instead of the enclosed dining structure fabricated from stucco, mortar, wood, and red clay tiles; and reproductions of vintage fountains and urns from big-box stores might have been substituted to save money.

Budget

The project's budget allowed up to U.S. $750,000, which matched the multimillion-dollar home's attention to quality and detailing.

Challenges Along the Way

Because of the required retaining walls, the engineering and permit processes were very time-consuming.

Key Design Details

- Tony tried to extend the original architectural details of the house into the landscape: columns, terra cotta pavers, and railings.

- The pool, with its pergola structure, copies the columns of the home's upper terrace while framing the views of downtown Los Angeles.

- The garden remains an open-floor series of spaces because of the limited amount of space—even after adding more flat land during construction.

The New Garden—An Epilogue

The homeowners are pleased with the success of the garden for large and private parties and their own personal use. They consider it their oasis after stressful days of working in metropolitan Los Angeles.

PROJECT AND TEAM CREDITS: Client Bruce Hatton and Tom Young **Location** Los Angeles, California **Landscape designer** Anthony Exter, Anthony Exter Landscape Design, Los Angeles, California, www.anthonyexter.com **Project duration** 12 months (mostly waiting for permits to be secured) **Completion** 2012

SPANISH COLONIAL REVIVAL MUSE

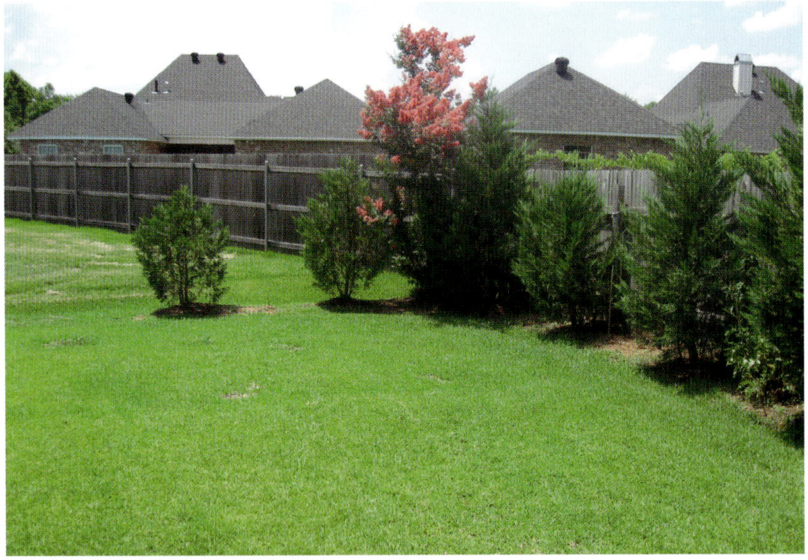

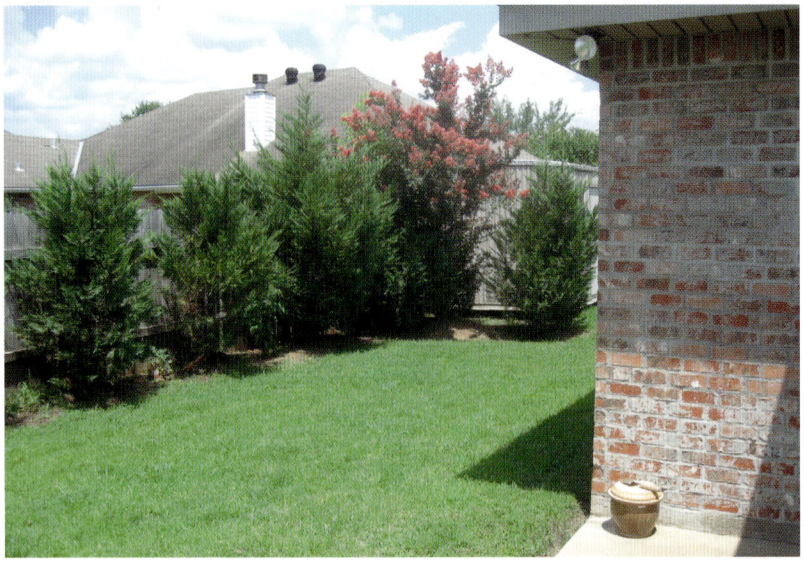

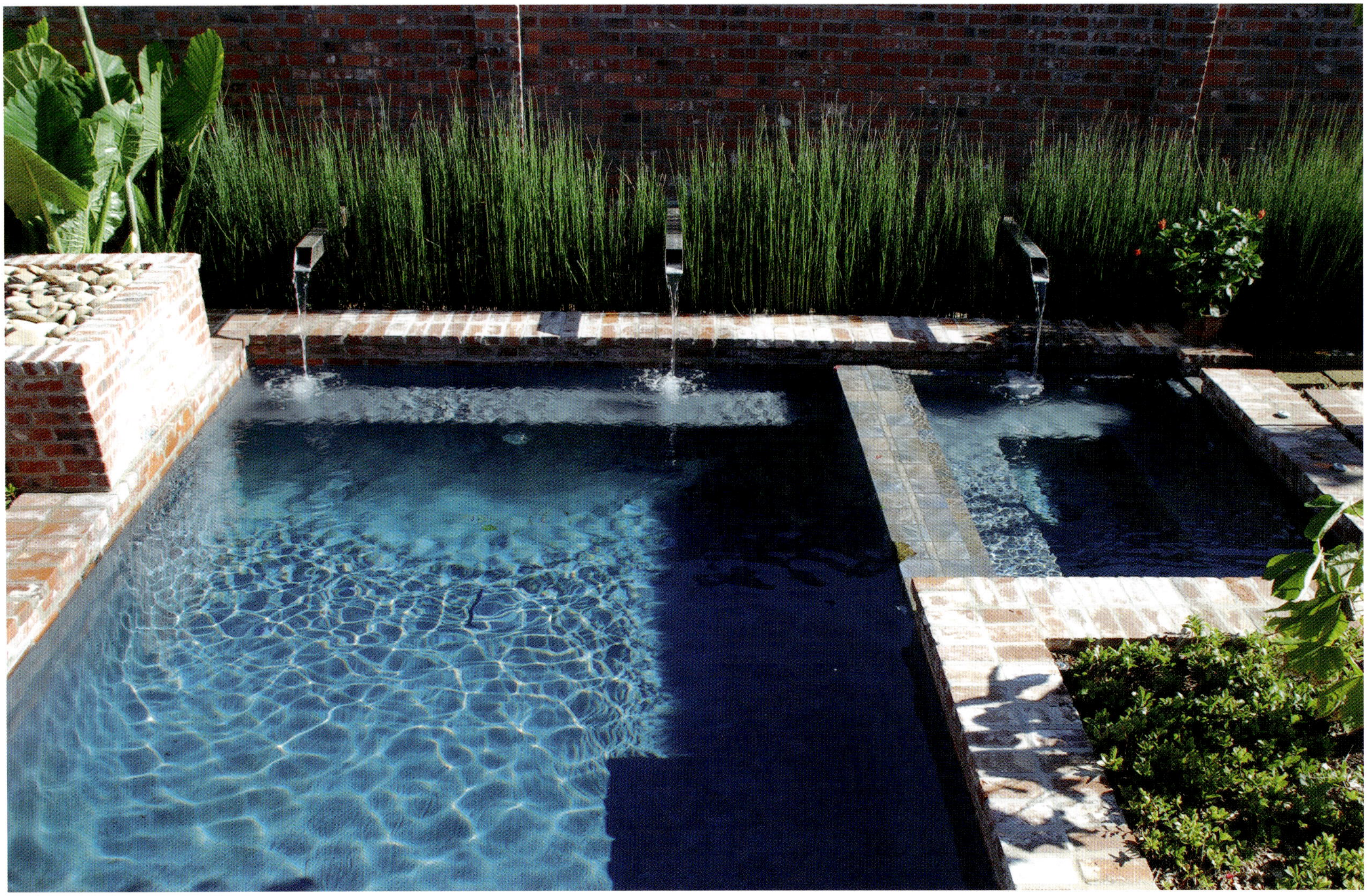

WATER RIGHT

Tony Tradewell has worked as a landscape architect for 12 years, and has seen what he thought were tough challenges, but a site in the central Louisiana city of Alexandria almost took the cake with its homeowners' many requests for a small site with poor drainage.

Site Problems

- Poor drainage in a densely developed neighborhood
- Compact site (measuring 70 feet by 22 feet [21.3 meters by 6.7 meters])

Wish List

- Swimming pool for dipping and adjacent spa
- Outdoor sitting area with fireplace
- Separate lounge area
- Resolve drainage problems and reclaim more of the site to be functional for entertaining
- Landscaped garden
- Significant, attractive water feature

Finding a Professional

The clients found Tony through word of mouth.

Project Challenges

- Site surrounded by brick walls with lower grade, creating places for standing water to collect
- Extensive list of amenities for such a compact site

Problem-Solving Solutions

The small site and the long list of amenities desired made the design quite a challenge. In addition to those cited, the property also sloped away from the house and created a 3-foot-wide (91-centimeter-wide) expanse against the perimeter brick wall, which created a low spot for standing water to collect. Tony's innovative approach was to capture the runoff by creating a dry well that would percolate naturally. He decided the most efficient way to do this was to construct a linear retention area along the entire rear of the space, and made it an attractive focal point by incorporating the water feature here. The water feature and bio-retention area now appear to be one completely seamless feature; Tony planted the retention area with Equisetum and projected nine stainless-steel scuppers through the plantings. The outlets pour water into a river-rock trough below. Water then travels down the trough and spills into the pool and spa at the far left side of a courtyard.

At the far right of the courtyard, opposite the new pool, a garden room has the desired outdoor fireplace with comfortable teak furnishings, providing the clients with the additional entertaining space and extending the use of the courtyard into the winter months. In the center of the courtyard sits a lounge area for the pool area that is connected to the garden room and pool through brick paving, which is broken up with a pattern of 4-inch (10-centimeter) gaps, each planted with groundcover. Beneath the paving gaps a gravel system directs captured runoff back to the retention area at the rear of the space, offering another environmentally smart solution.

Because of the tight site, Tony planted Chinese parasol trees that grow tall but not wide, adding a key vertical focal point. The Louisiana chapter of the American Society of Landscape Architects recognized the design professionally with an award for its attractiveness and environmentally responsible way of dealing with runoff.

Cost-Saving Alternatives

The swimming pool represented more than one-third of the total budget and could have been eliminated. The 7.5-foot-high (2.2-meter-high) brick wall was more a key to helping conceal the site and introducing a traditional southern courtyard feeling. But something less costly could have been used as a privacy screen such as a large stand of clumping bamboo or a cement block wall.

Opposite top left and right: Before: The small size of the space and drainage issues meant the site only included lawn and cedar trees.
Opposite bottom: After: Tony added the pool with fountain feature in the rear with scuppers concealed within horsetail reed. Brick was selected to suggest an old-fashioned New Orleans courtyard feeling.

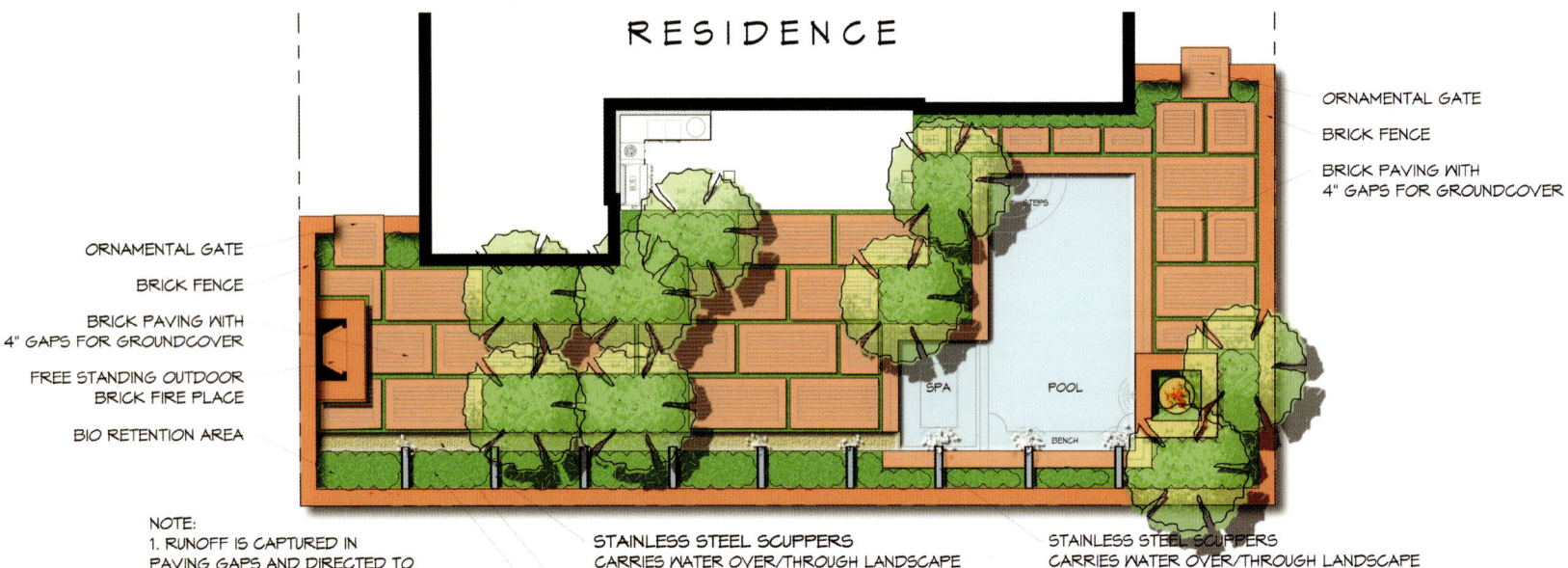

RESIDENCE

ORNAMENTAL GATE

BRICK FENCE

BRICK PAVING WITH
4" GAPS FOR GROUNDCOVER

ORNAMENTAL GATE

BRICK FENCE

BRICK PAVING WITH
4" GAPS FOR GROUNDCOVER

FREE STANDING OUTDOOR
BRICK FIRE PLACE

BIO RETENTION AREA

NOTE:
1. RUNOFF IS CAPTURED IN PAVING GAPS AND DIRECTED TO BIO RETENTION AREA AT REAR OF SPACE.
2. A SEPARATE POOL/FOUNTAIN SYSTEM HAS SCUPPERS THAT BRIDGE THE BIO RETENTION AREA AND CIRCULATES WATER BACK TO POOL.

STAINLESS STEEL SCUPPERS
CARRIES WATER OVER/THROUGH LANDSCAPE
INTO RILL

RIVER ROCK RILL CARRIES WATER TO POOL/SPA

BIO RETENTION AREA

STAINLESS STEEL SCUPPERS
CARRIES WATER OVER/THROUGH LANDSCAPE
INTO POOL AND SPA

Top left: Elephant ear growing in the foreground was selected to add bold texture and reflect more of the New Orleans courtyard feeling. **Top right:** Detail of the scuppers, which empty water into a runnel, a small narrow channel of water that goes from one end of the courtyard to another. **Above:** At one end of the site, a pool and at the other a fireplace, which are connected by a continuous water feature. **Opposite top left:** Room was left for a seating group by the fireplace, with one of the scuppers behind the chair. **Opposite top right:** One of the scuppers which recirculate water; all were fabricated from stainless steel and extend about 48 inches (122 centimeters) long. "They appear to grow out of the grasses," says Tony. **Opposite bottom left:** River rock lines the runnel, framed by sandstones, chosen because it's a local material. **Opposite bottom right:** The pool is used to dip and cool off, and has an attached spa.

Challenges Along the Way

The project did not involve many problems, except for rain, but this did allow the designer and homeowners to see how well the system caught and recirculated the rainwater.

Key Design Details

- The project's redesign captured rainwater at the back and made it work stylistically in the garden.
- The modern edgy stainless steel scuppers of the water feature are striking.

The New Garden—An Epilogue

The homeowners' enjoyment is the highest compliment: They spend less time traveling and more time at home. "It's their paradise now," says Tony.

PROJECT AND TEAM CREDITS: Location Alexandria, Louisiana **Landscape architect** Tony Tradewell, RLA, ASLA, Deville, Louisiana, www.tonytradewell.com **Project duration** Nine months **Completion** 2011

WATER RIGHT   131

Above left (top to bottom): Equipment was necessary to clean up the existing seasonal creek and to grade and grub out the brambly slope. Existing concrete slabs lead to "nowhere"; the existing lawn merged into a swampy slope full of thorny plants and weeds. The slope is contained by a gorgeous stone wall; bronze scuppers give the illusion of the existing groundwater being collected and spilling into the new water feature. A liner and placed boulders allow the seasonal creek to run cleaner and to be more defined. **Above right:** A peaceful pavilion reached by crossing the stone slab bridge expands the outdoor living areas into what was once unusable space.

SERENITY EVOLVED, WATER BANISHED

When Scott and Stephanie looked for a house and garden, the goal was an outdoors that would suit their lifestyle. Prior to the home's construction, a well-known local landscape architect had sited it with two sleek concrete patios at the back. After the home was built, steps and concrete pillars from the construction took up a large chunk of the space, making the patios almost unusable. The couple wanted a better solution, but the site presented a challenge. The property extended about 20 feet (6 meters) from the rear of the home, then sloped up slightly. A seasonal creek at the bottom of the slope created a bog environment on the edge of their lawn, and overgrown brambles and weeds choked the slope, creating an eyesore from the inside of the home, and making for a very unwelcoming outdoor living environment as well. After a year or so of getting settled, the couple was ready to tackle the back yard with the goal of making it beautiful, relaxing, and a place to recharge from their busy schedules. They hired Laurie Van Zandt to take better advantage of the location: high on a hillside in Pleasantview, Utah, with stunning city and mountain views from portions of the back and from the front of the property.

Site Problems

- Seasonal creek that ran across the entire back of the property, and close to the back of the home, which made for continually wet and boggy lawn in the back yard
- Slight slope behind the creek also made for a large amount of groundwater seeping out of it
- Very wet, boggy soil in the entire back yard

Wish List

- Entertainment areas
- Clean up the slope and add outdoor living space by terracing
- Clean up seasonal stream
- Create a water feature
- Add fireplace or fire pit
- Add chicken coop and vegetable garden
- Add a pergola to provide shade
- Retain existing concrete patios
- Keep a traditional, organized layout

Finding a Professional

The homeowners found Laurie through her website, but coincidentally she had designed and coordinated gardens for their neighbor across the street. They were able to easily take a look at her work. She referred the landscaper, concrete contractor, stonemason, and carpenter.

Project Challenges

- Copious amounts of groundwater, creating a bog environment in the back yard, complete with bugs
- Slope at the back of the property that visually and effectively cut off the use of the back yard
- Overgrown brambles and invasive weeds had taken over the slope and were encroaching across the seasonal stream into the back yard

Problem-Solving Solutions

The two biggest problems were finding a solution for all the groundwater, and deciding on the configuration of the water feature. Beus Landscaping designed a system to capture the slope's groundwater in culverts that would then direct it on to an existing seasonal steam. The stream was temporarily dammed up during the construction, debris and mud were cleaned out, a weed barrier was put down, and new cobble introduced to keep it cleaner. The existing stream was then allowed to flow. It remains a natural course until it hits the water feature, where it is piped underneath the ground, and resurfaces on the other side of the water feature. A rubber liner under the water feature needed to be covered up, so Laurie sandwiched the liner between the stone wall and a sandstone veneer set on a ledge. Because of the near-vertical walls on either side of the water feature, it was necessary to build additional "sandwich" walls with stone caps to hide the edge of the liner. Laurie designed the aesthetics of the feature; a consultant designed its plumbing, with pipes located on the feature's rear side and valves to control the flow.

Cost-Saving Alternatives

Instead of sandstone, concrete would have been cheaper. Laurie could have dredged and put down a weed barrier and new rocks in the seasonal creek instead of creating an entirely new water feature. A boulder wall could have been built on the back of the stream to separate it from the new water feature. A portable fire pit could have been used instead of a custom-built one with a seat wall.

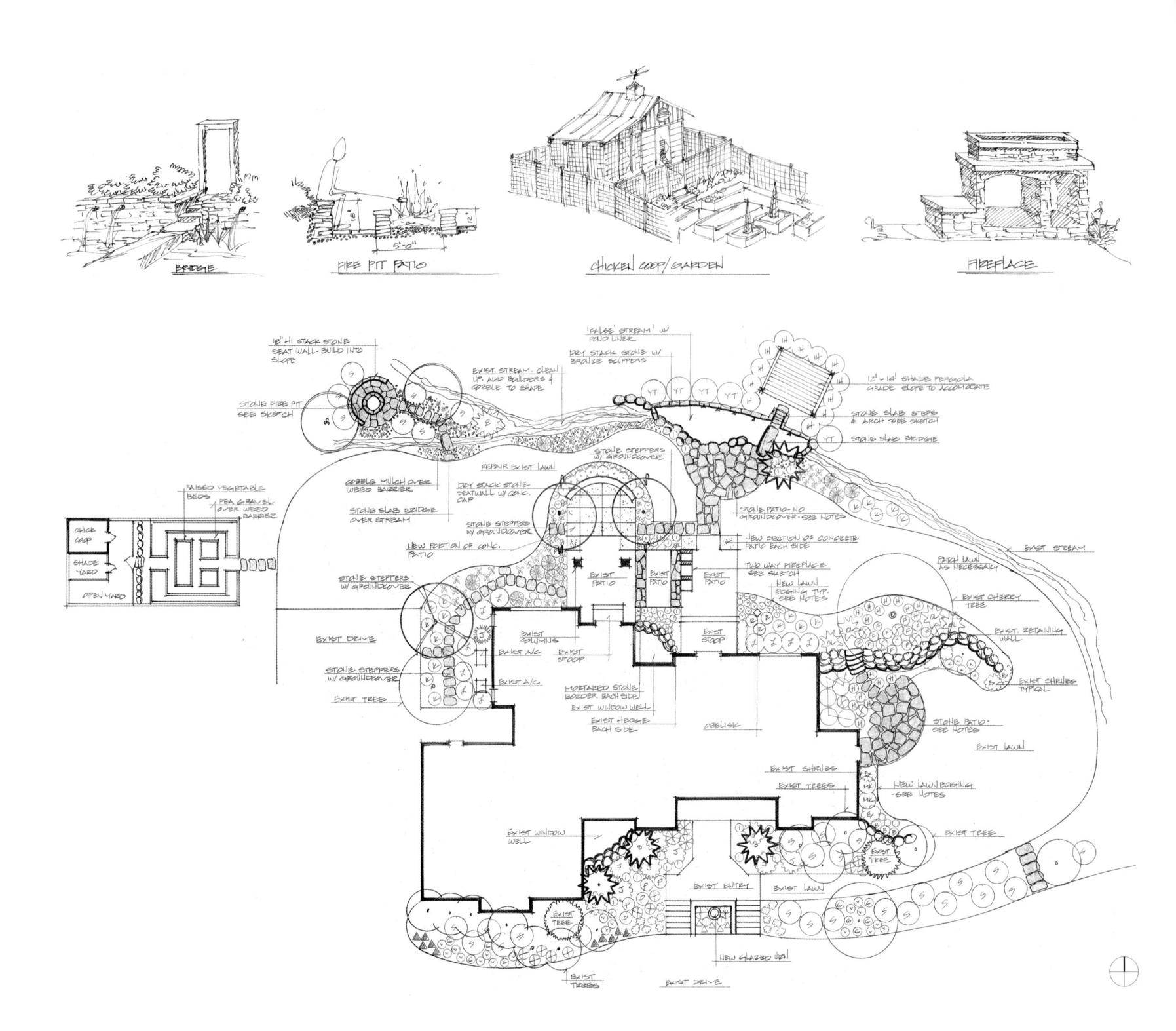

Above: A scaled plan and numerous sketches allowed the finished design to be accurately visualized and executed. Potential issues were able to be anticipated in the planning stages. **Opposite top left:** Planning out even the details of the chicken coop/vegetable garden allowed for a beautiful, functional aesthetic. **Opposite top center:** A stacked stone wall retains the slight slope and is the perfect height for built-in seating. **Opposite top right:** Simple plantings give a sense of peace, while extensive stonework ties the garden together. Quality workmanship assures the beauty of the vision.

The chicken coop could have been purchased instead of custom built. Having a landscape master plan in place prior to the construction of the home would have caught the problem of the patios being gobbled up by steps and columns; instead, they could have been resized from the get-go. It also would have saved costs if there'd been a master plan set out in a manner that let the homeowners do the projects in stages as their budget permitted, or so they could do some of the work themselves.

Budget

About U.S. $200,000 included water feature, stonework, pergola, chicken coop, garden, concrete work, and landscaping; the front and side gardens were redesigned later for an additional U.S. $50,000.

Challenges Along the Way

The biggest problem was how to contain the water feature. There were nearly vertical walls on all sides, and the rubber liner needed to be hidden. Sandwich walls were the solution, with the liner placed in between the walls; a cap was put on top to hide the edge. Other issues included making sure that all the work was covered in the bids. There were so many trades involved, and often they had to work together to achieve the desired result. Deer that were giddy with excitement at the prospect of all that new foliage, especially fruit trees, had to be deterred through the use of animal repellent.

Key Design Details

- The main design feature is the water element, and the extensive use of blond sandstone to tie all the pieces of the garden together.
- The flow of the water from the scuppers can be controlled through the use of valves.
- The overhanging stone patio and stone slab bridge allow the homeowners to feel that they are a part of the landscape. Everything is present—water, fire, and ambience.
- A fireplace near the house makes for intimate evenings, while a fire pit is located farther away from the home to take advantage of amazing city views.

The New Garden—An Epilogue

The homeowners now spend as much time outside as indoors. They have hosted weddings and fundraisers. Before the work had been done, the yard had caused a little anxiety due to all the water and the overgrown feeling of the hillside. Now, it offers nothing but serenity. The homeowners are spiritual people, and this is reflected in their garden. It is alive with bees, birds, chickens, and a bounty of vegetables. After the back yard was completed, they asked how soon they could start redesigning and constructing the rest of the gardens. Quite a compliment!

PROJECT AND TEAM CREDITS: Client Scott and Stephanie **Location** Pleasantview, Utah **Landscape designer** Laurie Van Zandt, The Ardent Gardener Landscape Design & Project Coordination, Huntsville, Utah, www.theardentgardener.net **Stonemasonry** Brion Taylor, BT Stone, Ogden, Utah **Concreting** Chad McInelly, CMC Designs, Ogden, Utah **Landscaping** Russ Beus, Beus Landscaping, Ogden, Utah **Water feature plumbing consultant** Duane Richards, Ewing Irrigation, Salt Lake City, Utah **Carpentry** Tad Judd, Huntsville, Utah **Project duration** 18 months with carpentry (including the chicken coop and pergola, completed last and much of it during winter) **Completion** 2012

136

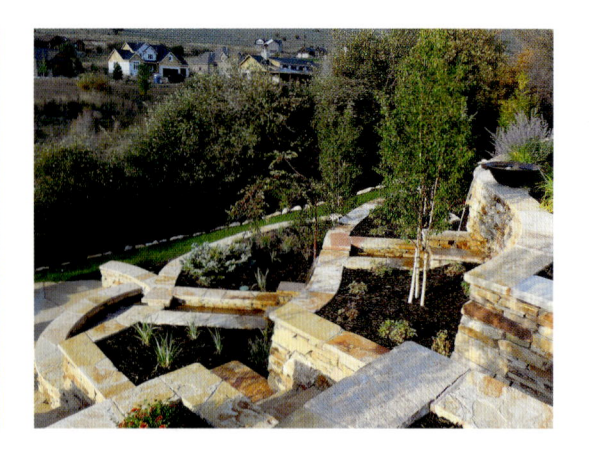

MULTITIERED MAXIMIZER

Casey and Haley are a young, professional couple with four children, who live in a single-family home in Eden, Utah, part of the Ogden Valley in the northern part of the state. They had purchased an existing home at a good price with terrific views of the local mountains, but with a steep slope in the back yard, so there was only about 15 feet (4.5 meters) of flat land. However, because of the good sale price, they were willing to spend money to gain a more practical and more beautiful landscape that would work for their family. At the time they first chatted with landscape designer Laurie Van Zandt, who was known in their area, the clients were adding a new handrail to their deck. She suggested instead they enlarge the deck to gain more living space and a better furniture layout, but also a spiral staircase to the ground level for additional outdoor living and play space.

Site Problems

- Very steep grade
- Clay soil
- Too little space for outdoor entertaining
- Limited access to the back yard from the front and also from the home

Wish List

- Fire pit
- Play area for children
- Classic, timeless design
- Low maintenance
- Space for entertaining
- Attractive outdoor areas
- Maximize site and how all spaces would be used

Finding a Professional

Landscape designer Laurie Van Zandt of The Ardent Gardener in Huntsville, Utah, was referred to this client by several others who lived in a different city but knew her work. Laurie, in turn, recommended the landscape contractor and stonemason, and the concrete contractor, whom she also knew from working together on many prior jobs.

Project Challenges

- Deal with steep slope in a safe manner
- Coordinate all subcontractors to be sure everyone knew who was doing what on the project—and when
- Construct a dramatic water feature with adequate water flow
- Create different areas that were pleasing when viewed from the upper deck, as well as from the lower-level entertaining areas
- Tie together all the outdoor areas visually using contiguous hardscape materials

Problem-Solving Solutions

Increasing the size of the family's existing deck was a primary goal that would allow for better traffic flow and maximize the outdoor area. Laurie suggested a cantilevered extension over an existing support beam to avoid constructing new post supports. She also suggested a spiral staircase that would consume little space and allow guests to access other areas of the garden without having to go through the home. On the ground level, she designed a new concrete patio where the stairway descended for additional entertaining space. Laurie added a stone garden wall with planter to surround this patio, and also designed three new steps to lead to the first level of this new multitiered garden, separating the levels with wide planters in front of stacked stone walls for safe landings. The stone was locally quarried, and the walls were designed with minimal thickness to allow for more usable space. Step lighting was also built into the walls for additional safety.

The highest level of the new back garden is the new concrete patio and the garden walls with plantings. Stone steps lead down 18 inches (45.7 centimeters) to a play lawn that stretches across the entire back of the home. Mass plantings of day lilies edge the lawn and soften the edge of the first tier of the stone wall. A copper bowl, which contrasts beautifully with all the stonework, sits on top of

Opposite top left: Before: Steeply sloped lot allowed for little usable space in the backyard for entertaining or play. **Opposite top center:** Before: The home felt a lack of integration with the site and gave off a sense of exposure, rather than intimacy. **Opposite top right:** After: New stepped walls allow a gradual transition through the slope and allow people to safely access the lower areas of the garden. **Opposite bottom:** After: Natural stone walls are beautiful when viewed from any angle, and blend with the earth tones of the home. Carefully placed native trees allow the wall to be the main attraction and help integrate the home to the site.

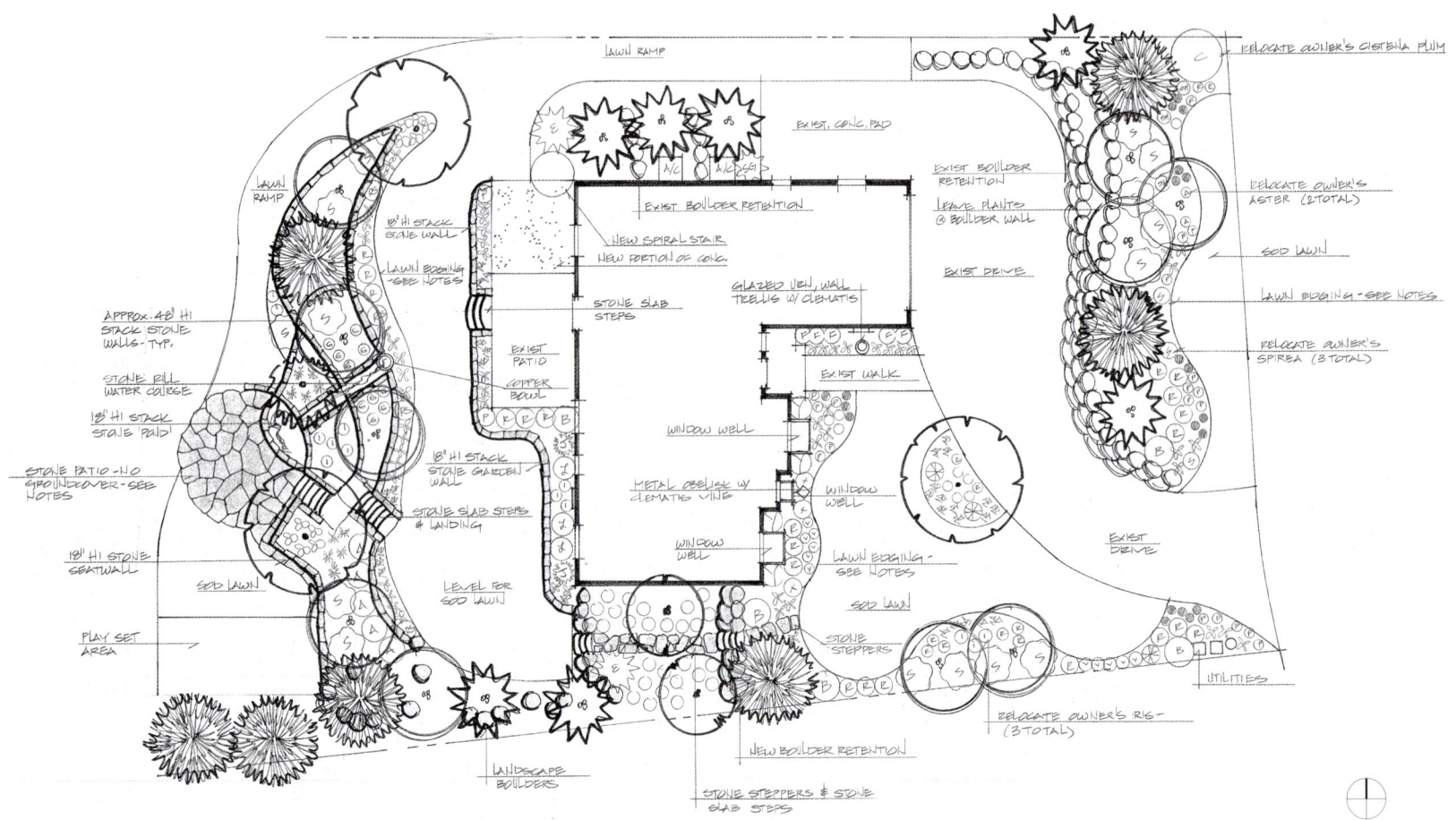

Top left: Gracefully curving walls create maximum space. The lawn ramp is an alternative path to the lower living space. **Top right:** Locally quarried stone blends beautifully with the natural environment and landscaping plantings. Boulders, pulled from the site, are incorporated into the stacked stone wall rather than being hauled off. **Above:** Detailed, scaled plan delineates the works to be completed and helps with budgeting. **Opposite top:** Stone slab steps lead from the front garden to the back. The same stone is used throughout the garden. **Opposite bottom:** A gorgeous copper bowl adds a contrasting element to all of the stonework. Stone rills have individual valves to control the amount of water flow in each level.

this wall. Water cascades from the bowl through the next two tiers of walls. These walls have wide planting beds at their bases, and are planted with textured masses of low-growing perennials and grasses. Sparingly planted aspen and spruce trees help break up the expanse of the wall, and allow it to star as the landscape's main feature. The lowest area of the garden, about 12 feet (3.6 meters) down, consists of a small lawn area, fire-pit patio, play equipment for the children, and the terminating pool of the water feature (the water flows from the copper bowl, drops through the planting areas where it flows through narrow stone rills, and then falls into this pool). LED lights illuminate the stone steps, which lead through the walls, casting shadows from the trees onto the walls, and bring a glow to the pool for nighttime drama. The entire wall and water feature can be viewed from the home's living area as if they are a giant sculpture.

Cost-Saving Alternatives

For more cost-conscious clients, they could have used boulders for the retention rather than the stack stone. This would have made for less usable space, however, since the walls would have taken up more room. A readily available water feature instead of a custom one would have been another less expensive choice. The spiral stair might have been eliminated and gravel or road base could have been used to extend the ground-level concrete patio. Another money-saving option is if a clients are willing to do the planting themselves rather than hire a professional.

Budget

The budget was about U.S. $150,000, or one-third of the home's value.

Challenges Along the Way

A big portion of the stonework was completed in the winter. Heated tents were erected around the site, and insulated blankets were placed on the ground to keep it from freezing. Laurie brought in a consultant to help with the design of the water-feature plumbing. The rills were narrow, with a fairly large drop, and Laurie needed to ensure that as little water as possible was lost to evaporation and overspray, yet a decent flow was still maintained into the lower pool.

Key Design Details

- The key design feature is the stone wall and water feature. Even though the walls and water feature are obviously manufactured, they have a very organic, natural feel to them.

- The space feels really good and spiritual, and is one you don't want to leave.

- Plantings of evergreen mugo pines and Bakeri spruce; a weeping crabapple tree over the water feature; and mass plantings of interesting grasses and perennials, such as Little Blue Stem, variegated iris, and Britt Marie Crawford ligularia allow for year-round interest, even in winter. The landscape looks like a giant still-life painting in winter, but there are interesting textures and colors in all seasons.

The New Garden—An Epilogue

The couple loves the garden and referred the designer and her firm to several other clients. The design took them from a steep, overgrown, dangerous, unusable space, to a garden that they and their children can enjoy year-round.

PROJECT AND TEAM CREDITS: Client Casey and Haley **Location** Eden, Utah **Landscape designer** Laurie Van Zandt, The Ardent Gardener Landscape Design & Project Coordination, Huntsville, Utah, www.theardentgardener.net **Stonemasonry** Brion Taylor, BT Stone, Ogden, Utah **Landscape installation** Dusty Poulson and Ron Sorensen, Western Landscaping, Eden, Utah **Concreting** Chad McInelly, CMC Designs, Ogden, Utah **Decking** Peterson Builders, Eden, Utah **Water feature plumbing consultant** Duane Richards, Ewing Irrigation, Salt Lake City, Utah **Project duration** 12 months (primarily because of the extensive stonework) **Completion** 2013

Top left: Before: Stakes set in the ground help lay out the pool's location and size on the 3-acre (1.21-hectare) site that landscape designer Howard Roberts purchased for himself and his family. **Top center:** Before: Howard designed an addition and designated the pool location. **Top right:** Before: The early stages of the pergola and the pool, the structure is covered in plastic, but showing more progress during the construction stage. **Bottom:** After: The pool and pergola are finished. The symmetrical pool is aligned with the center of the house. The pool is designed so it can be entered from either of the two shallow ends, with the deepest part in the center at 5.5 feet (1.68 meters). Brick paving all around mimics the home's brick façade.

EVOLVED LANDSCAPE, FROM BARREN TO MATURE

For a landscape professional, a clean slate with almost no plantings offers the ultimate challenge and delight; the sky's almost the limit. And for designer Howard Roberts, founder of Liquid Inc., a full-service pool and landscape design and build firm in New Jersey, he had another bonus with his own blank property he purchased 20 years ago—no difficult client homeowners—only himself. When he and wife Carol purchased a 3-acre (1.2-hectare) site with a Williamsburg-style brick colonial in New Jersey, surrounded by horse farms and cornfields, he found the challenge exhilarating: "It was a home with good bones and an architectural style to work with. While we were renovating the entire house, we were ready to transform the site as well," he says.

Site Problems

- No protection from heavy wind exposures
- No protection from sun, since no canopy of trees or structure
- No privacy from neighbors
- No landscape interest or scale on the site
- No outdoor living space
- Driveway not laid out properly
- Heavy deer pressure

Wish List

- Take a 3-acre-wide (1.2-hectare-wide) open property and turn it into a park-like environment
- Redesign existing gravel driveway and pave it to meet new needs
- Renovate detached barn
- Add walkways of brick that would complement house
- Construct brick patios and pool deck
- Renovate house with new front portico, rear bump-out addition, new windows, bathrooms, kitchen, overall interior layout and flow, which would transition with all new outdoors to follow
- Add pool house, pergolas, fencing, gates, arbor, etc., and make all additions a destination to experience the changes

Finding a Professional

Howard knew he would tackle the design, construction and plantings himself, but he also knew family would prove to be the toughest critics in any case. Although he stresses the importance of a master plan for clients so everyone is on the same page, in this case when his family inquired, "Where's the plan?" he replied, "In my head." He worked that way for himself because he wanted to start slowly and let the transformation evolve in tandem with the house, which he and Carol also changed, as well as with the wildlife that came to visit and nibble, and with the new ecosystems that developed due to his choices.

Project Challenges

- Provide protection from wind since cold northwest breezes pounded one side of the house
- Offer screening and separation from neighbors to eliminate a lack of privacy and undesirable views
- Add relief from the sun in hot weather via structures and a canopy of green to permit sitting outside in warm weather, since there were no structures or trees

Problem-Solving Solutions

This was a big project that took more than a decade to bring to fruition. Howard felt it was important to plant trees early in tthe process, so they would be established, mature and have an impact on the overall renovation once completed. "Taking this approach gave the trees a big head start. They can actually function the way I needed them, provide shade for our new patios, screening for privacy, and a barrier from the harsh winter winds." He planted a variety of trees—red and sugar maples, pin oaks, willows, redbud, dogwood, crabapple and London plane—more than 160 altogether, along with evergreens (Norway spruce, Dawn Redwoods, etc.) for winter interest, and creating wind screens and privacy.

The design serves two functions and purposes: there's a more casual, native and natural setting around the perimeter of the property, and more structure and symmetry around the house to respond to the architectural lines and style. The home was the focal point of the property and the center of the design, with outdoor spaces and rooms playing off the circulation and layout. The gravel driveway proved impractical when snow and ice needed to be plowed, so Howard changed it to paving. He added brick walks throughout to complement the house, along with brick patios and a pool deck, which he laid in a running-bond pattern to cut labor costs and waste. The outdoor features were designed to become pleasant destinations to experience the grounds from different views and perspectives.

Plantings that might tempt deer were planted closer to the house but within confined areas; these include hosta and hydrangea. Howard took notice of the grazing habits of the deer during the course of the year. He also chose some materials to attract birds, squirrels and butterflies, and by so doing changed the site's ecosystem. "Birds and wildlife now flock and live within the property to nest and eat because of the shelter and food supply from such plantings as crabapple, dogwoods, and oak trees," Howard says. He decided to paint the home, structures and remaining architectural details to play on the tones of the brick, lawn and meadow areas within the landscape.

Cost-Saving Alternatives

Using this project as a case study, the goal was to plant a large quantity of trees. However, going with smaller trees would have allowed this owner to economize and stretch the budget. Patience and good planning will pay off long term because allowing trees to acclimatize at a very early stage in their development produces more ideal results. Case in point, Howard planted 3-inch to 4-inch (7.6-centimeter to 10-centimeter) caliper pin oaks along the street and front property line, which took the brunt of the northwest winds. Once the trees were installed, they expended the energy on growing a larger flare and root system (an anchor), to withstand the winds opposed to a canopy (sail). Plants are like people; they adjust to their environment. Another savings and choice Howard made was to go with boxwood hedges rather than brick masonry walls. Hedges are a good alternative for creating the framework of an outdoor room!

Top: The darker color of the plaster in the pool creates a more reflective color to the water, says designer Howard Roberts. A more substantial roof was added to the pergola several years after the pool was finished to offer more of a sense of destination and coverage. **Bottom:** The pool house is in the distance, with purple smoke bush in the foreground, opposite deutzia and catmint in front of American boxwood. **Opposite:** The plan reflects a symmetrical design, playing off and repeating the home's symmetry, which reflects a colonial-style Williamsburg design.

a. Front drive entry
b. Circular drive and front brick walkway
c. Detached barn
d. Front play lawn
e. Main house
f. Rear pergola
g. Main brick terrace
h. Pool
i. Pool house/storage
j. Freestanding open and covered pergola
k. Screening (which was selectively positioned for closing undesirable and framing desirable views)

Budget

Howard and his wife viewed their home as a long-term investment for their family as they planned to bring up all three of their children there. He also used the property as a place to experiment his landscape design ideas and theories, which he shared with his clients. He estimates he put U.S. $300,000 to U.S. $400,000 into the pool, hardscapes, structures, and landscape in the property, with the house originally valued at U.S. $250,000. Another U.S. $300,000 was used to modify and expand the home and barn, which makes a collective total of U.S. $850,000 to U.S. $950,000 with all the improvements. "We always intended to live here until all three kids were done with college, so we looked at our costs spread over a 20-year period from 1995 when we bought the site," he says. The enjoyment was creating something from almost nothing and equally gratifying is seeing and experiencing years of enjoyment and memories.

Challenges Along the Way

None, except for the need now to replace some plant materials that have died or that no longer thrive. Spaces that had direct sun originally are now in shade, due to the growth and maturity of the tree canopy. "We truly changed the environment, which is partially the joy and evolution of every garden," Howard says.

Now that his 160 trees have matured, he's thinning and opening the understory plantings to open up space and views, just as he's also opening up the interior of his traditional home for a more open modern layout. "Tastes, functions and influences change," he says.

Key Design Details

- The colors of the house are striking and complement the coziness and warmth of spaces.
- Open land with surrounding cornfields and farms in the distance was changed to more manicured clusters closer to the home.
- Howard worked hard to maintain attractive/appealing views, such as his neighbor's 1728 farmhouse and barn and cornfields, but hide/screen unsightly views of another neighbor's unkempt property. "Though our property is 3 acres (1.2 hectares), it really feels and appears to be 15 acres (6 hectares) to enjoy," he says. "I call it the push and pull in design, grab and frame the desirable views, and push out and screen the undesirable ones," Howard explains.

The New Garden—An Epilogue

"Creating the site's changes represented my greatest enjoyment; along with seeing how much others enjoy using it," Howard says. "We've used the property for so many great events and parties, with years of memories; I've brought contractors and clients here to see, enjoy and become more informed; so they can experience the same success, value and enjoyment we have. My wife had certain personal favorites she desired, so we incorporated, for example, lilacs, peonies, and other plants for cuttings she loves or that remind her of her mom, along with privacy—so she can enjoy and entertain comfortably—and trees she loved for their graceful form, like weeping willows and cherry trees to create the overall oasis," Howard says.

PROJECT AND TEAM CREDITS: Client Howard and Carol Roberts **Location** Pittstown, New Jersey **Landscape designer** Howard Roberts, Liquid Inc., Pittstown, New Jersey, www.liquidscapes.net **Project duration** 10 years (intensive work went on for seven years, from 2000 to 2007 for major renovation, with more casual tweaks and maintenance over the next three years) **Completion** 2010

144

STAYCATION SHOWCASE

Landscapes need remodeling, just as the interiors of homes do. And although Rick Rudie had lived in his suburban Chicago home for more than 15 years, he planned to stay longer and wanted to make it more livable as a place to unwind and entertain. Located adjacent to a golf course, the site had an old Trex (composite) deck and hot tub. He hired landscape designer Jim Bertrand, who worked nearby, to turn the property into the equivalent of a resort where he could relax, watch TV outdoors, cook, eat, enjoy sunsets, and entertain, often with his golfing buddies. He also asked for his front property to become more colorful and alive. Says Jim, "He wanted to fall in love with his home again rather than move or just make do."

Site Problems

- No curb appeal
- No ample space for relaxing, cooking, and eating
- Drainage challenges due to land sloping toward house in the back
- No privacy because of noisy neighbors

Wish List

- Be outdoors and entertain golf buddies with the sound and TV systems
- Be on adjacent golf course and enable access for taking a break at his house
- Cook and eat outdoors
- Add color at the front with mostly annuals
- Tie together the interiors and exteriors with similar materials and palette

Finding a Professional

Word of mouth and landscape architect Jim Bertrand's website led Rick to the firm, located just 30 minutes away.

Project Challenges

- Expectations high despite the site problems
- Permit release limitations by the village and subdivision committees made the wish list difficult, if not impossible, to fulfill

Problem-Solving Solutions

Because the site had almost nothing, except a small rear deck, Jim's approach was to start anew with a master plan. Despite concern that the village and subdivision committees would never approve a fence or wall unless there was a pool, and certainly not one taller than 5 feet (1.5 meters), Jim was determined, and he succeeded by making the plan extremely detailed, as well as attending village and association permit meetings with his client. "We stressed that all that we were doing would enhance the site and neighborhood and property values. They ended up agreeing," he says. The focus of the plan is a 1,000-square-foot (93-square-meter) rear patio that stretches across the entire rear with Italian tile pavement, which would hold up the best in the tough Chicago climate and be something different from brick, slate, or gravel. The patio was large enough to have areas designated for different functions, including watching TV (with two sets), sitting by the fireplace, and enjoying a fully equipped kitchen, eating area, and bar.

The plan also dictated a colorful palette of annuals, some perennials, and evergreens, particularly in the front to greet visitors; an irrigation system on zones for watering annuals in the ground and in pots, with minimal water waste. Jim wanted to unify the interior and exterior, so he used the same granite from the inside kitchen for the outside bar; and he carefully illuminated the house, patio, walks, and trees for nighttime use and safety. To eliminate drainage problems, he graded the site and installed PVC piping attached to gutters and the sump pump to send water to the lowest point on the property, and to eventually drain into the municipal sewer system.

To make outdoor time as pleasant as possible, he also installed a mosquito-management system that has an organic spray that repels the mosquitos and sends them flying, plus a fan under the newly constructed rough-sawn cedar pergola, whose beams imitate those of the house. To achieve

Opposite top: After: The terrace constructed from porcelain tiles from Italy extends 50 feet (15 meters) and includes areas for sitting, cooking, eating, relaxing, and watching TV and sunsets. **Opposite bottom left:** Before: A composite deck with its railing obstructing views of the yard. **Opposite bottom right:** Before: Showing the railed deck and few plantings.

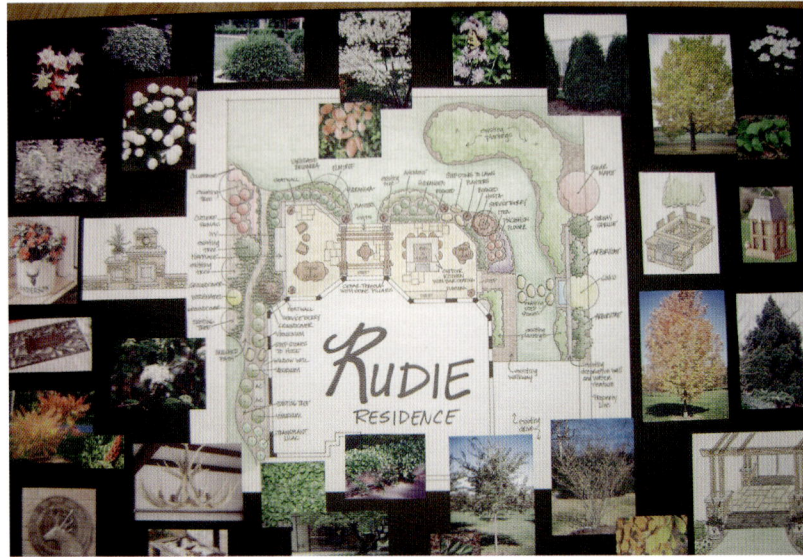

Top: A rough-sawn cedar pergola adds a sense of intimacy, shade and structure. This space is a perfect area for enjoying fires or relaxing. A fan helps keep mosquitoes and other flying insects away. **Above left:** A hand-drawn plan to scale required collaboration among three designers at Jim Bertrand's firm. **Above right:** A brick wall with fountain was built to provide visual and noise privacy. Wisconsin flagstone from a local quarry was used as 2-foot by 2-foot (60-centimeter by 60-centimeter) steppers. **Opposite top:** An outdoor TV that can remain outdoors was framed and painted to match the home's façade. **Opposite bottom:** To link indoors and outdoors, Jim used the same type of granite for the outdoor cooking area that is used inside. The person grilling offers entertainment for those sitting at the bar and can see the golf course beyond; a second TV was installed above the chef's head.

privacy, he screened the house with many large trees, including maples, swamp white oak, flowering pears, an assortment of Norway and Colorado spruce, and Techny and Nigra arborvitae. A masonry water feature with plantings blocks noise and the views from neighbors.

Cost-Saving Alternatives

Rick could have used pine for the pergola, concrete pavers for the walkways and the terrace, eliminated the irrigation, mosquito, and lighting systems, planted with less mature materials and waited for them to grow.

Budget

The budget was one-third of the value of the home.

Challenges Along the Way

None, except getting it done on time, with maximum value.

Key Design Details

- The main features include the overall structures that were added—pergola, patio, and kitchen.
- The thick vegetation and the colors of the annuals.
- There's an overall feeling of spaciousness despite the small site because of how it's laid out and its position adjacent to the open golf course.

The New Garden—An Epilogue

Rick uses his outdoor areas much more than he ever did or thought he would, and entertains frequently; he also enjoys the views from inside during winter.

PROJECT AND TEAM CREDITS: Client Rick Rudie **Location** Orland Park, Illinois **Landscape designer** Jim Bertrand, Jim Bertrand Landscape Design, Monee, Illinois, www.jimbertrand.com **Project duration** Six months **Completion** 2015

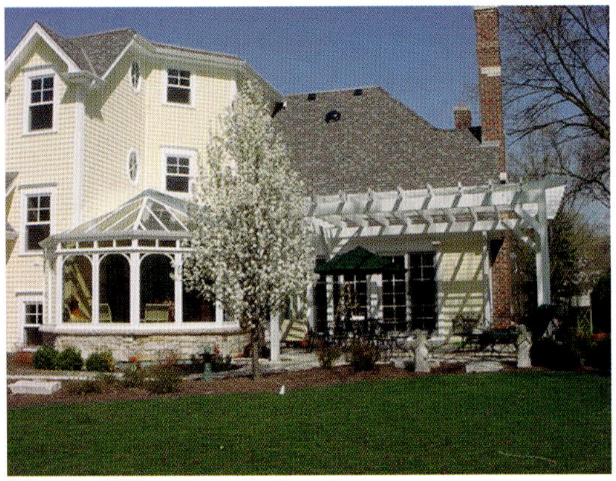

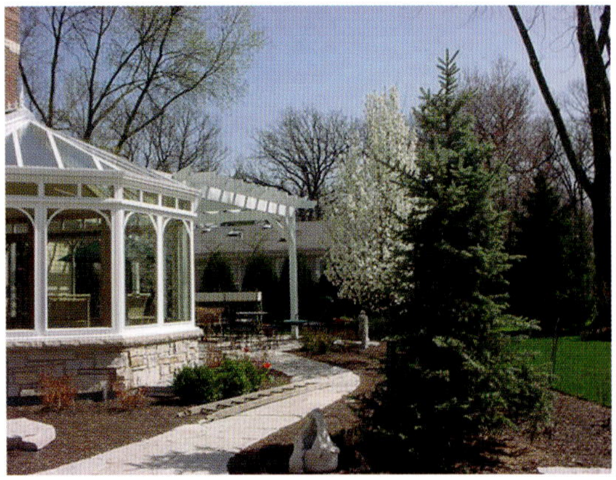

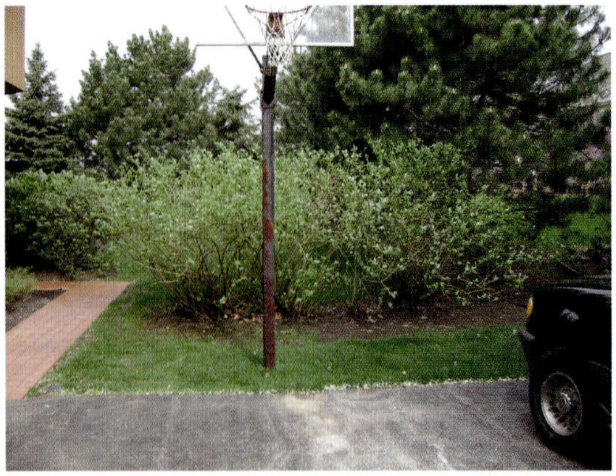

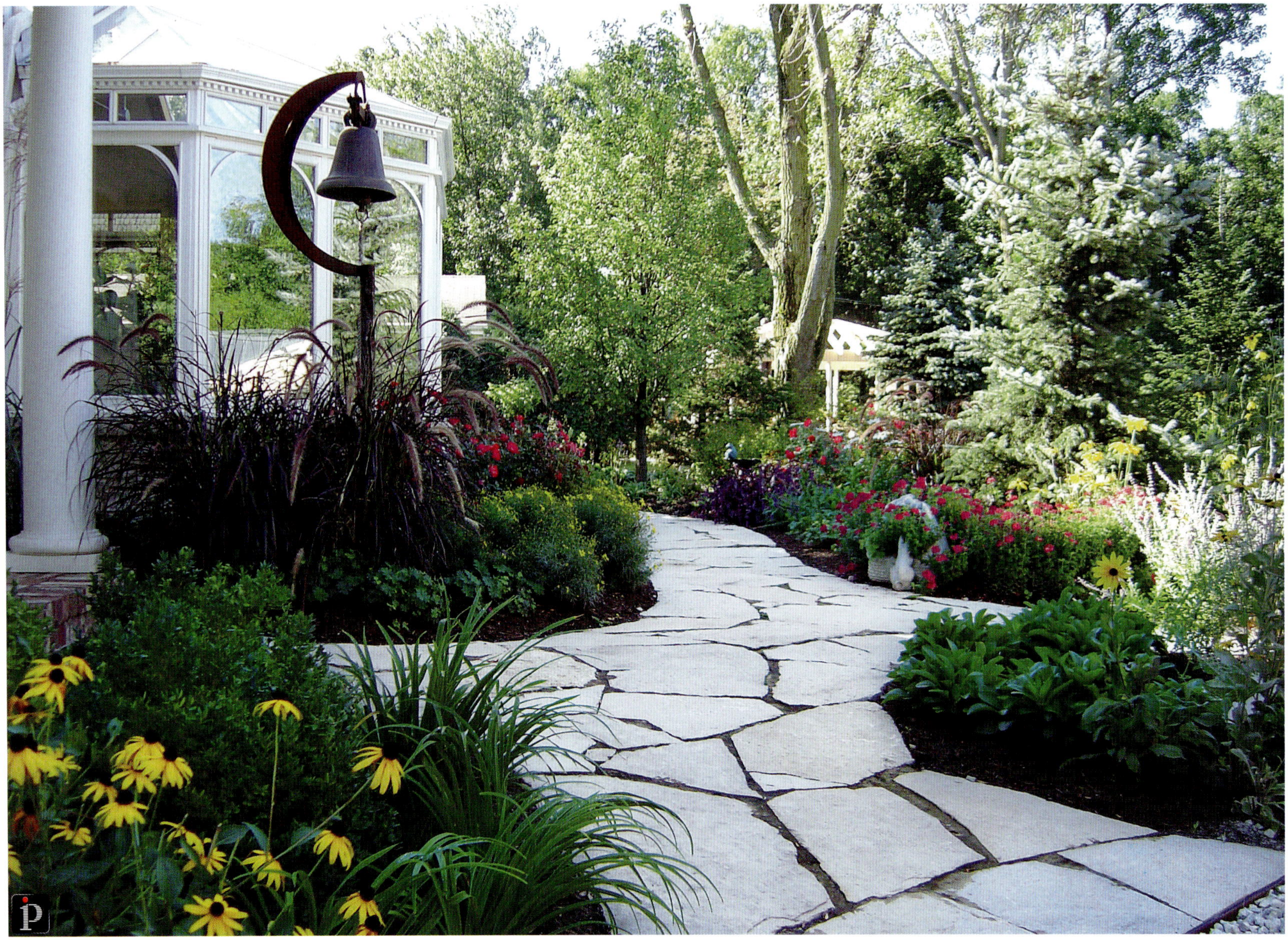

COHESIVE CLARITY

Constructing a house and the surrounding landscape at the same time can provide greater design unity and save time, but having two separate crews working simultaneously on each major project requires flexibility on the each team's part. This was the major challenge for homeowners, Tom and Loretta Volini with their new house near a forest preserve in suburban Chicago.

Site Problems

- Drainage
- Brand new, barren site without plantings
- Sloping site with limited flat terrain for entertaining
- Lack of privacy due to the proximity of two houses near the half-acre (0.2-hectare) site

Wish List

- Privacy
- Driveway that worked well for traffic, since the large family had a lot of cars that needed to be parked both in the garage and on the site
- Back yard that could be used for entertaining, even weddings, which meant the need for flat areas
- Good security that would prevent the house from being easily accessible to break-ins
- Low-maintenance plant materials and lawn

Finding a Professional

Word of mouth led the homeowners to Jim, at Jim Bertrand Landscape Design.

Project Challenges

- Wanting landscaping to be done at the same time as the house, so landscape crew had to work around house construction
- Creating a classic-style, old-world design when it would be brand new
- Coping with utility lines, and having some destroyed during construction, which required repair

Problem-Solving Solutions

Because of the drainage problem, Jim knew it was critical to develop a plan that included regrading the site, and installing downspouts and a sump pump. He needed to get the neighbors' and municipality's approval to drain the water to the edge of the property and into a natural pond. He selected crushed granite for the driveway and limestone with large joints between stones for the patio, both of which allow water to percolate through rather than add to the runoff. Antique Chicago street pavers that match those on the home's chimneys were used to pave the entry walk. To solve the privacy issue, Jim planted large arborvitae and left existing foliage that was already planted between his clients' and neighbors' homes.

He also regraded the site and added local mushroom compost, pulverized top soil, and sand from Lake Michigan. For a more personal touch, Jim went hunting, often with his client, for eclectic antiques that could withstand the cold, from a cooking stove found in New York to an Amish copper candy-making bowl from Kansas City to a bell that he found in Atlanta; each item became a planter. To enjoy the outdoors even at night, Jim installed lighting throughout the site. Both the sod and the planting materials were chosen to give the homeowners a low-maintenance design that requires only pruning, mulching, and applying a weed inhibitor a few times a year.

Cost-Saving Alternatives

Using less-mature plants, and cheaper materials for walkways and the patio area.

Budget

The project was budgeted at 25 percent of the value of the house and land.

Challenges Along the Way

New utility lines were broken, including a gas line, and had to be repaired.

Opposite top left: Midway during the construction, a work in progress. **Opposite top center:** Another shot of the work in progress with the English conservatory and pergola completed. **Opposite top right:** Before: shot before the house was demolished. **Opposite bottom:** After: Jim planted tons of perennials with lots of visual interest, and a good pathway structure to the house and detached garage. The bell came from a pre–Civil War church in Atlanta.

Key Design Details

- It's very clear that the work makes the house and landscape both look like they've existed for the last 80 years, with classic, understated elegant lines, as well as a homey, inviting feeling.

- All four sides of the property present visual interest. "Every area is vibrant," says Jim.

The New Garden—An Epilogue

The homeowners hadn't yet experienced living there, but they quickly found that their wish list was fulfilled. The landscaping offered privacy and joy. Although he has worked on countless projects, Jim found during this process how important it is to hand-select plants and hardscape for the exact look desired, and that good scheduling of work keeps the process going smoothly for all the trades, particularly when work on a home is happening simultaneously.

Above left: An antique well pump from Jim's father's farm in Illinois was recycled to this project and became a water feature. **Above right:** Antique Chicago street pavers line the walk; antique benches and trellis grouping offer a wonderful place to sit opposite the front porch. "Two choices to hang out," says Jim. He planted the trellis with wisteria and trumpet vines, and surrounded it with red bud trees. **Opposite top left:** Curb appeal comes from layering of plants, a garden fence and charming brick walk that matches the brick in the chimney. **Opposite top right:** Detail of perennials and annuals mixed together with the water pump. **Opposite bottom:** A meandering path along one side of the house with evergreens screening a neighboring home.

PROJECT AND TEAM CREDITS: Client Tom and Loretta Volini **Location** Oak Brook, Illinois **Landscape designer** Jim Bertrand, Jim Bertrand Landscape Design, Monee, Illinois, www.jimbertrand.com **Project duration** Five months **Completion** 2003

COHESIVE CLARITY

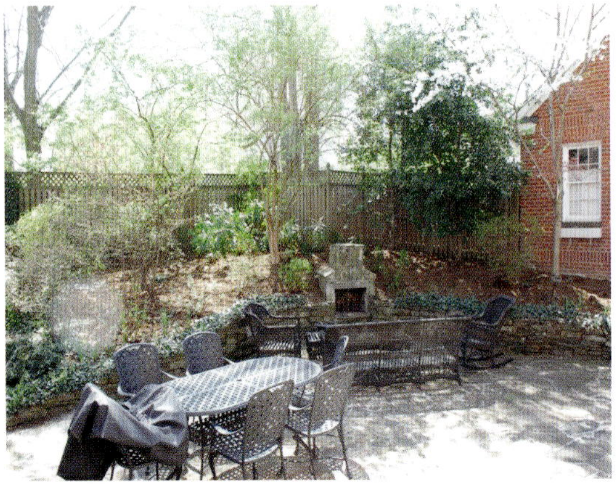
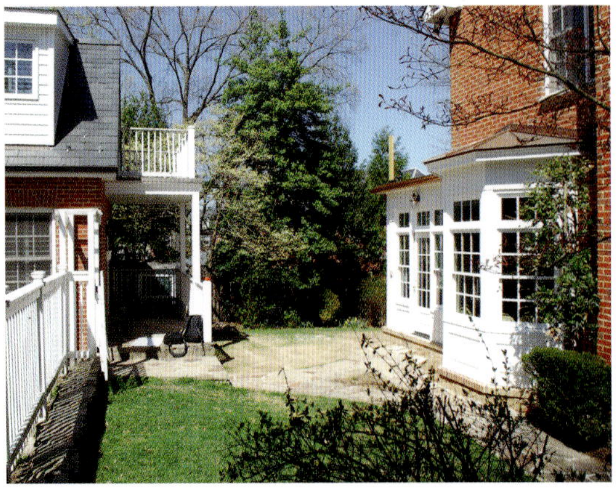
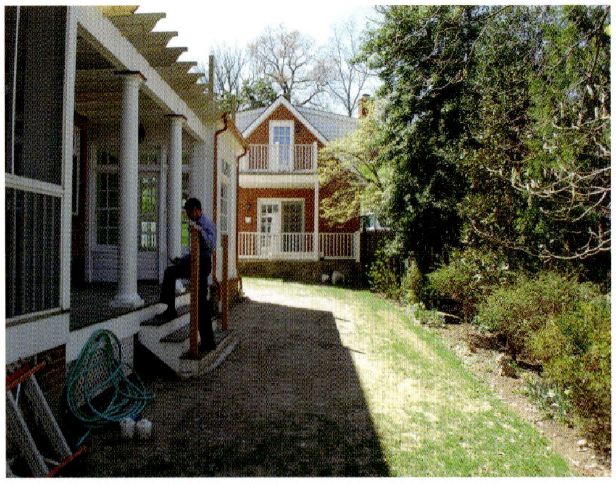
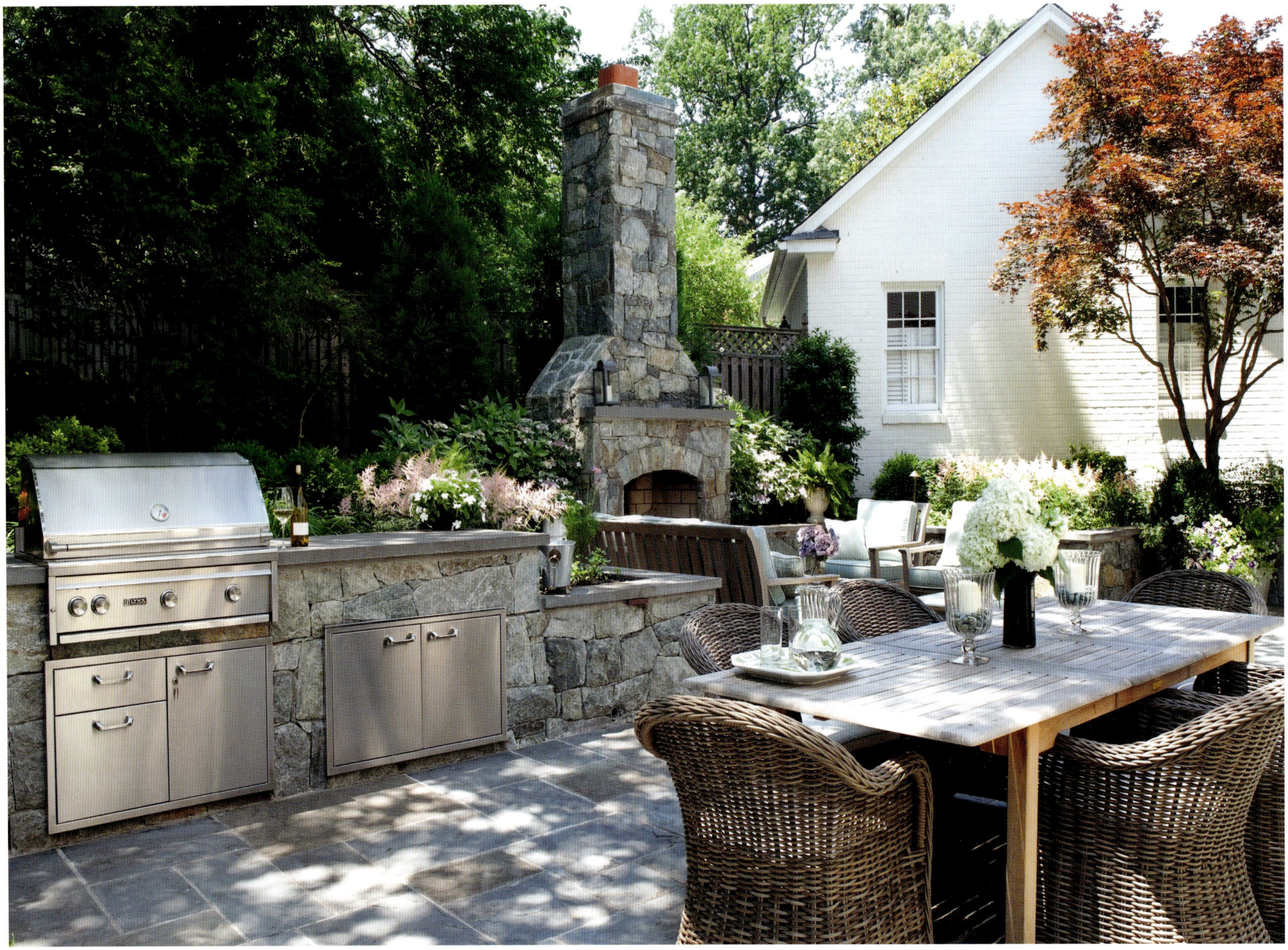

TRIFECTA OF DELIGHTS

Close to bustling Washington, D.C. but far away in terms of ambience and serenity, a small site in Alexandria, Virginia, shows how a property can use a new vision to work and flow better, similar to remaking an interior. The new owners of a Colonial-style house purchased the quarter-acre (0.10-hectare) property with the idea of spending more time outdoors with their two daughters and entertaining more frequently. But their challenge was that they weren't sure how they would meet that goal since the lot was small, disjointed because of small disconnected parts, and not level. Brian Hahn, who oversaw the work for his design/build firm Botanical Decorators in nearby Olney, Maryland, aided by colleague Christopher Cahill, quickly recognized upon walking across the site that they would need to regrade, plant more shrubs and flowers, and renovate the two outbuildings and existing patio to improve functionality and flow. "There was really no driveway to park, the front of the house sat on a busy street, most of the access to the freestanding garage was in the back near a separate guest house, which left little lawn area for socializing except on the sides," Brian explains.

Site Problems

- Tight property
- Grade changes
- No connection between main residence and the two outbuildings due to disconnected small parcels and because of renovations through the years that brought in different palettes and materials

Wish List

- Nice welcoming entrance to home at rear/side so it has an enhanced sense of arrival
- Outdoor fireplace and dining/grilling areas for large family events where an existing but deteriorating patio stood and where there was a small fireplace
- Introduce a flower palette of soft blues, pinks, and whites that are low maintenance, as opposed to those needing high levels of care or thirsty options, and a more simple range of choices

Finding a Professional

The owners found Brian Hahn by word of mouth.

Project Challenges

- Fashion three defined spaces with different purposes, but have similar walkways, plant materials, and lamps, which connect them physically and visually
- Improve an existing but deteriorating patio area and give it greater purpose
- Fix an existing porch and deck and make them more important, so they'd be used more often
- Improve the rear area of the property since it would serve as the day-to-day entrance to the home
- Make the very tight backyard feel more inviting and spacious
- Update all three buildings and give them a unified design motif

Problem-Solving Solutions

The designers' first decision was to give the rear entry at the side a more significant role, since it was used more frequently than the front door. Then they transformed the site into three distinct zones, each with its own personality and purpose, yet part of a cohesive whole. Having Botanical Decorators in charge of all work—landscaping, hardscaping, painting, furniture choices, and even accessories, such as pots—made coming up with a cohesive look much easier than it would have been if the homeowners had hired different contractors and subcontractors.

It was clear that the mostly empty spaces in between each of the three buildings didn't function as well as they could, and a greater sense of space was needed for the rear of the property.

Brian approached each of the three parcels as a distinct entity, even though they were small. He tied the spaces together by selecting similarly colored plants but with some different textures and leaves; using similar Pennsylvania flagstone with a natural

Opposite top left: Before: Backyard terrace where a small fireplace once existed and was replaced. *Opposite top center:* Before: Existing entrance where a new walkway was constructed. *Opposite top right:* Before: Unused lawn where a new lawn space was installed as a secondary entertaining space. *Opposite bottom:* After: The new dining patio was built using flagstone; the space also includes an outdoor kitchen with a 5-foot-long (1.5-meter-long) serving counter and a 14-foot-tall (4.27-meter-tall) fireplace built from quarry stone that's a focal point for a seating area.

cleft for walks; Pennsylvania bluestone for wall caps, fireplace mantel, and hearth; old-fashioned gray New England cobblestones for detailing and inlays; similarly styled furnishings and pots throughout; similar lighting along paths and walls of buildings; and a similar palette of off-white on all three buildings, rather than having the different brick façades left as is.

At the same time, Brian gave each area a distinct use. By the side off the kitchen and dining room and near the new side-door entry, he repaired and painted the existing deck and screened porch; the deck also gained a pergola for shade and which also connected it to the existing architecture. The lawn a few steps down was leveled for better drainage and usability, then given a detailed border of mini-granite cobblestone to add structure and visual appeal. This side of the house is used mostly for small gatherings with the owners serving cocktails from tables set up on the lawn. The larger area on the other side of the house off the home's living room became the family's main gathering space. An existing patio that sat too low, collected water, and had a non-functioning fireplace was transformed into an extended entertaining area with oversized dining patio, grilling station, and sitting/conversation patio with a tall, majestic fireplace as the centerpiece. The sitting walls and grilling station hold back the grade in a much understated fashion that allows homeowners and guests to feel nestled into the garden while it also took back critical space from the hillside. Because the sun is the strongest on this side in the morning, this area is used mostly in the afternoon and evenings.

In the area between the garage and guest house that was formerly used for parking, Brian introduced plantings to perk it up and a long curved walkway that leads around to the front door for a more gracious journey. He also removed a small porch

Top: The new lawn area has a cobblestone border; the circle motif became a contrast to all the rectilinear lines and is used for entertaining. **Above:** The owners use a new entrance to a mudroom on a daily basis since the home's main entrance sits on a busy road. **Opposite top left:** A view of the fireplace patio at night with low-voltage landscape lighting and uplighting in trees. **Opposite top right:** A view of the walkway and the entrance used daily are complemented by lush new landscaping. **Opposite bottom:** The plan shows how the main entertaining area was angled; doing so was because of the topography and grade changes but also because angling a layout can make it seem larger visually.

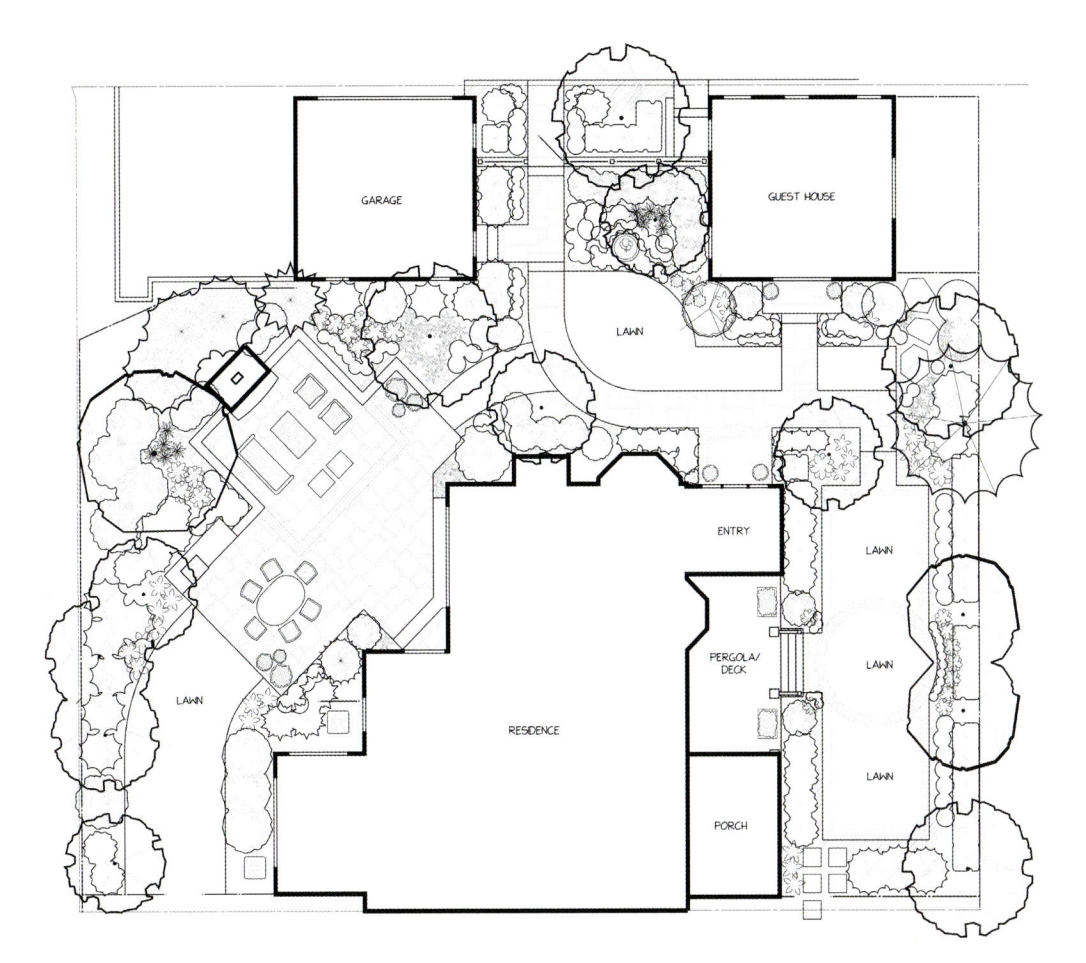

off the guest house that jutted into the area and produced an unpleasant claustrophobic feeling. The other side of the garage became the main parking area. Because the homeowners didn't want to spend a lot of time caring for plants, Brian went with traditional boxwoods, several types of hydrangeas, azaleas, and three groundcovers—pachysandra, liriope, and periwinkle, which provide different textures, leaf sizes, and floral colors. At the clients' request, he also incorporated kitchen herbs in this area, which are easily accessed by the client due to the kitchen's proximity.

Cost-Saving Alternatives

To suit a smaller budget, Brian suggests smaller plantings and less mature trees, and switching out flagstone for a less costly aggregate. "Those two changes would cut costs by as much as 40 percent," he says.

Budget

The budget was between 15 and 20 percent of the value of the home, and included landscaping, painting, and carpentry work.

Key Design Details

- Each space has a different feel and look yet there is a clean cohesiveness to the outdoors with the stone fireplace and low stone walls capped with flagstone to yield a classic, timeless feeling, suitable for a Colonial-style house.

The New Garden—An Epilogue

The homeowners went from having a tired yard to a beautiful fresh-looking garden with distinct spaces; they also gained better views and architectural focal points from inside to outside through large doors and windows.

PROJECT AND TEAM CREDITS: Location Alexandria, Virginia **Landscape designer** Brian Hahn and Christopher Cahill, Botanical Decorators, Olney, Maryland, www.botanicaldecorators.com **Project duration** The project was done in two phases for budgetary reasons as well as to see how the materials and areas evolved. First came the changes between the garage and guest house, which took between two and three months; then 1½ years later the firm returned to renovate the entertaining patio off of the family room, enlarge the fireplace, and add a grilling station and walls, which altogether took another one to two months **Completion** 2012

TRIFECTA OF DELIGHTS   155

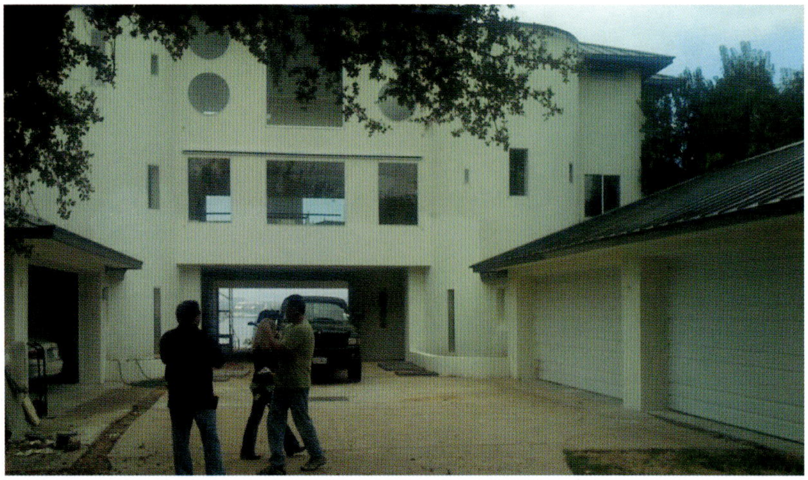
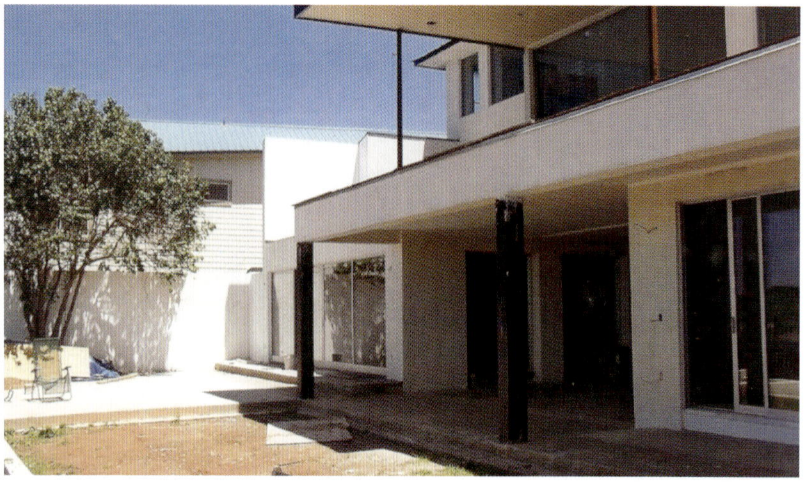
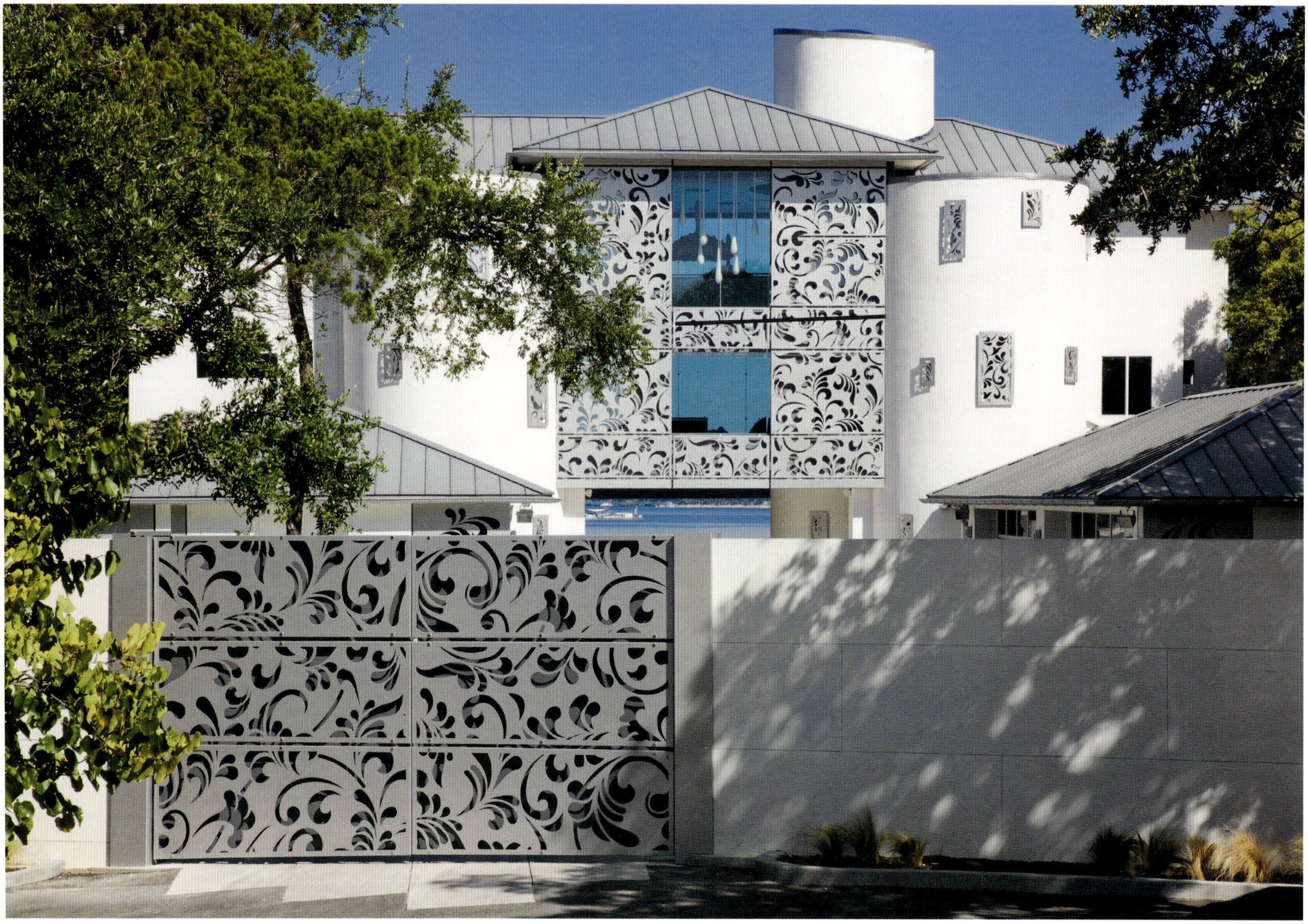

HIP REVIVAL

Things happen for a reason, or so the saying goes. When architect Winn Wittman met with a diamond dealer at a local Starbucks to replace his wife's engagement gift, area executive Milton Verret was grabbing some java, and heard Winn say he was an architect. "We struck up a conversation, and he said he needed an architect," says Winn, whose eponymous firm is based in Austin, Texas. And so it went serendipitously. After signing a contract and working on the house for 1½ years, Verret's large 1990s, weekend house—more than 10,000 square feet (929 square meters)—became a much more contemporary, dramatic, and sustainable design. His site also gained major improvements of a vanishing-edge pool styled after a swank hotel design in Miami that the homeowner liked, hot tub and cold plunge spas at the pool's corners, and landscaping that works in the hot Austin climate. Two garages were redesigned for climate control and to house the owner's collection of cars and rock 'n' roll memorabilia.

Site Problems
- Steep site on the side of a cliff

Wish List
- Vanishing-edge pool that would mimic the pool at the Delano hotel in Miami, Florida, a favorite resort of the owner
- Enlarge the garages and make them climate controlled
- Add to landscaping
- Improve the home's façade

Project Challenges
- Build a vanishing-edge pool with adjoining hot and cold tubs, and cantilever the new pool along the cliff
- Remove inferior work undertaken by a former plumbing contractor
- Select landscaping that would thrive in the hot Austin climate
- Figure out a solution to screen the home for more privacy and shade on one side as well as at the front of the residence
- Develop a solution to cool the house's interior from the hot afternoon sun
- Develop a way to traverse down the hillside as an alternative to the existing tram system
- Provide better guard rails along the steep slope
- Make better use of an existing breezeway that served no function

Problem-Solving Solutions

The steeply sloping site and an existing breezeway led to two novel solutions and some Herculean construction efforts. Because the breezeway bisected the house but didn't connect any structures, Winn decided to make greater use of it by building the desired pool adjacent to it to provide views of Lake Travis, a reservoir on the Colorado River. The property was so steep that the construction team wore rappelling gear, which allowed them to hang off the cliff's side to chip away for the pool's foundation. To make the pool as dramatic as the house, Winn designed it as a sculptural 40-foot by 50-foot (12.1-meter by 15.2-meter) body with a vanishing edge and two corner spas—one a hot tub and the other a cold plunge spa. To make the pool appear even more natural and mimic the owner's favorite Miami Beach resort, he lined the sides in glass tile and constructed a shallow end where lounge chairs could be placed. Between the breezeway and pool, new limestone tile paving runs in a random-width pattern with gravel between stones for sustainability. Winn also designed oversized steps with built-in lighting for more drama and safety, and used glass handrails along the walkways on the low-slung terraces to add a more contemporary edginess.

Everything was constructed to withstand strong hurricane-force winds. Along the slopes, Winn planted grassy areas with a turf that can withstand the hot climate and help with erosion—Tif Sport Bermuda, which is what many golf courses in Texas use. For privacy from neighbors on one side, he planted 20-foot-tall (6-meter-tall) giant timber bamboo that has now grown to 50 feet (15.2 meters). To get down to the lakefront where Verret docks his boats, visitors and family use a tram that Winn updated with a new railing and interior appointments.

Opposite top left and right: Entry façade before the remodel and before the pool was added. **Opposite bottom:** Entry façade after the remodeling with custom aluminum panels designed by the architect to provide visual interest and solar shading; a gleaming contemporary duo of white and aluminum.

1 Lake Travis
2 Cliff
3 Pool

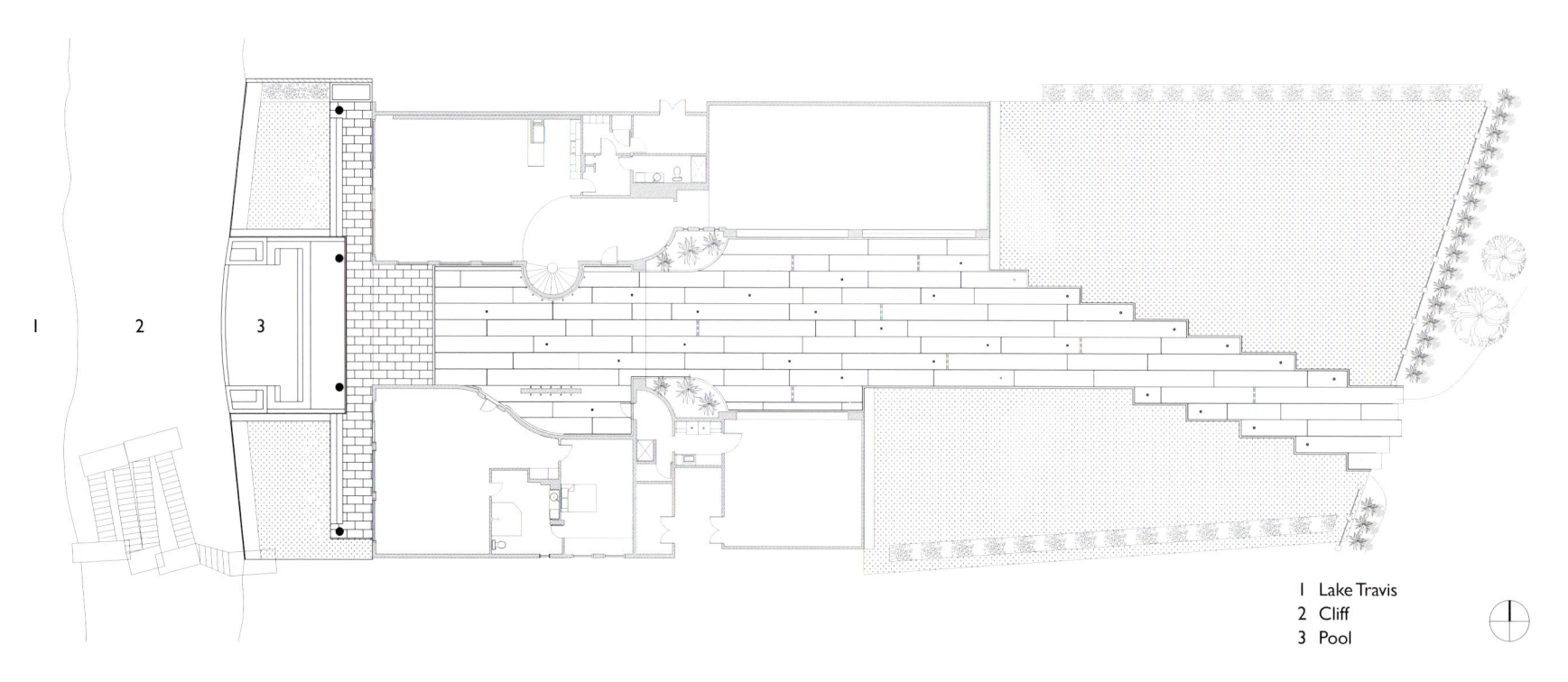

Top left: View of lakeside façade with stone decks and custom glass railings that don't impede the view. Note color-changing LED lights.
Top right: Living room with silver-leafed ceiling and zeppelin lights by Marcel Wanders. **Above:** The plan of the house shows how a central breezeway divides its two wings and frames a view of the lake. **Opposite:** View of rear façade with new glass-tiled vanishing-edge swimming pool, decks and custom-designed shading device overhead.

At the front of the house, the façade was flat and lifeless, and also had unattractive round, porthole-style windows. Winn improved the curb appeal with decorative panels constructed from powder-coated aluminum that he had etched with a giant floral pattern. He repeated the pattern on the front gate and inside the house. These panels do more than just improve the home's aesthetics: they also help by keeping the house cooler. This idea helped the firm win the 2010 Best Green Innovation award in the Dream Home contest. Landscape architecture student Andrew McConnico, who helped on the project, came up with the idea of incorporating mounds of colored glass in several of the landscaping beds. Throughout the site, succulents such as Mexican feather grass and agaves were planted. These have a low-water requirement. An efficient drip irrigation system and heavy mulch were also installed.

The redesign offered an additional benefit from within: new windows in the 25-foot-high (7.6-meter-high) living room provided more expansive views.

Cost-Saving Alternatives

The budget could have been decreased by using less expensive steel rather than glass railings; instead of glass tiles, plaster; instead of custom colored lighting, more conventional bulbs; instead of polished concrete strips on the driveway to emphasize the home's axis with the lake, crushed gravel or asphalt. While the front panels were costly in the short term, Winn projects they will save money over the coming years because of their cooling capacity.

Budget

This project was estimated at 50 percent of the value of the house.

Key Design Details

- Custom screens with floral motif
- Colorful LED lighting in steps and throughout landscape
- Vanishing-edge pool with twin tubs
- Five giant chandeliers made from 1,000 sheets of silver leaf installed in the living room

The New Garden—An Epilogue

"My client used to have a very bare suburban lot—now he has a lush landscape with privacy," Winn says. And he learned in the process that although all the detailing might not reflect his style, it appeals to the client, who wanted a very personalized site. "It taught me to be flexible in my design approach and accommodate everyone's individual taste," he says.

PROJECT AND TEAM CREDITS: Client Milton Verret **Location** Austin, Texas **Architect** Winn Wittman, Winn Wittman Architecture, Austin, Texas, www.winnwittman.com **Landscape architect** Andrew McConnico, Swift Company, 304 10th Avenue, East Unit A, Seattle, Washington **Project duration** 1½ years **Completion** 2010

160

NATURAL WILDNESS BALANCES CULTIVATED TURF

After having gone to college by the ocean in New Hampshire, a business executive was determined to enjoy regular visits there from his other home near New York City. "It was initially to be a weekend and vacation house, but a place that he and his wife eventually would use as a retirement home," says landscape architect Terrence Parker, whose firm Terra Firma Landscape Architecture in Portsmouth was awarded the assignment. The specific goals, which were extensive, were to help transform the 6-acre (2.4-hectare) site into a visually rich, layered landscape with innumerable amenities. Living near his clients' home, Terrence understood the climate well, which was a big consideration—salt air, wind, summer sun, and an extremely cold winter. Terrence was enthusiastic at the chance to alter the very flat terrain with a modest mansard cottage, some evergreen hedges, and lawn right up to the sea wall—it "was all lawn with no context," he says. "We needed to make the landscape much less monotonous and more textural, as well as fit into the context of the site with all the amenities my clients wanted—the cottage expanded, outbuildings introduced, and a number of other architectural features."

Site Problems

- All lawn
- Bland and uninspired without any discerning landscape features

Wish List

- Open, uninterrupted views to the ocean while still maintaining some privacy from neighbors
- Interesting modern pool house, and pool
- Maximize exterior spaces with terraces, breezeway, porches, decks
- An open area left for pitching and putting, since husband is an avid golfer
- Adequate vehicular circulation and parking for large gatherings

Finding a Professional

The architect provided the reference for Terrence; they had worked together before.

Project Challenges

- Integrate the architectural extensions and additions, including breezeway, porches, pergola, barrel-vaulted pool house, and pool into the landscape
- Manipulate the site's topography with grade elevations that made sense and worked with the house so they all flow together seamlessly
- Create context and visual interest on a formerly uninteresting site

Problem-Solving Solutions

The project required extensive work and a team consisting of a landscape architect, architects, engineers, and interior designers to transform both the building structure and terrain into a more interesting site experience, as well as introduce architectural features, including an expanded house with porches and decks, breezeway to a pool house and pool, pergolas, and walkways. Terrence also worked to minimize the impact of the parking on the site and pulled it away from the house and relocated it to another area behind a spruce hedge row and outbuilding.

On top of those goals was to blend everything—new and old, both the site and buildings. In manipulating the flat property, Terrence's goal was to vary the landscape for greater visual appeal with a trio of looks appropriate for a New Hampshire coast, but have them segue from one to the next logically: a rugged wild coastal feeling by the ocean, low-grass meadow with masses of perennial plantings, and some flat lawn left for the husband, a golfer, to pitch and putt to his heart's content. To accomplish this, in fact, he removed some of the perimeter lawn for the meadow to increase the sense of being on the coast with wild grasses, which he terms "rewilding." "I wanted to create the right context that would normally exist by the ocean," he says.

Opposite top left: Before: The front of the lawn shows where the future pool was constructed, looking back at the house before its renovation.
Opposite top right: Before: Another elevation, the ocean side at the back of the house, with another view of the existing architecture before changes were made to the house and landscape. **Opposite bottom:** After: The non-ocean side view of the architectural renovations made at the front of the house with newly installed landscaping create a cohesive, attractive whole. Double rows of viburnum shrubs are seen in early October when their fall colors are almost at their peak. The shrubs offer privacy but do not block the great views of the site.

Top left: This photo showcases the view from the house toward the newly installed pool house, pergola, and dining terrace. The paving is a custom-dyed and ground aggregate concrete, which made it affordable, since there was a large expanse of paving. **Top right:** Large stone stepping pads made from native granite lead from the meadow garden to the pool. **Above:** The view from the pergola and pool toward the newly renovated house showcases a fence that meets code but is also an elegant meandering serpentine style to match the curve of the stone walls. **Opposite left:** This view from the lower meadow highlights the pool and pergola and shows how the irregular granite steps blend with the natural setting of the property. **Opposite right:** The rectangular pool has an elegant simple shape, surrounded by a mix of concrete and granite that blend seamlessly; the pool was designed on an axis with the new pool house.

Terrence also added variety through vegetative texture and patterns that would be visible in many seasons, rather than overly focusing on floral displays. In addition, there are perennial berry plantings—beach plum, blueberry, raspberry, and elderberry, which all grow well in the low grassy meadow. For the big lawn area, he planted different fescue grasses.

Because Terrence knew that his client wanted to retain unobstructed views to the Atlantic Ocean right beyond—and who wouldn't want such front-row seats—and privacy from neighbors, he carefully sited some features lower and others higher. The pool fence and stone retaining wall meander at a low height, yet are high enough to offer safety. The pool area itself is elevated above so swimmers and loungers enjoy views, and that area is now seamless with the home's elevation. He planted native deciduous trees such as tupelo, shagbark, and other hickory specimens at the periphery of the property to frame views to the ocean; they also happen to screen the neighbors' house. The hardscape materials have a rugged elegance, which also provide a contrast in textures and patterns to enchant the eye.

Cost-Saving Alternatives

Dyed aggregate concrete, which mimics natural stone, was used for a terrace, and was about one-fifth of the cost. In another area a meadow was planted with seeds in masses, which also cuts costs since they tend to multiply and colonize.

Budget

The project budget was estimated at about 15 percent of value of house and site.

Challenges Along the Way

None, since the clients were determined to have excellent communications with the design team and asked very detailed questions.

The timetable was extended but primarily because the clients kept expanding their goals and scope of the project.

Key Design Details

- Seamless integration of views out toward ocean
- The overall feeling of an interesting natural site with a wild coastal setting married to meadows and lawn

The New Garden—An Epilogue

The clients are ecstatic and want to be there more and more of the time. For the architect, the project represented an enriching design experience, since he had a beautiful site by the ocean to work and make better with a context at the end that looks like it has always been there. "I honed a style and found that I could use lush native plantings in a large scale that would create long-term visual interest and survive the ocean climate," Terrence says.

PROJECT AND TEAM CREDITS: Location Seacoast, near Portsmouth, New Hampshire **Landscape architect** Terrence Parker, Terra Firma Landscape Architecture, Portsmouth, New Hampshire, www.terrafirmalandscape.com **Architect** CJ Architects, Portsmouth, New Hampshire, www.cjarchitects.com **Builder** Chinburg Builders, New Market, New Hampshire, www.chinburg.com **Interior designer** Paula Daher Interior Design, Boston, Massachusetts, www.daherinteriordesign.com **Civil engineering** Altus Engineering, Portsmouth, New Hampshire, www.altus-eng.com **Landscaping** Piscataqua Landscaping, Eliot, Maine, www.piscataqualandscaping.com **Woodwork** Salmon Falls Woodworking, Dover, New Hampshire, www.salmonfallswoodworks.com **Project duration** 18 months **Completion** 2011–2013

Top left: Before: Front of the house. **Top right:** Before: Back yard. **Above left:** After: A loggia sits on the new rear lawn, supported by large impressive stone pillars. **Above right center:** After: Stream and spa water features run into the pool, with a retaining wall holding up the plantings constructed from western Maryland fieldstone. **Above right:** After: Looking down on the spa feature from the raised terrace above the loggia.

WOODLANDS STAR

Finding a secluded site in a Maryland suburb close to Washington, D.C. was no easy feat. But the homeowners were determined to secure land and privacy for their new family home and outdoor living spaces. The 4-acre (1.6-hectare) site that they purchased from a developer certainly offered seclusion nestled amid a poplar grove and surrounding woodlands, and with a long driveway setting it back far from the road. All the stars seemed to align, except that the site was so steep that it necessitated a large retaining wall to provide a flat expanse for the house and the outdoor areas. The wall provided one downside: it bisected the property. Landscape architect Jeffrey Plusen of Plusen Designs, LLC, in Catonville, Maryland, resolved all the challenges and some that weren't part of the initial concept. At the front, he used the driveway as inspiration to design an interesting journey to the front door. At the rear, he found a way to incorporate all the architectural elements his clients wanted—pool, spa, entertaining space, lawn for children, dining loggia, and screened porch with fireplace, and he did so within one cohesive whole rather than divided parts. His results celebrate the property's naturalness while also providing an active habitat for humans.

Site Problems
- Steep slope that dictated the need for the developer to erect a retaining wall to provide a flat surface

Wish List
- Swimming pool that would fit into the wooded site but be long enough to swim laps
- Adjacent spa
- Dining loggia
- Lawn space for kids to play
- Ample guest parking
- Seating terraces
- Bucolic site left intact as much as possible with minimal pool surround

Finding a Professional
The landscaping design firm was found through a referral from friends of the homeowners.

Project Challenges
A retaining wall bisected the site and separated the house and garden from the woodland, so a design challenge was developing a way to celebrate the woodland yet also tie all of it together.

Problem-Solving Solutions
Jeff had his work cut out for him in this project. At the front, he designed a long asphalt-paved driveway to wind up to the house, crossing a drainage area, which he played up as an asset by designing a stone bridge with piers to span it, creating the equivalent of a resting spot that brings the three-story traditional farmhouse into view. The piers are on an axis with the home's front door. The journey continues on to an arrival court paved in pea gravel and framed by five hornbeam trees in a row, the American version of a French allée. The driveway also jogs off to the left of the home, extending into a garage court.

To make the pool and spa look more natural, Jeff designed the pool in a free-form shape and nestled both in the rear, close to the woods and property line. He also constructed them with thick walls and coping of local Western Maryland stone, and added a diving rock. The spa spills water into the pool, which is recirculated. A second water spill into the pool comes from a 50-foot-long (15.2-meter-long) artificial stream, adding even more to the site's natural feeling. To tie it all together and keep the emphasis on the natural beauty, Jeff repeated the native Western Maryland stone in a minimally terraced area on one side and left the other all to newly planted fescue lawn. For accents, there are new large boulders all about, embellished with spots of color from native coneflowers, black-eyed Susans, and milkweed.

Other additions include a screened porch with fireplace that opens to an upper terrace, a dining loggia under the upper terrace off the home, and a pavilion to enjoy vistas of the site.

Cost-Saving Alternatives
The asphalt driveway and pea gravel court reflect less costly choices; and the five hornbeam trees could have been selected smaller (i.e. less mature).

Top left: The plan shows the large walls that were needed to make the site level. **Top right:** A diving stone is at the deep end for a fun way to enter the pool; the fieldstone coping was used to fashion the lounge terrace. **Above left:** A big lawn area was planted using a fescue mix; poplars stand tall in the distance. **Above right:** A water feature flows into the pool and connects the pool to the woods behind. **Opposite top left:** A dining area under the loggia can be used even in inclement weather and has an intimate feeling. **Opposite top right:** An elegant mahogany gate with arched top leads to the pool area in back, flanked by stone piers made of Western Maryland fieldstone, all with an aged patina look. **Opposite bottom:** The stream feature flows into the pool using pool water. Jeff's advice: "Work with the grade you have to avoid a stream looking fake."

Challenges Along the Way

Bringing in large equipment to place boulders and construct the pool terraces; Jeff did this and his team also worked their way out by starting at the bottom of the hill.

Key Design Details

- The swale is celebrated with a large bridge with piers at the front.
- The five hornbeam trees that frame the arrival court.
- A long pathway that leads to the back of the house past a mahogany gate and down stone steps.

The New Garden—An Epilogue

The homeowners gained several new outdoor rooms: a screened porch, pool and terrace, lawn; and they are so pleased they are thinking of more changes and are discussing these with Jeff. "We're talking about a getaway more in the woods," Jeff says.

PROJECT AND TEAM CREDITS: Location Bethesda, Maryland **Landscape architect** Jeffrey Plusen, RLA, ASLA, Plusen Designs, Catonville, Maryland, www.plusen.com **Project duration** 1½ years **Completion** 2009

Top left: Before: Back door to the house with driveway to the garage court. **Top right:** Before: View of the garage court.
Above: After: A seating area beyond the back door reached by a gravel pathway. The little patio was constructed with bluestone rectangles fringed with dwarf acorus, a groundcover.

HISTORIC INSPIRATIONS FOR FOOD, FLOWERS, COMPANY

During much of the 20th century, William Roy Wallace played an important role in architectural design throughout Winston-Salem, North Carolina. Many of his Beaux Arts–inspired designs are still visible today.* When a now-retired couple was ready to work on the rear garden of their property at Wallace's well-known Meade Willis house, they retained landscape architect Jeff Allen, also a Winston-Salem resident. Sensitive to the home's history, they wanted to respect the 1940s architectural integrity and instructed Jeff to ensure that the gardens reflect its classical style. During his research for this project, Jeff found inspiration from prominent landscape designer Ellen Biddle Shipman, whose workmanship is on view at the famed Bayou Bend Gardens (Houston, Texas), Longue Vue Gardens (New Orleans, Louisiana), and Duke University's Sarah P. Duke Gardens (Durham, North Carolina), to name a few of her projects. For the couple, the immediate challenge was filling a large hole that was created when an oak tree fell abruptly by their back porch. But they didn't stop there, and gave Jeff a long list of additional requests—common in design work indoors and outdoors. As long as they were doing some work, why not now introduce, as well, gardens to grow food and flowers in a walled space that animals couldn't enter, a grilling station, a modest-sized terrace for alfresco dining and socializing, garage court, garden paths, rear entry porch, and improved drainage. Jeff designed all into the master plan and work began.

*More information about William Roy Wallace's architecture is available from the North Carolina State University Libraries, which acquired his papers.

Site Problems

- Poor drainage with water entering the garage due to insufficient system to address the volume of water during rainy times
- Erosion also due to water not running off the site properly
- Unsuitable soil in the main garden area

Wish List

- Working vegetable and flower cutting gardens for the wife, an avid gardener
- Compost area
- Outdoor kitchen with two grills for the husband
- Sitting area
- Improve porch
- Better access to back door, gardens, and eating area

Finding a Professional

Jeff was referred by a mutual architectural friend.

Project Challenges

- Improve drainage problems
- Conceal trash cans within attractive enclosure
- Appropriate design for prominent historic home

Problem-Solving Solutions

The first issue was to address the problematic drainage. Jeff designed the garage court using granite cobblestone curbing, dyed concrete paving, and a series of decorative iron drain inlets to catch the stormwater and direct the flow to a suitable part of the site. The gravel paths in the garden have subsurface drain pipes that collect rainwater and tie into the larger drainage system. The overall 37-foot by 33-foot (11.2-meter by 10-meter) garden is designed with brick walls that were engineered to retain the lower portion of the garden and raised above the finished height of the garden to protect the owner's flowers and vegetables from pests. Specially ordered, handcrafted brick was used for the walls and detailed to match the home's brickwork. Brick pillars and white period gates with wrought-iron hinges mark the two entrances to the garden, and all together lend an appearance compatible with the original design. Gravel paths and garden beds are organized in a classic pattern for ease of access, circulation, and function. An ornamental urn at the center of the garden works as a focal point. A teak bench sits at the back edge of the garden for the owner's respite and to enjoy the fruits of her labor.

Instead of designing a large outdoor kitchen, which has become a trend in garden design, Jeff kept this couple's cooking area modest to fit their needs; more important was access to the house and porch nearby. Yet, it still features two grilling stations—charcoal and gas. Close by, Jeff designed a small patio with a mix of gravel and bluestone stepping stones placed in a running bond pattern for resting furniture firmly, and fringed in a groundcover of dwarf acorus, which grows well in sunny areas. A bigger bluestone slab

Top left: The small outdoor kitchen, seen from the back porch. **Top center:** An urn found by the homeowner works as a focal point because of its size and scale, surrounded by lettuces and blue and yellow pansies. **Top right:** An overview of the garden in early spring; small river rock was used to pave the area because of its color that matches the brick mortar and was locally available. **Above:** To protect the plantings from rabbits, Jeff enclosed the garden with a 3.5-feet-tall (1.07-meter-tall) brick wall, which matches the brick of the house and was finished with an historic-style cap. **Opposite:** The garden plan is visible as soon as visitors enter the garage court; axial views were important for visual organization and as a wayfinding system.

placed on a diagonal provides a transition to other areas—straight ahead past hydrangeas to the left, and granite steps to the upper rear lawn area, or right to the garden gate and vegetable and flower gardens.

The eyesore of the trash bins was resolved with an enclosure. And despite its historic look, Jeff used vinyl instead of wood on the fencing and gate structures to help the homeowners avoid frequent repainting and replacement.

Cost-Saving Alternatives

Suitable compromises were made along the way to fit the owners' budget. Jeff's original plan for the design was scaled back once the job was bid. Instead of using bluestone for all walkways, he established a "hierarchy" of paths, incorporating gravel in less formal areas; bluestone was selectively used in high-traffic and formal areas only. The garden was also reduced in size, and extruded vinyl was used in lieu of iron gates at garden entrances. Dyed concrete was another affordable solution in the garage court, in keeping with the historic aspect of the project. Other considerations were to lower the height of brick walls and use wooden or iron fencing to enclose the garden.

Budget

Jeff estimated the amount at 7 percent to 8 percent of the home's value.

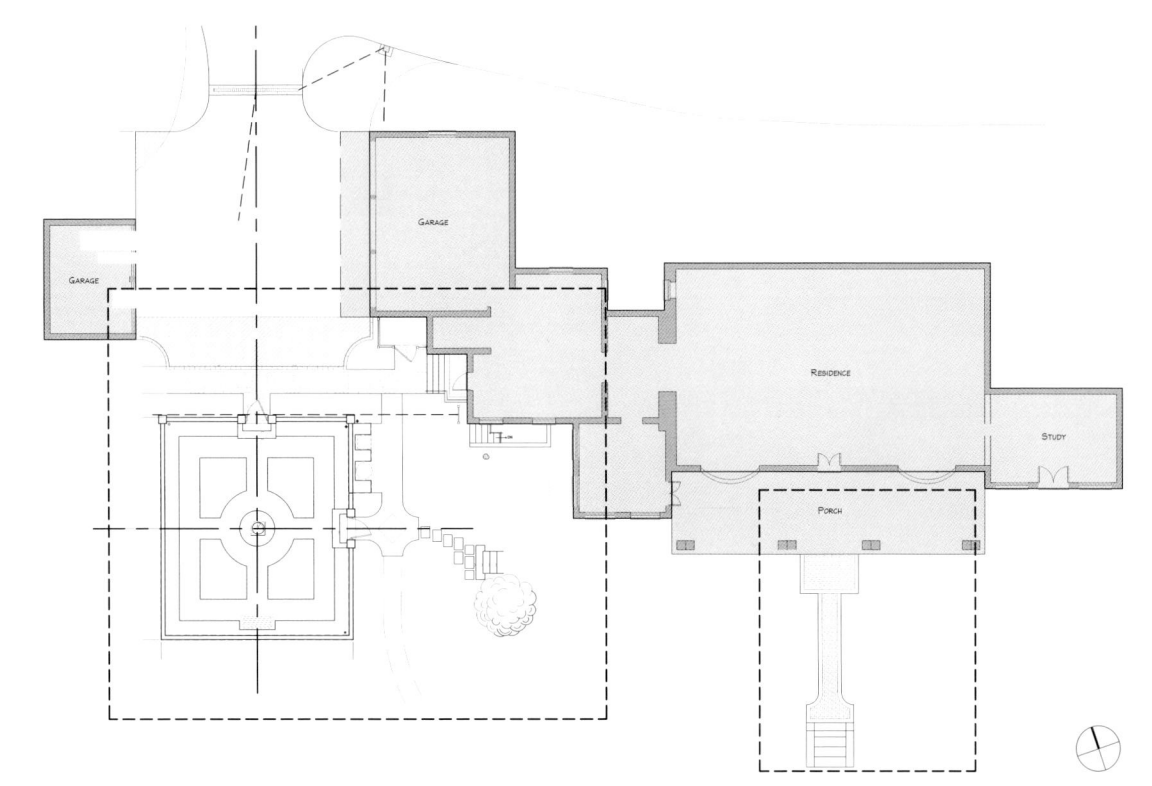

Challenges Along the Way

Utilities running underneath the garden demanded consultation with the local power company to find a way to build over them. The type of brick used for the garden walls was a specially ordered handcrafted brick, which took additional time to manufacture.

Key Design Details

- The brick walls and entry gates provide the first landmark when visitors drive onto the site.
- The next landmark is a large urn that's spotted as visitors move into the gardens, planted with culinary and flower perennials and annuals, including tomatoes, peppers, chard, catmint, and climbing roses.
- Eight boxwoods add a formal lush note, which Shipman was known for in her period designs.

The New Garden—An Epilogue

Not only have the new garden areas provided the homeowner with areas to pursue her passion, but she is excited that she will be able to show and teach her young grandchildren the joy of working with nature and its bounty. She also found that the new gardens are convenient to the side and back entries, making garden work and access in and out of the home and garden much easier. For Jeff, the completed gardens represent the type of collaborative teamwork with a knowledgeable client extremely satisfying. "The couple has been a wonderful steward of the property and home, as well as a great patron to design and fine gardening. Jeff notes that, "Garden design is an ongoing process that keeps evolving as the garden grows and develops."

PROJECT AND TEAM CREDITS: Location Winston-Salem, North Carolina **Landscape architect** Jeff Allen, Jeff Allen Landscape Architecture (JALA), LLC, Winston Salem, North Carolina, www.jalallc.com **Contractors** Brett Sipe, QFC INC, Winston-Salem, North Carolina, bsipe77@gmail.com; Brent Talley, LandPlus Landscape Design, Winston-Salem, North Carolina, landplus@bellsouth.net **Project duration** The design process started in July 2011 with construction running from April to November 2012 **Completion** 2012

Top left: Before: An existing messy slope where a checkerboard terrace and bocce ball court were added. **Top right:** Before: Front of the house with a mish-mash of plantings that dwarfed the scale of the house; all were removed. **Bottom:** After: At the street, a wall constructed of flagstone was inspired by an artist's work and a "river of succulents," which includes deer-proof plantings.

RULE NO 1: BAG THE MASTER PLAN

Rules are meant to be broken … at times. And that's just what landscape architect Jarrod R. Baumann did in designing a dozen separate gardens for a couple's recently purchased 1.3-acre (0.5-hectare) property in Los Gatos, a small city south of San Francisco. Jarrod may have won the proverbial lottery with the project. His clients gave him almost free rein to transform the very hilly site with an existing pool and tennis court, but little else noteworthy, into a series of very different, highly personalized garden delights. "They wanted to make the site much more modern in feeling, so it would better complement their 1990s house, and they also wanted better views of the city and hills," he says. Others might have considered the steep slopes a negative, but Jarrod turned them into positives with several novel terraced outdoor-style rooms. And because of the large budget and the clients' willingness to let Jarrod be innovative, even playful, he designed the entire site as he might his own garden—space by space, letting each completed area inspire the next rather than be tied to a preset plan. "I was told, and it's really true, that a garden is like a musical composition. The piece may be written, but every time you play it—or in this case work on the garden—it changes," he says. And this has and continues to, even five years after its start.

Site Problems

- Mish-mash of plantings—one of everything without any organization or relationship to the house
- Sloping hillside
- Existing pool and tennis court made it impossible to bring large equipment onto the site, so all terraces had to be dug by hand with wheelbarrows and shovels

Wish List

- More modern garden with structured plantings
- Variety of different gardens, almost like rooms
- Gardens that would reflect what is special about the Californian climate and vegetation

Finding a Professional

Jarrod was referred by a contractor colleague.

Project Challenges

- Getting to know clients who are very busy, making it hard to have face time together to understand their priorities and explain decisions
- Working with a contractor Jarrod had never worked with before, which requires a steep learning curve
- Provide places where the clients' young daughter would enjoy playing

Problem-Solving Solutions

Jarrod and the contractor, James Everett, started working at the front of the house back in 2010, designing a stainless-steel flax garden along the 100-foot-long (30.5-meter-long) portion of the garden. All around and on the site, the resulting gardens, akin to outdoor rooms, show off their distinct personalities:

- Spiral labyrinth
- Aviary with chicken coup
- Terraced garden with Inari shrine–inspired lower garden with repetitive arches
- Pebbled water trough
- Terrace with bocce court
- Contemporary-style Japanese teahouse
- Terrace with contemporary tapestry garden with checkerboard motif
- Shade garden
- Glass accent rivulet
- Pizza oven and barbecue area near pool
- Stainless-steel and glass arbor and wind screen
- Concrete raised vegetable garden
- Stacked-stone serpentine wall inspired by sculptor Andy Goldsworthy's work

Within these areas, Jarrod showed his creativity by mixing hard- and softscape materials—more than 450 different plants with sometimes 200 in a single mass, plus varied colors, and textures, and repeating patterns for greater emphasis. He also introduced native California succulents and fruit trees where possible since the clients, who were from Scotland and who still maintained a home there, wanted their California garden to reflect their newly acquired roots. But they also wanted some features inspired by Scottish architect and designer Charles Renni Mackintosh. A tapestry garden was inspired by yet another influence—the parterre gardens at Versailles outside Paris, which consist of a diagonal-shaped checkerboard motif fashioned from grass and crushed white gravel.

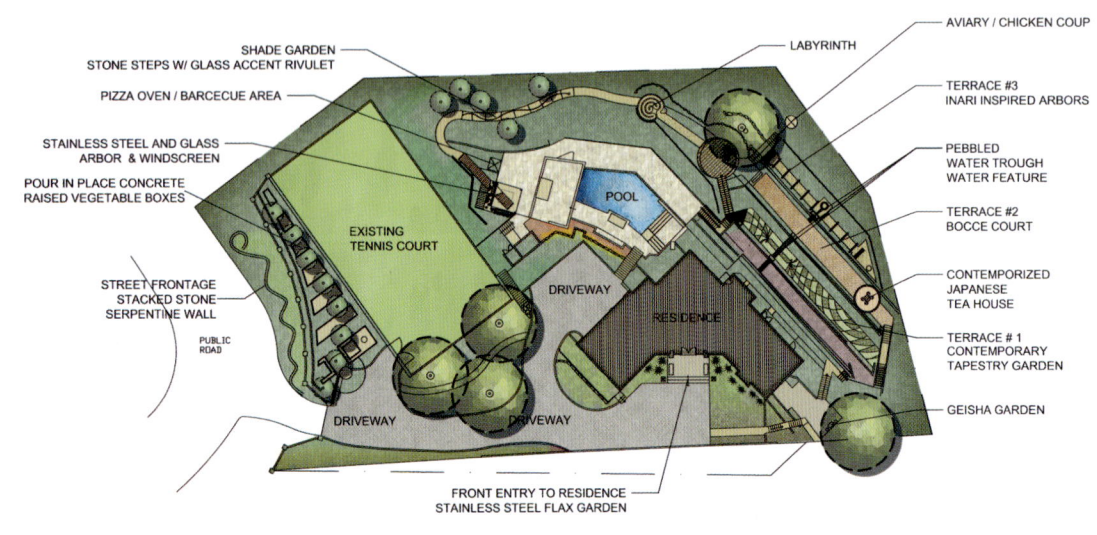

Top: Flagstone steps lead down, past a small seating bench and down more to a wildflower meadow. "This is one part of the garden that's not contemporary; we decided to make it a fern-woodland garden to see how they'd do in this climate," Jarrod says. **Bottom left:** The overall master plan was designed more for explanation since it was drawn afterward. **Bottom right:** The Zen garden in a contemporary style with stainless-steel bamboo edge and its shape is an abstraction of San Francisco Bay. **Opposite from left to right:** The contemporary tapestry garden; labyrinth; Inari-inspired arbors, a Japanese influence; Japanese blood grass–edged staircase.

174

One of the three terraced gardens comprises a series of rectangular arches with a Japanese flavor that Mackintosh might have conceived, marrying two cultures. Jarrod also took into account the site's microclimates by enclosing a small sitting area with glass barn-style doors on sliders that protect sitters from strong winds; an adjacent fire pit helping to warm them up, and a water feature offering pleasant sounds. Jarrod even left his mark on the existing pool by changing the planting out to a more modern and warm palette. He also went to great lengths sometimes with labor-intensive work. Case in point: the stones that make up the serpentine stone wall were stacked by hand without mortar, like a puzzle, for a more interesting look. The gardens can be enjoyed from different levels: the spiral labyrinth was designed to offer visual interest to those standing on an upper pool terrace, perhaps sipping cocktails.

Cost-Saving Alternatives

The checkerboard garden did incorporate a concrete paver instead of limestone, which saved money, but this is not a garden overall to duplicate on more modest funds.

Budget

The budget was set at 50 percent of the value of the house and land.

Key Design Details

- Long serpentine wall is visible immediately as people approach the house, and as they enter the site they catch glimpses of different gardens and architectural elements.

- All the right touches were so important to Jarrod that he even designed the curvilinear teak and stainless-steel lounge chairs.

The New Garden—An Epilogue

The owners, who had done well financially because of a technological invention, took off a year to enjoy their house and garden. The wife, who trained as a plant botanist, now spends a lot of time in the garden, and Jarrod designed an app so she knows all 450 plants he introduced on the site. "This wasn't a series of gardens for show or for entertaining, which they rarely do," he explains, "but just for them and their daughter to savor the experience of being outdoors and all it has to offer," says Jarrod.

PROJECT AND TEAM CREDITS: Location Los Gatos, California **Landscape architect** Jarrod R. Baumann, Zeterre Landscape Architecture, San Francisco, California, www.zeterre.com **Contractor** James Everett (now retired) | **Project duration** Five years **Completion** 2015 (but still working on the gardens)

176

CELEBRATING THE LAND

With 3½ acres (1.4 hectares) of oak-peppered rolling grass, a flowing river, historic pedigree of agriculture and horses, and sloping terrain, it doesn't get much better than this site. But time had taken a toll. The barn was in ruins, sheds were scattered about, and the site had become a tumbled-down, overgrown hillside with vines and weeds. Yet, a couple from a northern California community recognized its potential as an active contemporary, agrarian retreat for themselves, their children, and friends, as well as a place to keep horses. They set to work to transform it back to its original roots—and into something very special. They worked with Arterra Landscape Architects and architect Russ Dotter of Dotter & Solfjeld Architects + Design, who remodeled the barn and constructed a pool house. The family hired Arterra, based in San Francisco, to tackle the entire site, and to capture its natural beauty, which involved developing a master plan to focus on short- and long-term goals. "The clients wanted to use the property to host parties and events, and we had so much potential to work with—a site studded with oaks, beautiful topography, and panoramic views," says landscape architect Vera Gates. She graded the site to respect the natural siting of the oak trees and developed a series of intimate terraces to meet the family's varied recreational goals with special views visible from each; these spaces open to one greater area for larger events.

Site Problems

- Many existing mature oak trees at various elevations

Wish List

- Bocce ball court
- Infinity swimming pool
- Fire element
- Water features
- Vegetable garden
- An overall site that felt intimate and comfortable for the family yet could accommodate many people for special events
- Equestrian area

Finding a Professional

This was a professional referral; one of the clients' friends referred them to the firm.

Project Challenges

- Make a cohesive, logical whole from what had been a derelict agricultural site with barns and sheds. "There was no rhyme or reason to how it worked in a meaningful way when we started," says Vera.

Problem-Solving Solutions

Vera's overall mantra was to honor and celebrate the evolving site with thoughtful design decisions. To do so, she decided a combination of rustic hardscape materials would be suitable—decomposed granite that also offers a crunchy sound, sandstone, and concrete, even in the largest terrace area. For the terraces, she mixed all three materials, and for the walls and steps used just concrete stucco or sandstone. For a secondary water feature, a fountain, she used concrete to give it more impact and structure with decomposed granite framing on either side of the fountain.

Because the site faced west, she favored low-water native species where possible, grasses such as Berkeley sedge (Carex tumulticola), evergreen feather grass (Miscanthus transmorrisonensis), evergreen maiden grass (Pennisetum), a lot of perennials, including daylily (Hemerocallis), Iris douglasiana, Pacific Coast iris, catmint (Nepeta X faassenii), beardtongue (Penstemon), New Zealand flax (Phormium tenax), and new trees such as a native dogwood hybrid (Eddie's White Wonder), which were planted in a grove. Rocks on the site were reused and more were brought in to form retaining walls, and act as a transition where two materials came together. Paths meander through the site, connecting the various areas, including the bocce ball court, the pool, the pool house, and an indoor/outdoor fireplace.

Opposite top: After: Taking full advantage of the natural topography and native oak trees, Arterra Landscape Architects helped site the pool house and designed a series of terraced hillside garden spaces and an infinity-edge pool. **Opposite bottom left and right:** Before: The site had endured years of overgrazing and neglect but retained a stand of beautiful oak trees and panoramic views. The old barns, originally scattered all over the site, were moved to create the equestrian area at the front of the property.

Top left: The bocce ball court rests just above the pool and well above the barn. Its elevation was determined by the existing topography, ensuring that the big oak (seen at right) was preserved. **Top right:** The rustic pool house (Dotter & Solfjeld Architecture + Design) sits quietly in a stand of great oaks and provides shade during the midday heat, as well as a cozy gathering area on cool evenings with a fire ablaze.
Above: The gardens are illuminated in the evening, providing a magical beauty and extending the use and enjoyment of the gardens. This terrace provides an expansive space for large gatherings, as well as everyday play. **Opposite:** Two plans; the design team developed a series of conceptual studies conveying the look and feel of the proposed garden; the top plan shows the trees, and the bottom master plan shows the cohesive and harmonious arrangement of spaces throughout the estate.

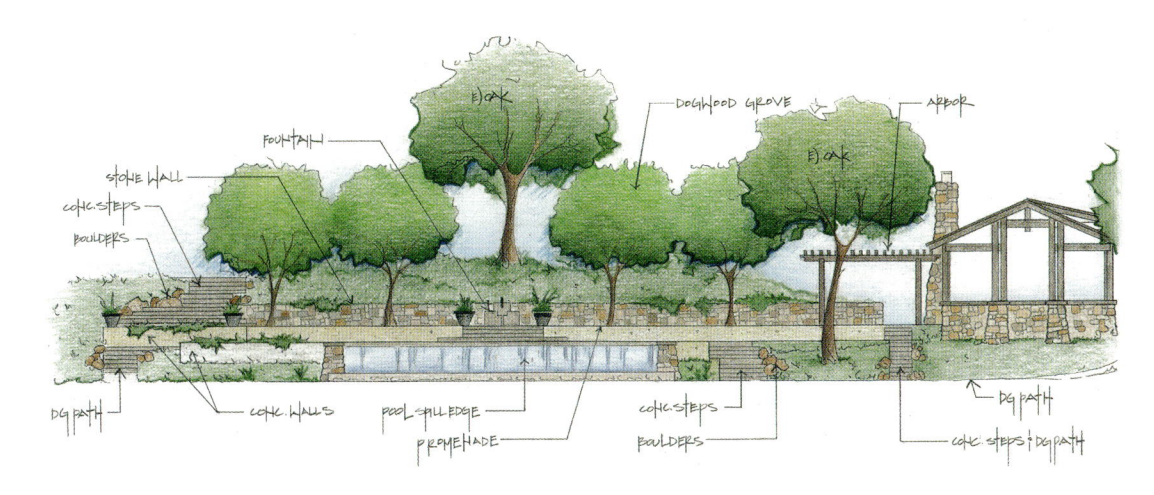

Key Design Details

- Each individual terrace creates an intimate space for the family with well-placed retaining walls and greenery, yet as a whole the site now caters to larger groups for entertaining and functions.

- The site showcases the large feature oak trees.

- The infinity-edge pool sits within its own secluded terrace that overlooks a verdant, green hillside valley.

The New Garden—An Epilogue

Arterra transformed a tumbledown, overgrown lot into a gracious and comfortable series of garden rooms. The landscape firm retained trees and built into elevations terraces as well as the features the homeowners sought for gathering and entertaining—a swimming pool with infinity edge, sun shelf, bench and waterfall, pool house, fireplace, fountain, soccer field, bocce court, horse rings and stables. The architect summarized the experience with the lesson learned: to listen carefully to our clients who are very creative, imaginative, and playful in their thinking. "I want to find ways to fulfill their dreams," Vera says.

PROJECT AND TEAM CREDITS: Location Los Gatos, California **Landscape architect** Vera Gates and Scott Yarnell, Arterra Landscape Architects, San Francisco, California, www.arterrasf.com **Landscape contractor** Elements Landscapes, Menlo Park, California, www.elements-landscape.com **Architect** Russ Dotter, Dotter & Solfjeld Architecture + Design, www.dottersolarchitects.com **Project duration** Four years **Completion** 2010

CELEBRATING THE LAND 179

Top left: Before: Front of the house hidden by a large spruce tree and a circle driveway added too much pavement. **Above left center:** Before: Back patio that had deteriorating pavers and overgrown shrubber. **Top right:** After: Front of the house with the spruce removed and new plantings of boxwoods, yews, viburnums. **Bottom left:** After: Lounge chairs on a new master bedroom terrace with 'Little Lime' hydrangeas in the foreground. **Bottom right:** After: The courtyard planters and a brick wall built to match the home; the walkway was paved in bluestone.

FAMILY FUN

When a Chicago couple with three children contacted landscape designer Bob Hursthouse, it was to rework an awkward transition in grade between their driveway and an adjacent sports court. The solution was to build a flight of stairs and plant some additional materials on their half-acre (0.2-hectare) suburban site. Nothing big or time-consuming, everyone thought. But as so often happens, once Bob walked the site with his clients, both enthusiastic gardeners, a discussion ensued about making "some" additional improvements, and one thing led to the proverbial other. "A patio in the rear showed deterioration since its pavers had shifted. Soon, I was drawing a master plan that we would work on in as many as five or six stages. We initially focused on circulation since the home has many doorways that cried out for adjacent meaningful outdoor spaces," he says. After deciding where everything on the couple's new expanded wish list would go, Bob first fixed the patio and installed more plantings around the sports court.

Then, it was on to the rest of the back yard, with an outdoor kitchen and adjacent dining area framed with a pergola to define the area; new master bedroom patio; small private patio with fire pit down a few steps with better views from it toward an existing pond; an enclosed courtyard; privacy screens around the property's rear border; changes in the front yard, too, so the house would show better since it was camouflaged at points; greater cohesiveness between the back and front yards so they'd look like they were completed at the same time; and, finally, a much more sophisticated lighting plan. Bob refers to this project as one all about family fun, since the homeowners spend so much time outdoors together, regularly handling a lot of the work. "Rick takes care of the maintenance and Brenda the planting. It's a great team effort," says Bob.

Site Problems

- Fix the grade change adjacent to an existing sports court so it's less awkward
- Repair the deteriorating rear patio area
- Connect the home's various external doorways to a specific destination point

Wish List

- Better circulation from indoors to outdoors with doors from the house each leading to a designated space
- Comfortable outdoor living, dining, and cooking areas with materials commensurate with the details and materials in the home's interior
- Nice fire pit with views toward an existing pond
- More color and texture in new plantings
- New, sophisticated lighting plan
- Improved deck off master bedroom with masonry materials
- More views from indoors to outside year-round
- Removed front circle driveway so house would show better
- Nice extra touches—small water feature on the back of the garage by the sports court, and new trellises and vines

Finding a Professional

The clients saw neighborhood work that Bob had completed.

Project Challenges

None, other than to decide where all new hard- and softscapes should go and to provide greater cohesiveness between the back and front yards so they'd look like they were completed at the same time.

Problem-Solving Solutions

Right from the start, Bob knew that getting to the outdoor areas needed to be improved since the house had been constructed with numerous doors on various sides, with none of them connecting to a specific destination point. He designed the master plan so that each door leads to a related space for a logical sequence: a door from the kitchen to the new outdoor cooking area; a door from the dining room to the outdoor eating area; and

Top left: The gardens that adjoin a dining terrace with the pergola framing the design. **Top right:** Looking from the fire pit toward the cedar pergola, which defines the dining terrace. **Above:** Arches under the pergola are repeated for support of the back porch. The overall look sought was "lush, green and colorful, with pockets of annuals," says Bob. **Opposite:** The plan was done in stages, initially with a dining terrace and fire pit, then a sport court, then the front yard, and finally the rear border plantings. "By working that way, the design evolves as the homeowners' style becomes evident," says Bob, who has worked that way on his own home over the past 27 years. "It's all evolutionary."

from the front door to a porch with bench and a meandering walk to the driveway. He selected plant materials for a soft, classic palette that works with the brick house: walks paved in bluestone, laid horizontally; brick step risers to match the house; and pergolas and beams clad in cedar to offer a sense of shelter but not feel claustrophobic.

As the owners and guests move beyond the house, spaces are more open for expansive views of the site. The new fire pit by the pond was set deliberately at a distance from the house to be a secret getaway. Plant materials arranged in curved borders and masses for greater impact were also chosen for four-season interest. "Even with winter snow there are conifers and branches, and landscape lighting illuminates trees softly," Bob says. Come spring, there's a huge bulb display of tulips, plus serviceberry, forsythia, hydrangeas, and other perennials. In the front, there are boxwood, more hydrangeas, pachysandra and liriope groundcover, and annuals replanted to evoke the spirit of the moment. "One year it might be all pinks and purples, another year oranges and yellows," he says.

Budget

The budget was set at 25 percent of the value of the house and property.

Challenges Along the Way

The architect needed to correct the grading for better use, and to resolve some prior improvements that hadn't been done properly.

Key Design Details

- Strong cohesiveness of materials to give the hard- and softscaping areas the feeling they've always been there
- A gracious circulation plan all around and between the indoors and outdoors
- Seasonal blooms that draw visitors throughout the site
- A grove of small trees and daffodils by the fire pit

The New Garden—An Epilogue

The clients wanted a house that they would use all the time with their three children as they grew up, and now that they're empty-nesters it's a place that works for them as well as for large fundraisers and other events. The project highlighted the importance of circulation all around, between indoors and outdoors, and how a site can be improved to make it work better. "What's most exciting is the peace and tranquility that the new design connotes and how it blurs the lines between inside and outside," says Bob.

PROJECT AND TEAM CREDITS: Client Rick and Brenda **Location** Chicago, Illinois **Landscape designer** Robert Hursthouse, Hursthouse Landscape Architects and Contractors, Bolingbrook, Illinois, www.hursthouse.com **Project duration** Eight years (started in 2005, making changes in phases throughout the project's duration) **Completion** 2014

Top left: The pergola with a louvered metal roof has a fan, gas fireplace, and a travertine floor. This gives the space the feeling of a room.
Top right: The site was regraded with a slope so natural stone steps could lead up to a spa with a gas fire bowl and a cascading waterfall.
Above: A zigzag path of 1-foot by 3-foot (30-centimeter by 91-centimeter) stones with a contemporary vibe winds past a colorful planting border to the pergola in back or up to an outdoor kitchen and dining terrace.

WATER TIMES THREE

The first challenge that landscape architect Marc Nissim, founder of Harmony Design Group in Westfield, New Jersey, faced in designing the pool and outdoor living spaces was deciding where to place all the features that the clients requested. Their suburban lot in a cul-de-sac in New Jersey offered little space at the rear since it backed up to wetlands and woods. After walking the site, studying the topography, and photographing what he saw, he decided that an ample and sunny side yard would accommodate their wish list of swimming pool, spa, koi pond, dining/sitting terrace with fireplace, and outdoor kitchen. The second, almost tougher, challenge was coming up with a design aesthetic that would please both the wife, who loved an organic natural look, and the husband, who favored a more contemporary style. In addition, their house was based on a traditional Colonial style.

Site problems

- Irregular-shaped lot with most of the open land to one side
- Wetland and woods at the rear
- Orientation of house on the site
- Some slope to the yard

Wish List

- Raised dining terrace with adjacent outdoor kitchen close to house
- Lounge area with fireplace, shaded from heat and rain
- Swimming pool with adjacent spa
- Level lawn area
- Koi pond
- Connection with the driveway

Finding a Professional

A landscape contractor that Marc had worked with introduced him to the homeowners.

Project Challenges

- Differences between the wife's and husband's aesthetic preferences
- Placement of elements within a confined side property

Problem-Solving Solutions

After his initial site visit, Marc did what he always does in developing a program: he checks what the city, town, or municipality zoning regulations are, so he knows where he can place different features—how close or far from property lines and how high fences and other required or desired structures can go. Also key in this case was coming up with a design that would appeal to both clients, whose tastes diverged. The first element that Marc decided needed to be determined and placed was the largest—the swimming pool. He designed it in a free-form, natural shape to nestle into the site and suit the wooded setting behind. To make it a focal point, he added a natural stone waterfall with dive rock, boulder seat bench, and fire feature, and he placed the spa a few steps above with a natural outcropping so water could flow down into the pool and be recycled back. He paved a contoured patio surrounding the pool on three sides in a handsome travertine that matched the organic look of the pool, but edged the coping in brown stone.

The dining/sitting terrace with fireplace became the second feature to be sited, and this he decided should be a separate unit, shielded from elements by a pergola with aluminum louvered slats to prevent water from coming in, as well as shading anyone sitting there. "People tend to use a fireplace area for much longer periods than a pool—even into colder weather," Marc says. But to add a contemporary touch—a nod now to the husband to balance the aesthetics, yet make the area work with the pool—Marc paved it in the same travertine, but surrounded the area beyond in a much more contemporary brownstone, which he repeated on the walkway leading to the driveway. He also bordered the entire area in river rocks to act as a drain for water to collect and percolate into the ground. Marc introduced yet another material, but sparingly in this area: ledgestone for column bases, which further define the dining/sitting area.

He placed the third main area, the outdoor kitchen, close to the homeowners' back door, as requested, and just a few steps up from the outdoor living room under the pavilion. Whether anyone's cooking or sitting, they can enjoy the sight and sound of the koi pond, which was nestled in between. All around, new plantings—evergreens, hydrangeas, crepe myrtle, purple moor ornamental grass—help screen neighbors' homes, and offer visual pleasure from indoors or outdoors. More than 25 tons of boulders were brought in to create more of a natural and contemporary flavor—a true blending of two different, but compatible design traditions. Landscape lighting adds a nice touch and safety feature at night. Both the budget and time lines were met, helping the entire job become a success. And for Marc, who has designed more than 500 projects over 10 years, this remains one of his favorites.

Top left: At night the gas fire bowl makes the secluded spa come alive. **Top right:** A 3-D model shows what the dining terrace will look like when built. **Bottom:** A natural koi pond was constructed near the pool and softened with natural-looking plantings. **Opposite top:** Curtains can be closed to keep out mosquitoes in the pergola for greater enjoyment and kept closed with a magnetic closure. **Opposite bottom:** The plan and a 3-D rendition of the pergola show the relationship of all the elements to give the owners what they wanted, including three different water features—a pool, spa, and koi pond.

Cost-Saving Alternatives

The project could have featured smaller and less complicated water features and boulders, less travertine, smaller plantings, and readily available (rather than custom) pergolas; also, the project could have been phased in in several stages.

Budget

Set at 20 percent of the value of the house and property.

Challenges Along the Way

Trying to create a contemporary design with a natural looking site; she wanted more natural and he wanted more modern so it needed to be combined.

The house sat on a cul-de-sac, and the backyard was limited so it had to go to one side, which led to the need for three distinct "rooms" with the pergola area acting as a hub.

Key Design Details

- Blending of contemporary and natural aesthetics.
- The use of the pergola and fireplace as the transition between other areas.
- There are three distinct living spaces.

The New Garden—An Epilogue

Both owners were pleased with the results and felt that Marc satisfied each of their design aesthetics and came up with a cohesive whole.

PROJECT AND TEAM CREDITS: Location Denville, New Jersey **Landscape architect** Marc Nissim, Harmony Design Group, Westfield, New Jersey, www.hdglandscape.com **Contractor** Rich Cording, CLC Landscape Design, Ringwood, New Jersey, www.clcdesign.com **Pool installation** Marson Pools, Oakland, New Jersey, www.marsonpools.com **Project duration** Six months **Completion** 2012

Top left: Lavender, westringia, and dwarf manzanita are the backbone of the drought-tolerant hillside planting. **Bottom left:** A Zen-like composition of rocks harmonizes with the warm yellow gray Chinese limestone walls, the buff gravel and warm tones of the wooden gate. **Above right:** Aeoniums, grasses, Luma apiculata (from Chile) and elfin thyme offer contrasting greens and textures in this relatively flower-free garden.

MINIMALIST SIGNATURE

Some landscape designers and architects have a definite style; you can spot their handiwork just as you would artwork by certain artists, interior rooms by some designers, and buildings by architects. Any architectural aficionados would recognize a Frank Gehry versus a Richard Meier versus a Robert Stern, for example. San Francisco landscape designer Stephen J. Suzman takes a unique approach. His guiding principle is that his own style and that of his firm, now Zeterre Landscape Architecture and formerly Suzman Design Associates, are inspired by the site, climate, and client needs and taste. To start the process, he sends his homeowners a questionnaire and familiarizes himself with the architecture and topography. Such was the case with a young couple with children who hired Stephen to landscape their 1-acre (0.4-hectare) property in northern California with water views. The site included a half-finished Spanish-style McMansion that architect Peter Pfau of Pfau Long Architecture, also in San Francisco, was hired to redesign in a much more contemporary, minimalist vernacular. The family planned to use it for vacations. They have since sold the property.

Site Problems
- Sloping site with one neighboring home close by
- Little on-site except for a lot of weeds, a small group of coast live oaks and a few scrubby shrubs
- Strict water restrictions

Wish List
- Stone fire pit
- Play areas for children with basketball hoop and separate fort area
- Spa designed by architect
- Lookout point for water views

Finding a Professional
The client was introduced by colorist James Goodman.

Project Challenges
The project required the use of reclaimed Chinese limestone from the façades of buildings and old granite slabs salvaged from streets across villages drowned by the Yangtze River dam. The materials appealed because of their texture, patina of warm gray with a bit of green, and absence of shiny particles. "We wanted to create a Zen garden feeling with rocks, boulders, gravel, and plantings that would offer serenity and a contrast to the family's busy lives," Stephen says. Limestone also would be used throughout the garden for walls.

Problem-Solving Solutions
The goal was to make the house and garden flow in an "intelligent" or logical visual and physical manner by developing areas for use on the sloping site for an active family; screening of neighboring homes, especially one close by; and selecting a palette of drought-tolerant materials where possible, as well as a limited palette of hardscape choices that would work in sync together and also reflect the home's contemporary lines and predominantly monochromatic palette.

In introducing trees and some shrubs, Stephen digressed from all-native choices to avoid monoculture so that they would survive best in the climate. Among his choices were cork oak trees from the Mediterranean, since California's live oaks have suffered sudden oak death, Italian stone pines because local Monterrey ones are also dying, plus some Mediterranean and South African shrubs with foliage that offer color. "I wanted a fairly monochromatic, virtually flower-free garden with a subtle color scheme based on a variety of different greens, and accenting textures of foliage. Flowers are nearly always diminutive and subtle in soft lavenders, pale pinks, pale blues and white," he says. He also introduced sweet-smelling citrus and lemon scents, vines such as creeping fig and silvervein creeper, and groundcovers ranging from Manzanita to wild ginger, Irish moss, baby's tears, and Korean grass.

Monolithic granite slabs for steps and pathways contrast with much smaller gravel paving and both work well with the limestone walls, and all form a sophisticated pairing with the contemporary home.

Cost-Saving Alternatives
A limited palette of hard- and softscape choices offered an economy of scale, along with using plant choices in masses for both economy of scale and greater visual impact. Consider using gravel for paving of driveways and terraces, and drought-tolerant materials where possible.

Top left: Monolithic slabs of Chinese granite wind gracefully up a hill through a planting of pennisetum grasses. **Center left:** Simplicity and serenity reign with gravel, grasses, and stone. **Bottom left:** Corten steel, granite steps, limestone walls and gravel welcome guests to this peaceful haven. **Above right:** Native Monterey pines and Coast Live oaks form the backdrop for a stone fire pit; seat walls eliminate the need for cluttered furniture. **Opposite top left:** An elegant, simple spa is rimmed by a terrace, accented with a stone wall. **Opposite top right:** Stephen designed a Zen-like, raked gravel path and graceful grasses as an effective foil for walls clad with Chinese limestone, formerly façades of villages drowned by the Yangtze River dam. **Opposite bottom:** The plan reveals the different special zones of the property, including a fire pit, spa and viewing area.

Challenges Along the Way

"The clients were very decisive about their choices, which made the project much easier along the way," Stephen says. The only serious challenge was screening the house from neighbors.

Key Design Details

- What's most noticeable upon stepping onto the site is the richness of textural materials, including Corten steel, gravel, limestone, and the warm simplicity of the contemporary style house. "When you have a contemporary house, you can't hide any mistakes," Stephen says.

The New Garden—An Epilogue

After the work was done, the family could use all parts of their site, whereas before it was blank except for weeds and some scrubby trees. It is worth noting that the new owner changed almost nothing in the garden. Some of the lessons learned were about the importance of being a team player and collaborating with the architect. "We used traditional materials in a contemporary way; and repeated the plant and hardscape palette for simplicity and cohesiveness," says Stephen.

PROJECT AND TEAM CREDITS: Location Pebble Beach, northern California **Landscape designers** Stephen J. Suzman, Zeterre Landscape Architecture, San Francisco, California, www.zeterre.com **Architect** Peter Pfau, Pfau Long Architecture, San Francisco, California, www.pfaulong.com **Landscape contractor** Roark Craven, Craven Landscaping, Seaside, California, www.cravenlandscaping.com **Project duration** 2½ years **Completion** 2001

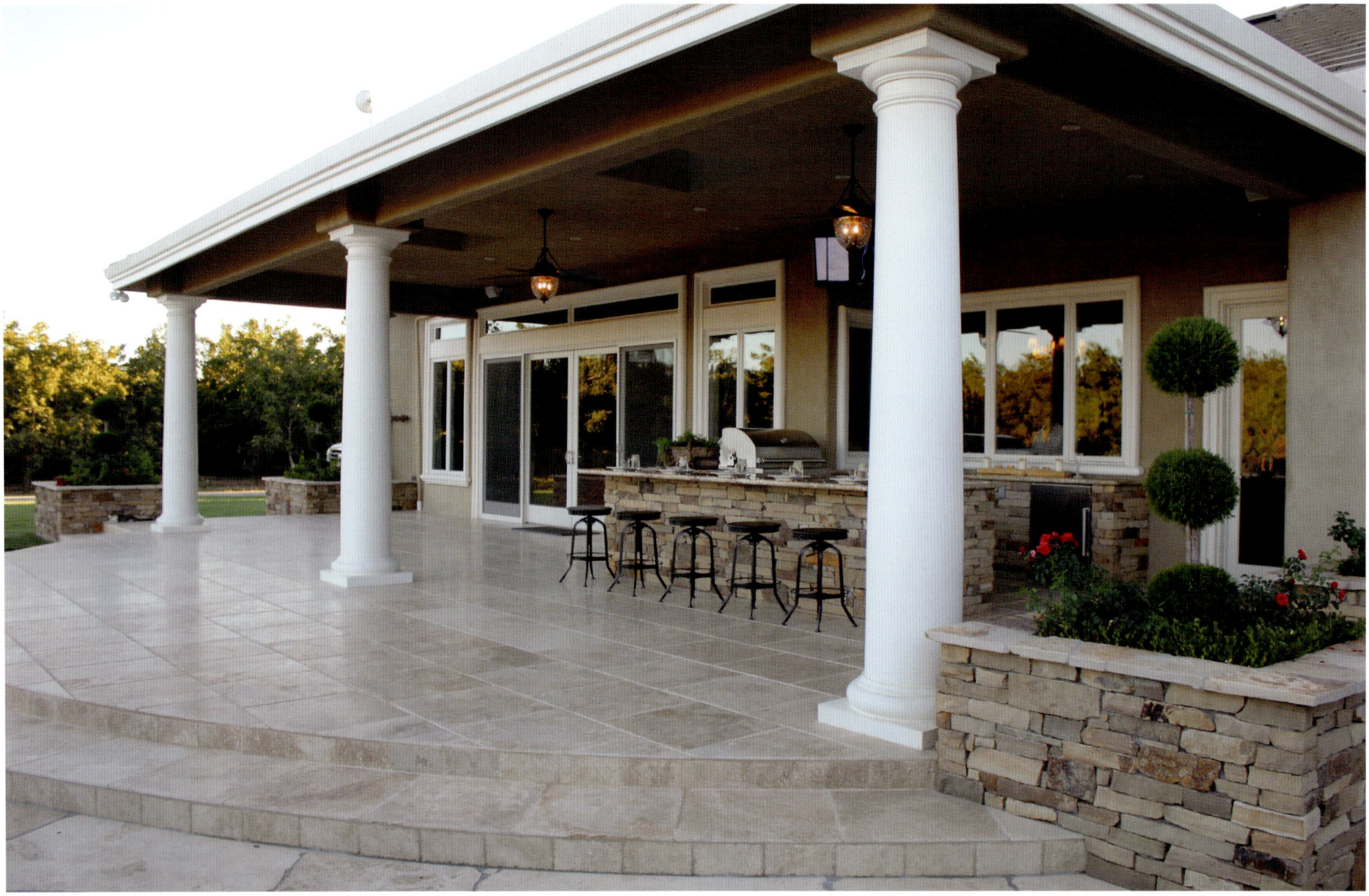

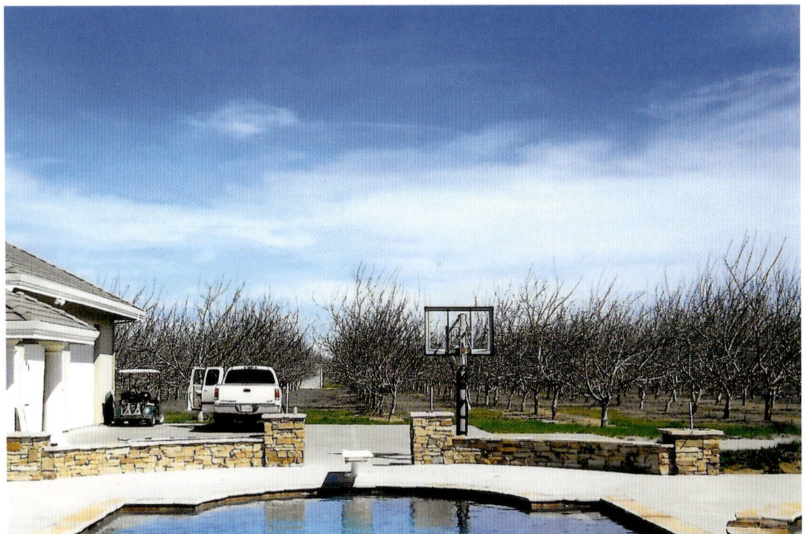

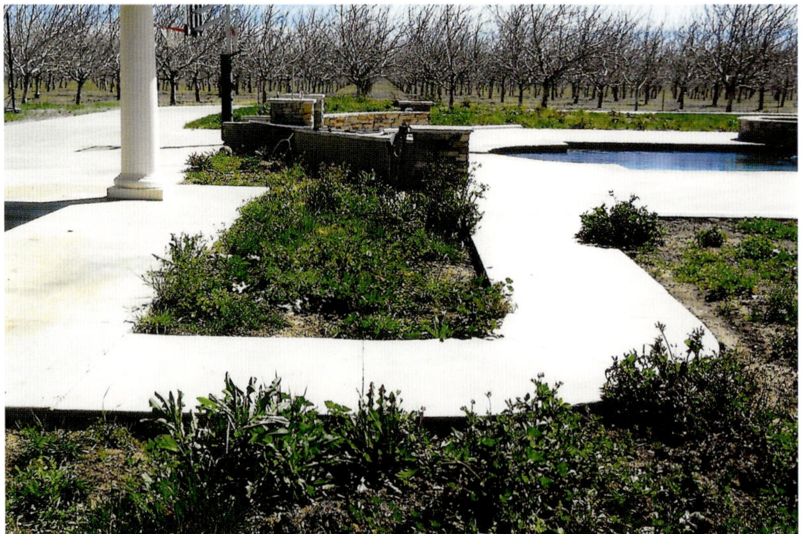

NUTS INSPIRE A HOME RESORT

When your family owns one of the largest nut-processing companies, it would make sense that you might buy 160 acres (65 hectares) and plant walnuts. After purchasing and planting the property just outside of Winters, California, in 2003, Shannon and Mark decided that the setting of walnut trees was the perfect place to build their dream home. "Our landscape was incomplete. We built our house but did not have the money to do what we wanted with the yard," says Shannon. "We never worked with a designer at first so we wasted time and a lot of money doing the wrong things."

Site Problems

- Everything was flat
- No shade
- View from the windows along the back of the house was cluttered with a shed, dog kennel, driveway, and garage
- No entertainment area
- Existing landscape built in 2009—a pool, spa, and lower paved area—needed to be incorporated into the new design

Finding a Professional

Several friends referred Michael Glassman to Shannon. They liked his vision, and hired him to design a master plan for their property that was then built in several phases. In turn, Michael recommended Greg Mehl, co-owner of Empire Construction Company Inc.

Wish List

- An outdoor entertainment area with fireplace
- Some elevation variation to give the yard greater visual interest
- Sense of enclosure
- Overall feeling of a resort

Problem-Solving Solutions

Michael worked in phases. For the first phase, he designed a series of raised planters faced in natural stone that he placed behind the pool. The center planter contained a 7-foot-tall (2.1-meter-tall) formal cascading wall fountain flanked by topiary privets to block the view of the driveway and provide a sense of enclosure. Michael filled the planters with boxwood hedges, multistem red crepe myrtles, and red carpet roses. He also constructed raised planters at the entrance to the pool for structure that also provided a change in elevation to the flat yard. He then bordered the pool area with two large grass areas to give the yard a more stately resort feel. For the second phase, Michael enlarged the upper patio and loggia, and covered all with travertine tile to match the home's interior. He built a large outdoor kitchen under the loggia, which he outfitted with a barbecue, stainless-steel hood, refrigerator, sink, warming drawer, granite countertop, and TV. Next, he moved onto working on a lower patio, which he paved in large random flagstone pieces of the same colored travertine used elsewhere. At this level, Michael also designed a custom gas fireplace for a focal point for a sitting area, which could be seen from the living room. Large rock-faced planters flank the fireplace and were filled with white crepe myrtle trees, juniper teardrop topiaries, red carpet roses, dark blue agapanthus, and boxwood hedges.

Cost-Saving Alternatives

Instead of facing planters in stone, they could have been stuccoed and painted; patios could have been constructed of stained concrete rather than travertine; a prefabricated fireplace and kitchen would have been less costly than custom design; and planting could have been done at ground level rather than in raised planters.

Challenges Along the Way

There were few due to the phasing in of work.

Budget

This was set at 20 percent of the house and property value, but that percentage will grow as the clients add more to their setting, including a redo of the front of the house and security fence all around the perimeter.

Key Design Details

- The custom fireplace, ledgestone used on planters, walls, and the kitchen make a special visual statement.
- The layout of the landscape is very open and private, yet spacious.

Opposite top: After: A travertine-tiled loggia and terrace provide a traditional and functional entertainment space.
Opposite bottom left: Before: The uninteresting yard had no shade or elevation change, and a direct view into the garage and driveway. **Opposite bottom right:** Before: Few plants grew well in this poor rocky soil.

Top: The custom rock-faced fireplace provides a great space for relaxing. **Above left:** The counter of the outdoor kitchen is oriented to allow guests to interact with the cook or watch an outdoor TV. **Above center:** The pool area now has privacy. A tall arched fountain wall and the raised planters give the pool its enclosed feel. **Above right:** From the elevated spa the homeowners can look out to the golden light shining on their walnut orchard. **Opposite left:** The master plan of the back yard showcases all the elements of design, including the long elegant pool. **Opposite far right top:** The pool scape now offers a relaxing, functional space. **Opposite far right bottom:** The custom fireplace is nestled in front of white crepe myrtle trees planted in the flanking raised planters.

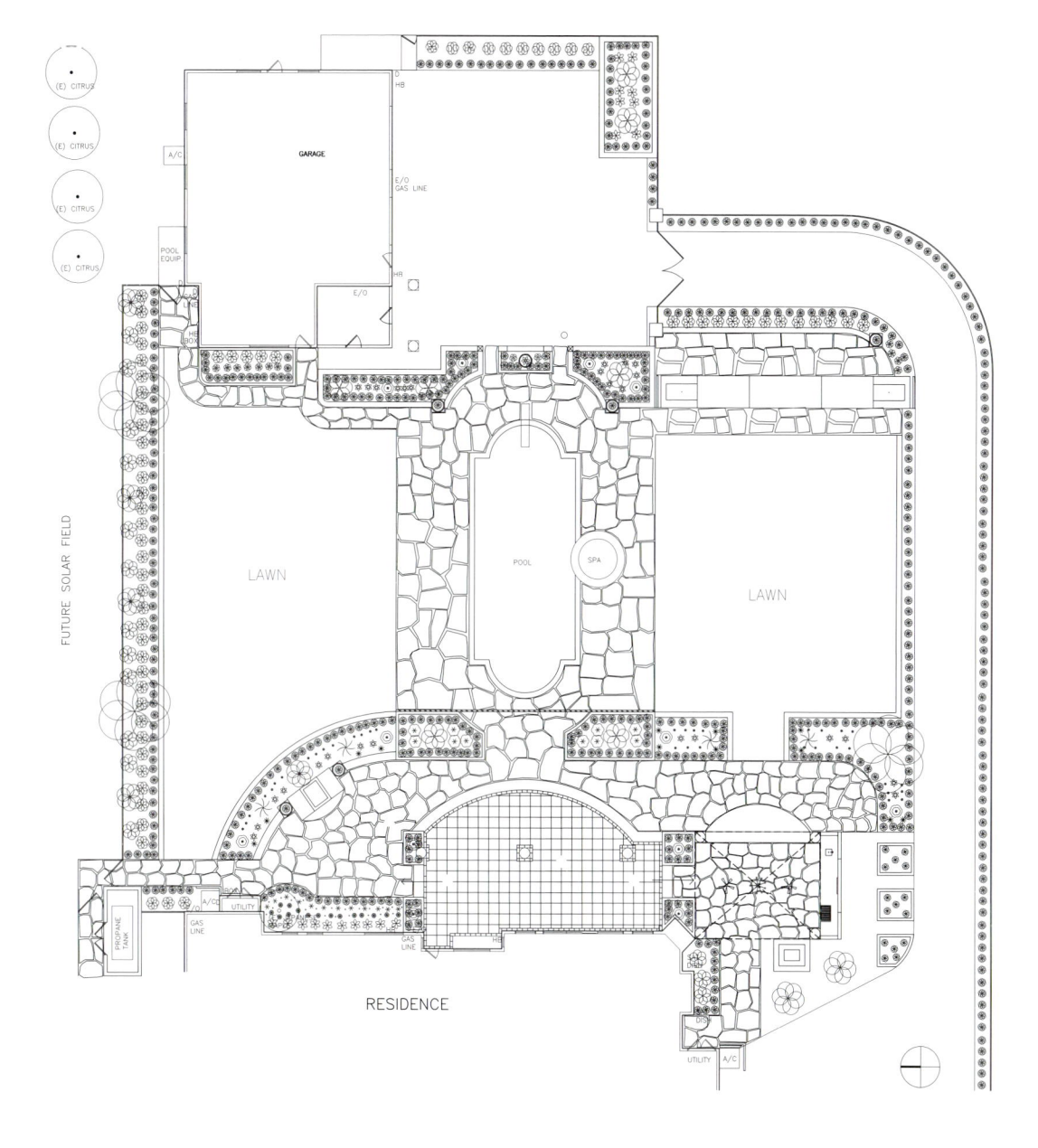

The New Garden—An Epilogue

The couple now uses their yard for regular outdoor parties and fundraisers. They love coming home to the design where they spend a large portion of their time in good weather. They were pleased that the result so far has provided a resort feeling—a vacation destination right at home.

PROJECT AND TEAM CREDITS: Client Shannon and Mark **Location** near Winters, California **Landscape designer** Michael Glassman, Michael Glassman & Associates, Sacramento, California, www.michaelglassman.com **Contractor** Greg Mehl, Empire Construction Company Inc., Winters, California **Project duration** Six months **Completion** 2014

Chapter 8

FIND INSPIRATION—GARDEN TOURS, COMMUNITY GARDENS, AND GARDENS AROUND THE WORLD

How do your neighbors' gardens grow? There's one good way to find out. A residential garden tour can provide quick answers and inspiration to help you fine-tune your wish list for your property.

Seeing neighborhood gardens can provide ideas about what will grow in your climate, and what will not, present amenities you hadn't thought about—maybe a bocce or badminton court—or suggest styles that might complement your house, and expose you to the work of area professional designers and contractors to hire. (For extra resources, such as blogs and books, see also page 208.)

There can be additional social benefits of going on a local or regional garden tour. You can expand your network of fellow gardeners, and even start to share ideas and to trade plants. In addition, if you are interested in growing vegetables as part of your landscaping plan but have never grown edible plants, visiting community gardens in your area can also be beneficial to see what thrives and what doesn't grow so well.

And wherever you live, there are likely great botanical gardens, arboretums, landscape and art centers, annual flower shows, or homes with gardens open to the public. When you travel, there are more gardens to visit and worth a detour. Every garden usually has some outstanding feature or features that are worth viewing. Some are known for specific plants, such as the Buffalo Botanical Gardens in northwestern New York State, which has the world's largest public display of ivy, or Kirstenbosch National Botanic Garden in Cape Town, South Africa, which has an amazing collection of proteas.

In St. Louis, the Missouri Botanical Garden draws visitors for its 14-acre (5.6-hectare) Japanese garden and its annual orchid show. The Chelsea Flower Show in Great Britain has unusual landscape displays, and although it's not a garden per se, this is a great annual show that's worth touring. The Fairchild Tropical Botanical Garden in Coral Gables, Florida, displays a rare collection of tropical plants. Longwood Gardens near Philadelphia has the most beautiful Christmas display featuring lights among the snow-covered landscape.

All these places can inspire new ideas. Barbara discovered her love of rose bushes and peonies during her many visits to the Missouri Botanical Garden and then found sunny patches to plant these in her own yard. As a child, Michael was inspired by displays of prehistoric plants at the La Brea Tar Pits (www.tarpits.org) in Los Angeles. He also loved visiting the Japanese Gardens at the University of California, Los Angeles, and the Huntington Botanical Gardens in nearby Pasadena.

Opposite top left: An unconventional front garden on Garden Walk Buffalo incorporates large slabs of marble. **Opposite bottom left:** Lush, tightly planted, narrow urban spaces abound on Garden Walk Buffalo. **Opposite far right:** Grassless front yards are incorporated into the impressive, diverse architecture found throughout neighborhoods of Buffalo, New York, which can be visited on its annual garden tour.

197

Above: A popular Victorian garden on Garden Walk Buffalo like this Delavan Avenue garden will attract nearly 10,000 visitors in the tour's two days.

Residential Neighborhood Garden Tours

Stars of the shade and sun shine at a surprising garden tour in Buffalo, a city in northwest New York State, which boasts the largest neighborhood garden tour in the country, despite its reputation for rough winters with piles of snow. In 2014, with almost 400 gardens to visit and 60,000 visitors, **Garden Walk Buffalo** (http://gardenwalkbuffalo.com/), celebrated its 20th annual tour. In 2015, the tour featured 416 gardens and brought out between 60,000 and 70,000 visitors.

It started as a simple self-guided block tour of 29 gardens by homeowners and amateur gardeners, Marvin Lunenfeld and Gail McCarthy, after they attended a garden tour in Chicago. Their own front porch became their first tour's headquarters, and anybody could participate without having judges scrutinize their garden or paying any fees. The couple's main goals were to encourage neighborhood beautification and promote community pride.

Garden Walk Buffalo quickly became an annual event with the couple's original guidelines preserved: anyone who lives in downtown Buffalo can participate, and the tours are still self-guided and free. Contributions from individuals and corporations permit the group to provide more than 70 grants for community gardening projects.

Many other cities have followed suit; here are some examples.

- **Garden Walk Cleveland** (www.gardenwalkcleveland.org/) in Ohio showcases gardens in area neighborhoods in mid-July. Many garden clubs sponsor tours and use funds collected to promote garden beautification and related activities.

- **Cape Fear Garden Club** (www.capefeargardenclub.org/azalea-garden-tour/) in Wilmington, North Carolina, hosts its annual Azalea Garden Tour, dating back to the 1950s, as a way to reinvest profits in the community.

- **Hidden Gardens of Beacon Hill** (www.beaconhillgardenclub.org/tour.html) in Boston, Massachusetts, is the Beacon Hill Garden Club's major fundraiser; the club also has published books showcasing the gardens, *Hidden Gardens of Beacon Hill*.

- **Secret Gardens of Cambridge** (www.cambridgepubliclibraryfriends.org/secret-gardens), also in the Boston area, mixes together public and private gardens on its tour and benefits the Friends of the Cambridge Public Library.

- **Garden Conservancy's Open Days'** (www.gardenconservancy.org/open-days) program, a nationwide event, permits entry into private gardens at different times of the year throughout the country to benefit the organization, which works to preserve gardens and the landscape.

To find an area tour or one in an area you are visiting, it is best to search the web for the location, contact an area garden club through the **National Garden Clubs** (www.gardenclub.org/) organization, or ask your Chamber of Commerce.

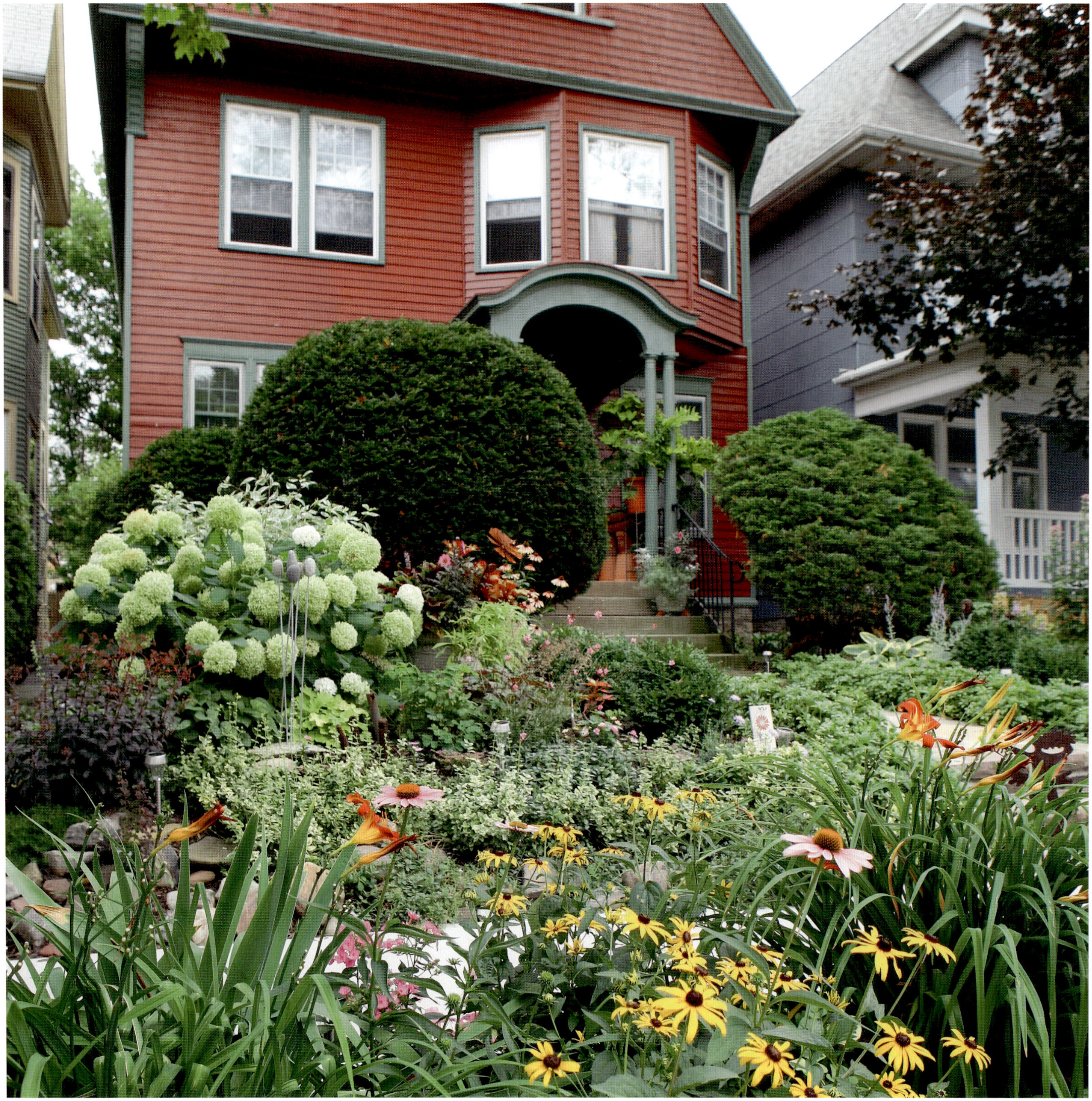

Opposite: Rejuvenated, more walkable streets, and improved home values are benefits of a neighborhood garden tour like Garden Walk Buffalo. **Top left:** Grassless front yards are a hallmark of Garden Walk Buffalo. **Top right:** In Buffalo, you can find small urban gardens that pack a big punch, including cheerfully brash juxtapositions of colorful perennials and unique annuals, minimal or no lawns, and creative uses of found objects and architectural artifacts as sculpture. **Bottom left:** This garden in Buffalo, New York, uses grass as a design element mimicking a checkerboard. **Bottom right:** Garden Walk Buffalo gardens have the patina of well-used, customized spaces, often with novel designs that ignore traditional garden design conventions.

FIND INSPIRATION—GARDEN TOURS, COMMUNITY GARDENS, AND GARDENS AROUND THE WORLD

Top left: In Cape Town, South Africa, an overview of the Kirstenbosch National Botanic Garden. **Top right:** Another shot of a protea garden at the Kirstenbosch National Botanic Garden in Cape Town, South Africa. **Above:** A photo of one of the formal gardens at the Durban Botanic Gardens in Durban, South Africa.

Many of the gardens and arboretums listed below offer guided tours and lectures; some sell plants and garden accessories. While this list is hardly definitive, it represents an outstanding cross-section of different gardens from around the globe that we and other experts consider worth visiting. In alphabetical order by country:

AUSTRALIA

Norfolk Island National Park, Norfolk Island
www.parksaustralia.gov.au/norfolk

Royal Botanic Gardens, Melbourne
www.rbg.vic.gov.au

Royal Botanic Gardens, Sydney
www.rbgsyd.nsw.gov.au/

AUSTRIA

The Gardens of Schonbrunn Palace, Vienna
www.gardenvisit.com/garden/schonbrunn_garden_vienna

BELGIUM

National Botanic Garden, near Brussels
www.gardenvisit.com/garden/belgium_national_botanic_garden

BRAZIL

Jardim Botanico de Curitiba, Curitiba
www.curitiba.pr.gov.br/conteudo/jardim-botanico/287

Jardim Botanico, Rio de Janiero
www.guiadorio.net.br/2006/09/jardim-botanico-rio-de-janeiro-dicas.html

CANADA

Butchart Gardens, Vancouver Island
www.butchartgardens.com/gardens

National Botanical Garden, Montreal
www.gardenvisit.com/garden/montreal_botanic_garden

CHINA

Master of Nets Garden, Suzhou
www.beautifulsuzhou.com/2012/02/29/master-nets-garden-suzhou/

Summer Palace, Beijing
http://whc.unesco.org/en

Yuyuan Garden, Shanghai
www.yuyuantm.com.cn/yuyuan/en

COSTA RICA

Pura Vida Gardens and Waterfalls, above Jaco
http://costarica.com/attractions/pura-vida-gardens-waterfalls/

ENGLAND

Bodnant Garden, Conwy, North Wales
www.nationaltrust.org.uk/bodnant-garden/

Chelsea Flower Show, London
www.rhs.org.uk/shows-events/rhs-chelsea-flower-Show

Hidcote Manor Garden, North Cotswolds, near Stratford-upon-Avon
www.nationaltrust.org.uk/hidcote/

Powis Castle and Garden, Wales
www.nationaltrust.org.uk/powis-castle/

Royal Botanic Gardens, Kew, London
www.kew.org/

Sissinghurst Castle Garden, Kent
www.nationaltrust.org.uk/sissinghurst-castle-garden/

Stourhead, Warminster
www.nationaltrust.org.uk/stourhead/

FRANCE

Chateau de Versailles and Gardens, Versailles
http://en.chateauversailles.fr/discover-estate

Chateau Villandry, Loire Valley
www.chateauvillandry.fr/en/

Claude Monet's Garden and Museum, Giverny
http://fondation-monet.com/en/

Courances Castle Gardens, near Paris
http://courances.net/en/

Gardens of the Villa Ephrussi de Rothschild, St-Jean-Cap-Ferrat, France
www.villa-ephrussi.com/en/

GERMANY

Sans Souci, Potsdam
www.spsg.de/startseite/

INDIA

Taj Mahal Garden, Agra
www.tajmahal.com/14/places/taj-mahal-garden.htm

INDONESIA

Bogor Botanical Gardens, Bogor
www.bogorbotanicgardens.org

Botanical Garden, Ubud, Bali
www.balibotanicgarden.org

IRAN

Bagh-e-Fin Garden, Kashan
www.orientalarchitecture.com/iran/kashan/bagh-e-fin_garden.php

IRELAND

Powerscourt Estate Gardens, Wickelow, south of Dublin
http://powerscourt.com/

ISRAEL

Bahá'í Gardens, Haifa and Akko (Acre)
www.ganbahai.org.il/en/

Jerusalem Botanical Gardens, Jerusalem
http://en.botanic.co.il/

ITALY

Boboli Garden, Florence
www.museumsinflorence.com/musei/boboli_garden.html

Isola Bella, Lake Maggiore
www.gardenvisit.com/garden/isola_bella

Villa Adriana (Hadrian's Villa), Tivoli, near Rome
http://whc.unesco.org/en/list/907

Villa d'Este, Tivoli, near Rome
www.villadestetivoli.info

JAPAN

Kyoto Gosho Imperial Palace Garden, Kyoto
www.gardenvisit.com/garden/kyoto_gosho_imperial_palace

Rikugien, Tokyo
www.gotokyo.org/en/kanko/bunkyo/event/kouyouteien.html

Ryoan-ji Temple, Kyoto
www.gojapango.com/travel/kyoto_ryoan-ji_temple.htm

MALAYSIA

Kuching Orchid Garden, Kuching
www.worldreviewer.com/travel-guides/garden/kuching-orchid-garden/

MEXICO

The Floating Gardens, Xochimilco, Mexico City
www.mexonline.com/history-xochimilco.htm

MOROCCO

Menera Gardens, Marrakech
www.jardin-menara.com

THE NETHERLANDS

Hortus Bulborum, Limmen
www.hortus-bulborum.nl/english

Keukenhof Flower Park, near Amsterdam
www.keukenhof.nl/en/

NEW ZEALAND

Aramatai Gardens
www.gardenstovisit.co.nz/private-gardens/aramatai-gardens.aspx

Hackfalls Arboretum
www.gardenstovisit.co.nz/public-gardens/hackfalls-arboretum.aspx

St Margarets Country Garden
www.gardenstovisit.co.nz/private-gardens/st-margarets-country-garden.aspx

NORWAY

Artic-Alpine Botanic Garden, Tromsø, near the Arctic Circle
www.nordnorge.com/en/?News=53

PAKISTAN

Shalimar Gardens, Lahore
http://pakistanpaedia.com/landmarks/shalamar-gardens_lahore.htm

SAINT LUCIA

Mamiku Gardens
http://caribya.com/st.lucia/mamiku.gardens/

SCOTLAND

Drummond Castle Gardens, Perthshire
www.drummondcastlegardens.co.uk

The Garden of Cosmic Speculation, Dumfries
www.charlesjencks.com/#!the-garden-of-cosmic-speculation

SINGAPORE

Singapore Botanic Gardens, Singapore
www.sbg.org.sg/

SOUTH AFRICA

Durban Botanic Gardens, Durban
www.durbanbotanicgardens.org.za/

Karoo Desert National Botanic Garden, Worcester, West Cape
www.sanbi.org/gardens/karoo-desert

Kirstenbosch National Botanic Garden, Cape Town
www.sanbi.org/gardens/kirstenbosch

KwaZulu-Natal National Botanical Garden, Mayor's Walk
www.sanbi.org/gardens/kwazulu-natal

SPAIN

The Allhambra and Generalife Gardens, Granada
www.travelinginspain.com/alhambra3.htm

SWEDEN

Bergius Botanic Garden, near Stockholm
www.stockholmmuseum.com/museums/gardens/bergianska-tradgarden101.htm

THAILAND

Jim Thompson's Garden, Bangkok
www.bangkok.com/product-reviews/jim-thompson-house-and-suan-pakkad-palace-review.htm

Suan Nong Nooch, Pattaya
http://pattayaspot.com/suannongnooch.html

Opposite top left: A flower bed from the Durban Botanic Gardens, Durban, South Africa. *Opposite top right:* A long shot of one of the formal gardens at Filoli Gardens, Woodside, California. *Opposite bottom:* A colorful knot garden at Filoli Gardens, Woodside, California.

FIND INSPIRATION—GARDEN TOURS, COMMUNITY GARDENS, AND GARDENS AROUND THE WORLD 205

Above: A close-up of the knot garden at the Filoli Gardens, Woodside, California.

UNITED STATES

Arizona-Sonora Desert Museum, Tuscon, Arizona
http://desertmuseum.org/

Arnold Arboretum, Harvard University, Boston, Massachusetts
www.arboretum.harvard.edu/

Asticou Azalea Garden, Northeast Harbor, Maine
www.acadiamagic.com/asticou-garden.html

Brooklyn Botanic Garden, Brooklyn, New York
www.bbg.org/

Buffalo Botanical Gardens, Buffalo, New York
www.buffalogardens.com/

Chicago Botanic Garden, Glencoe, Illinois
www.chicagobotanic.org/

Coastal Maine Botanical Gardens, Boothbay, Maine
www.mainegardens.org/

Cox Arboretum and Gardens, Canton, Georgia
http://coxgardens.com/nggallery/thumbnails

Denver Botanic Gardens, Denver, Colorado
www.botanicgardens.org/

Donnell Garden, Sonoma, California
http://tclf.org/landscapes/donnell-garden

Dumbarton Oaks, Washington, D.C.
www.doaks.org/gardens

Fairchild Tropical Botanic Garden, Coral Gables, Florida
www.fairchildgarden.org/

Filoli Gardens, Woodside, California
http://filoli.org/

The Getty Villa and Gardens, Pacific Pallisades, California
www.getty.edu/visit/villa/

Golden Gate Park, Japanese Gardens, San Francisco, California
www.japaneseteagardensf.com/

The Huntington Botanical Gardens, Pasadena, California
http://hometown-pasadena.com/resident-tourist/the-huntington-botanical-gardens

Ladew Topiary Gardens, Monkton, Maryland
www.ladewgardens.com/

Lady Bird Johnson Wildflower Center, Austin, Texas
www.wildflower.org/

Longwood Gardens, Kennett Square, near Philadelphia, Pennsylvania
http://longwoodgardens.org/

Memphis Botanic Garden, Memphis, Tennessee
www.memphisbotanicgarden.com/

Minneapolis Sculpture Garden, Minneapolis, Minnesota
www.walkerart.org/garden/

Missouri Botanical Garden, St. Louis, Missouri
www.missouribotanicalgarden.org/

National Tropic Botanical Garden, Kauai, Hawaii
www.ntbg.org/

New York Botanical Garden, Bronx, New York
www.nybg.org/frida/

Portland Japanese Garden, Portland
http://japanesegarden.com/

Sarah P. Duke Gardens, Durham, North Carolina
https://gardens.duke.edu/

UC Davis Arboretum, Davis, California
http://arboretum.ucdavis.edu/

United States Botanic Garden, Washington, D.C.
www.usbg.gov

FIND INSPIRATION—GARDEN TOURS, COMMUNITY GARDENS, AND GARDENS AROUND THE WORLD

Chapter 9

DIG INTO GARDEN BLOGS AND BOOKS

Whether it's simply inspiration from seeing gardens in far distant places or learning how another amateur garden was begun, these blogs and books are worth perusing; some books may be out of print but can be found online or in libraries. For more details on where to find innovative and creative ideas, see also Chapter 8: Find Inspiration—Garden Tours, Community Gardens, and Gardens Around the World (page 196). For books and other resources on edible gardens, see Edible Landscaping (page 48).

Blogs

Cyndi's Catalog of Gardening Catalogs (www.gardenlist.com/) helps you know which catalogs to save versus pitch, particularly for specific interests such as roses, daylilies, or fruit.

Dave's Garden (http://davesgarden.com/) offers articles, videos, and forums such as how to grow your own harvest decorations.

Garden Rant (http://gardenrant.com/) tackles subjects with humor in the categories of "shut up and dig" and "ministry of controversy" with a piece on kudzu that the blog's creator describes as the poster child for invasive plants or how death can enhance your garden.

Garden Web (www.gardenweb.com) offers a garden directory of online forums, experts, calendar of events, and blogs from around the world.

Kitchen Gardeners International (http://kgi.org/) is just what it says, a guide for those who want to grow their own food and be more sustainable. Start by joining online forums, securing recipes, and reading blogs about healing or community gardens.

The Royal Horticultural Society (www.rhs.org.uk) is not just for those living in England but offers helpful advice about picking and caring for plants, starting a school or community garden, or just visiting gardens.

Skippy's Vegetable Garden (www.carletongarden.blogspot.com/) is a charming blog written by a biochemist about gardening in her yard, which isn't large, an increasing challenge for many gardeners giving up big plots. It includes helpful tips, recipes, such as parsley pesto and a carrot martini, and lots of her wonderful photos of what she grows and the dog for which the garden is named, Skippy.

Tiny Farm Blog (http://tinyfarmblog.com/about-microfarming-101/) is for those who want to garden small, what's considered 2 acres (0.8 hectares), though to some that will seem gargantuan. The blog covers topics as varied as how to handle frost and different bugs, as well as hosting a farm stand.

Opposite top left: In Blanco, Texas, homeowners came to architect Lou Kimball and builder Grady Burnette of Burnette Builders seeking a house in the Texas Hill country that would seamlessly be part of the land and provide shelter and respite. It was built on part of their 26-acre (10.5-hectare) site near a grove of oaks and is open to summer breezes but turns its back on cold winter winds. The house also includes other green features, such as rainwater collection for potable water and irrigation, and a tight envelope with high R values. **Opposite top right:** An outdoor kitchen and living area is shaded by a canopy of live oaks with a view of the hills in another Texas landscape, designed by David Wilkes Builders of Austin, Texas. **Opposite bottom:** A weekend garden near Lake Michigan in Indiana designed by Leslie Rohrer of Carter Rohrer Co. from Canton, Georgia, features a gracious bluestone walk that leads to the front door on the side, designed so that it can be used as an additional patio. Stepping stones lead to a pergola in the back yard for dining or sitting, with another patio.

209

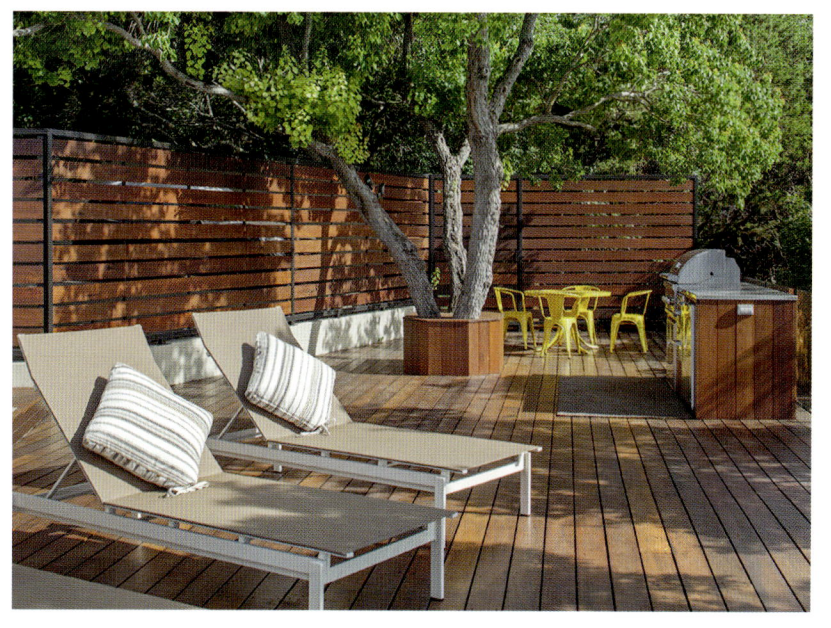

Books

Cultivating Garden Style by Rochelle Greayer (Timber Press)

The Defined Garden: Garden Design of Paul Bangay by Paul Bangay, Viking)

Down the Garden Path by Beverley Nichols (Timber Press)

The Essential Garden Design Workbook by Rosemary Alexander (Timber Press)

Four Season Harvest by Eliot Coleman (Chelsea Green Publishing)

Gardening Basics for Dummies by Steven A. Frowine (Wiley Publishing, Inc.)

Gardens in Detail: 100 Contemporary Designs by Emma Reuss (The Monacelli Press)

Making the Most of Shade by Larry Hodgson (Rodale Books)

The Most Beautiful Gardens in the World by Alain Le Toquin (Abrams Books)

Paul Bangay's Garden Design Handbook by Paul Bangay (Penguin Books)

Private Edens: Beautiful Country Gardens by Jack Staub (Gibbs Smith)

Remarkable Plants that Shape Our World by Helen and William Bynum (University of Chicago Press)

A Rich Spot of Earth by Peter J. Hatch (Yale University Press)

Royal Gardens by Mic Chamblas-Ploton (Abrams Books)

Seeing Flowers by Teri Dunn Chace (Timber Press)

Sissinghurst by Vita Sackville-West and Sarah Raven (St. Martin's Press)

Smith & Hawken: 100 Heirloom Tomatoes for the American Garden by Carolyn J. Male (Workman Publishing)

The Well-Tended Perennial Garden: Planting and Pruning Techniques by Tracy DiSabato-Aust (Timber Press)

A World of Gardens by John Dixon Hurt (Reaktion Books)

Above: A home built on 20 acres (8.1 hectares) of rolling meadow functions like a resort with a large pool, separate spa, pool house, brick pool deck and grounds that are mature and established. Due to the falling grades, New Jersey, designer Howard Roberts constructed four different levels or grade changes. **Opposite:** A rooftop deck in Washington, D.C. by Botanical Decorators' Morgan Washburn was designed to capture the city's beautiful skyline. Morgan constructed it using orchard-grown Ipe decking and carefully selected plant materials because of the rooftop location and area's sometimes harsh environment. Choices included ornamental grasses and drought-tolerant perennials.

DIG INTO GARDEN BLOGS AND BOOKS 211

Afterword

A PERSONALIZED GARDEN TEACHES A FINAL LESSON: REMEMBER TO PICK UP CLUES

I've been helping people create outdoor living spaces since Ronald Reagan was president. Ronald Reagan. That's a decade or two longer than I'd like to admit, but I feel truly blessed to have those years of experience under my belt. I've learned that no matter the style, size, or location there are essential elements of design that make a garden extraordinary. The good news is you don't have to be a professional to utilize these principles.

Start your design by spending time outdoors learning your "canvas." The landscape will show you things, such as how to divide the space into garden rooms, what to use as a focal point, and where to place paths. Before I started designing the gardens at my home at Moss Mountain Farm I strolled the property looking for clues on how to begin. I found an old oak to serve as the central axis, traces of old farm terraces for guiding the shape of the perennial gardens, and a grassy hill perfect for planting masses of daffodils.

Once you have established the outlines of your garden, you are ready to add color. When I design a garden I rely on 12 basic standards. The first six focus on building the framework of the garden:

- **Enclosure.** A garden room defined by borders of various materials.
- **Shape and form.** The contour and three-dimensional qualities of individual plants or groups of plants in the garden, as well as the outline of a garden room itself.
- **Framing the view.** Directing attention to an object or view by screening out surrounding distractions while creating a visually balanced and organized composition.
- **Entry.** A defined point of entrance into a garden enclosure.
- **Focal point.** Positioning an object to draw the eye and create a feature of attention.
- **Structure.** A variety of constructed features within the garden used to create enclosure, screen views, and anchor the garden.

The second six principles add decorative or finishing touches to your garden as well as personality, charm, and, last but not least, fun!

- **Color.** Orchestrating the color palette in the garden through the selection and arrangement of plants and objects.
- **Texture, pattern and rhythm.** Using surface characteristics, recognizable motifs, and the cadence created by the spacing of objects as elements of design.
- **Abundance.** An ample to overflowing quality created by the generous use of plants and materials, what some term "massing."
- **Whimsy.** Elements of lighthearted fancy.
- **Mystery.** Piquing a sense of curiosity, excitement, and occasionally apprehension through the garden's design.
- **Time.** Various garden styles representing certain ages of design.

I like to think of these 12 principles as a box of crayons. There is no right or wrong way to use them. Color to your heart's desire, and you will be well on your way. After 30 years of designing gardens, I've learned it's the act of creating a garden that matters the most.

P. Allen Smith
Little Rock, Arkansas
www.pallensmith.com

An author, television host, entrepreneur, and conservationist, he has a passion for the American style. He uses his Arkansas home, Moss Mountain Farm, which *The New York Times* hails as a "stunning estate," as an epicenter for promoting the local food movement, organic gardening, and preservation of heritage poultry breeds.

Top: The terrace gardens gently curve around the side of a hill and follow the contours of the original farm's garden. A mixed border of shrubs, roses, perennials, and annuals occupies the upper terrace while the lower terrace is planted with flowers for cutting, herbs, and fruits.
Bottom: This colossal oak referred to as the Sister Oak is the epicenter of Moss Mountain Farm.

AUTHORS

BARBARA BALLINGER

Barbara, a professional writer, author, speaker, and blogger, learned about gardens by writing about the topic for magazines and newspapers over the last 43 years, and interviewing experts such as Michael Glassman, a landscape designer with more than 37 years of experience designing for clients in diverse locations from California to New York to Wisconsin. Barbara has a wonderful, small garden at her home, including an organic vegetable patch of four raised planters with watering station, gravel floor, herbs surrounding it, and all framed by blue slate low "walls." This past summer, Barbara enjoyed the whiff of a delightful fragrance from her new lilac bushes and the taste of her first pears from four newly planted trees. She loves sitting in the back yard reading when it's not too hot. Or, she might move to her Victorian front porch in the late afternoon, reading a newspaper, sipping wine, eyeing her small vineyard, and watching the traffic move through her farm village. She had her front yard designed first, enabling her to carry out and afford her three- then five-year, now, maybe, seven-year plan. She keeps learning as she witnessed deer and rabbits devouring too many of her plants through the summer. This means some different selections next spring, and perhaps a fence.

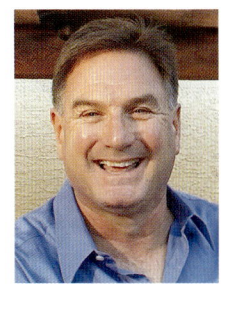

MICHAEL GLASSMAN

Michael is an award-winning landscape designer and also a serious photographer whose work has been published. He and Barbara currently write the widely-read blog, *The Bare Root* (https://glassmanballinger.wordpress.com/).

These days, Michael is enjoying more barbequed dinners with his wife and daughter in their outdoor dining room, surrounded by a bamboo privacy screen, listening to the trickling sound of their custom water-wall fountain. Michael's assistant at work calls their outdoor room "the palace" for its beauty, peace, and inspiring outdoor art. In the morning, through his bedroom window, he enjoys seeing hummingbirds come to his colorfully planted pots and bathe in an ideally placed fountain. He keeps learning, too, especially now that many of his clients must contend with California's terrible drought. His main solutions are to use native and drought-tolerant plantings that require little water, build raised planters around more functional hardscape, construct cisterns for rain and runoff water storage, and plant less lawn or use synthetic alternatives that fool the eye.

ACKNOWLEDGMENTS

There are so many to thank in helping this book go from an idea that Michael planted with Barbara after years of working together on magazine articles and a blog, *The Bare Root* (https://glassmanballinger.wordpress.com/). When we approached IMAGES' publisher Paul Latham, he loved the concept, but said, "Let's wait for the right time." We found it about two years ago as we witnessed continuing interest in gardening and living outdoors; among the biggest requests by homeowners worldwide is improving their homes and sites. However, there are so many others to thank who helped along the way.

To Elaine Waetjen, Michael's wife, who read every chapter with attention to detail and made wonderful suggestions. To Bruce, Barbara's significant other, who listened to her talk endlessly about gardens and learned—as she had learned from Michael—that gardens first sleep, then crawl, then leap. They saw together how wonderful it is to find new blooms emerge yet how sad it can make you to witness the results of deer trampling hosta, and squirrels taking away herbs, berries, and nuts. To Margaret Crane, Barbara's writing partner for more than 27 years, who read the copy to make it shine, as she always has.

To the staff of Images Publishing, far away geographically, but available daily, when needed, to advise and curtail words and an excess of photographs; thank you especially to senior editor Gina Tsarouhas, who added, deleted and questioned as the best editors do. And thank you again to Rod Gilbert and your staff for making the book look terrific, as you did with Barbara's earlier joint effort, *The Kitchen Bible: Designing the perfect culinary space*. Some day both of us will surprise the Images Publishing team with a visit down under to meet in person.

To the American Society of Landscape Architects in Washington, D.C. (www.asla.org), and in particular Terry Poltrack and Alexandra Hay, for sending out the word to landscape architects around the United States to share their best gardens; many did and showed us how other professionals do it!

To professional gardeners and enthusiasts: we thank James Hughes for writing our Foreword and P. Allen Smith for writing the Afterword.

To Michael's administrative assistant Carla who helped us schedule Michael's time to work on the book, as well as his associate Jennifer who helped arrange PDFs and "before" photos of his projects to be included.

Thank you to all the contractors and suppliers that made these projects a reality. While it may take a village to raise a child, it takes at least a hardworking team to build a landscape and see that it continues to flourish season after season, year after year.

To all the garden designers, landscape architects, and other design professionals who shared their handiwork, inspiration, and wisdom with us; you have taught us both the challenges of different sites, climates, budgets, design ideas, patience, and so much more. Thank you all, including your wonderful colleagues, staff and contacts, who assisted in securing images, plans, and information. And for anybody we neglected to include, we apologize profusely but know we appreciate your efforts:

John M. Algozzini
K&D Landscape Management, Inc.
Rockdale, Illinois
www.kdlandscapeinc.com

Jeff Allen
Jeff Allen Landscape Architecture (JALA), LLC
Winston-Salem, North Carolina
www.jalallc.com

Robin Amorello
Atmoscaper Kitchen Design
Portland, Maine
www.atmoscaperdesign.com

Tyler Arnold
Landis Communications
San Francisco, California
www.landispr.com

Sarah Barnard
Sarah Barnard Design
Santa Monica, California
www.sarahbarnard.com

Clara Couric Batchelor
CBA Landscape Architects
Cambridge, Massachusetts
www.cbaland.com

Jarrod Baumann
Zeterre Landscape Architecture
San Francisco, California
www.zeterre.com

Nicole Bemboom
Arterra Landscape Architects
San Francisco, California
www.arterrasf.com

Jim Bertrand
Jim Bertrand Landscape Design
Monee, Illinois
www.jimbertrand.com

Susan Brunstrum
Sweet Peas Design
Chicago, Illinois
www.sweetpeas-inspired.com

Grady Burnette
Burnette Builders
Wimberley, Texas
www.burnettebuilders.com

Christopher Cahill
Botanical Decorators
Olney, Maryland
www.botanicaldecorators.com

Cape Fear Garden Club
Wilmington, North Carolina
www.capefeargardenclub.org

Jim Charlier
JCharlier Communication Design
Buffalo, New York
www.artofgardening.org

Steve Chepurny
Beechwood Architecture, Landscape and Construction
Southampton, New Jersey
www.beechwoodlandscape.com

Chris Cipriano
Cipriano Landscape Design
Mahwah, New Jersey
www.njcustomswimmingpools.com

Scott Cohen
The Green Scene Landscaping Inc.
Northridge, California
www.greenscenelandscape.com

Christie J. Colville
Cipriano Landscape Design
Mahwah, New Jersey
www.njcustomswimmingpools.com

Brian Cossari
Hoffman Landscapes
Wilton, Connecticut
www.hoffmanlandscapes.com

John Cowen
John Cowen Landscape Associates
Sag Harbor, New York
www.jcowenlandscape.com

David Wilkes Builders
Austin, Texas
www.davidwilkesbuilders.com

Anne DiFrancesco
A&M Studios Inc.
Westport, Connecticut
www.am-studios.net

James M. Drzewiecki
Ginkgo Leaf Studio
Cedarburg, Wisconsin
www.ginkgoleafstudio.net

Joe Eisner
Eisner Design
New York City, New York
www.eisnerdesign.com

Terri Ervin
Decorating Den Interiors
Atlanta, Georgia
www.decdens.com/tervin

Anthony Exter
Anthony Exter Landscape Design
Los Angeles, California
www.anthonyexter.com

Jim Fogarty
Jim Fogarty Design
Malvern East, Victoria, Australia
www.jimfogartydesign.com.au

Amber Freda
Amber Freda Home & Garden Design
New York City, New York
www.amberfreda.com

Susanne Fyffe
Fyffe Landscape Architecture
Arlington, Virginia
www.fyffela.com

Garden Walk Buffalo
Buffalo, New York
www.gardenwalkbuffalo.com

Jean Garbarini
Damon-Farber Landscape Architecture
Minneapolis, Minnesota
www.damonfarber.com

Vera Gates
Arterra Landscape Architects
San Francisco, California
www.arterrasf.com

Michael Glassman
Michael Glassman & Associates
Sacramento, California
www.michaelglassman.com

Lya Gomez
Lya Gomez
San Francisco, California; Caracas, Venezuela
www.lyagomez.com

Christopher J. Grubb
Arch-Interiors Design Group
Los Angeles, California
www.archinteriors.com

Alec Gunn
Gunn Landscape Architecture
New York, New York
www.gunnlandscapes.com

Brian Hahn
Botanical Decorators
Olney, Maryland
www.botanicaldecorators.com

Ive Haugeland
Shades of Green Landscape Architecture
Sausalito, California
www.shadesofgreenla.com

Carol Heffernan
Heffernan Landscape Design
Chicago, Illinois
www.heffernanlandscapedesign.com

Charles Hess
Hess Landscape Architects
Landsdale, Pennsylvania
www.hessla.com

Staci Hill
Stock & Hill Landscapes Inc.
Seattle (Lake Stevens), Washington
www.stockandhill.com

Michael Hoffman
Hoffman Landscapes
Wilton, Connecticut
www.hoffmanlandscapes.com

James Hughes
James Hughes Landscaping
Tallahassee, Florida
www.jameshugheslandscaping.com

Robert Hursthouse
Hursthouse Landscape Architects and Contractors
Bolingbrook, Illinois
www.hursthouse.com

Claudia Juestel
Adeeni Design Group
San Francisco, California
www.adeenidesigngroup.com

Claire Kettlekamp and Ryan Kettlekamp
Kettlekamp and Kettlekamp Landscape Architecture
Evanston, Illinois
www.kandkla.com

Lou Kimball
Lou Kimball Architect
Harpswell, Maine
www.loukimball.com

Lana Korb
Foliage Landscape Design
Toronto, Canada
www.foliagelandscape.com

Leslie Markman-Stern
Leslie M. Stern Design
Chicago, Illinois
www.lesliemsterndesign.com

Andrew McConnico
Swift Company,
304 10th Avenue, East Unit A, Seattle, Washington

Joyce Means
Decorating Den Interiors
Charleston, South Carolina
www.decdens.com/jmeans

Jonathan L. Melvin
MRM Design Group
Battleboro, North Carolina
www.mrmdesigngroup.com

Above: Cipriano Pools & Landscaping designed this back yard with multiple water delights: a 1,000-square-foot (93-square-meter) vanishing-edge pool, 300-square-foot (27.9-square-meter) lower pool, 120-square-foot (11.1-square-meter) raised space, 5-foot-tall (1.5-meter-tall) waterfall/grotto, and a 45-foot (13.8-meter) waterslide, all to create unlimited fun!

Above: Concerned about rabbits, the client asked Jim Fogarty of Jim Fogarty Design Pty Ltd in Australia for a vegetable garden that the rabbits couldn't destroy. Inspiration was drawn from city skylines for the layout for the concrete pipe vegetable garden. The pipes take on a practical as well as a sculptural role, giving an industrial edge and creating an interesting mix of softness to the garden beds and the home's strong lines.

Renee Mercer
Mercer Landscape Design,
Kankakee, Illinois

Julie Meyers
Decorating Den Interiors
Waverly, Iowa
www.decdens.com/jmeyers

Elissa Morgante
Morgante-Wilson
Chicago, Illinois
www.morgantewilson.com

Marc Nissim
Harmony Design Group
Westfield, New Jersey
www.hdglandscape.com

Marie NyBlom
The Green Scene Landscaping Inc.
Northridge, California
www.greenscenelandscape.com

Terrence Parker
Terrafirma Landscape Architecture
Portsmoth, New Hampshire
www.terrafirmalandarch.com

Sue Pelley
Decorating Den Interiors
Easton, Maryland
www.decoratingden.com

Peter Pfau
Pfau Long Architecture
San Francisco, California
www.pfaulong.com

Jeff Plusen
Plusen Designs Landscape and
Architecture (RLA, ASLA)
Catonville, Maryland
www.plusen.com

Lisa Port
Banyon Tree Design
Seattle, Washington
www.banyontreedesign.com

Richard Poynter
Poynter Landscape Architecture & Construction (ASLA)
Ballwin, Missouri
www.poynterlandscape.com

Diane Purcell
Through the Lens Management Inc.
Wimberley, Texas
www.ttlmgt.com

William Renninger
William Renninger Associates
Greenville, South Carolina
www.williamrenningerassociates.com

James G. Robyn
BioNova Natural Swimming Pools
Chester, New Jersey
www.bionovanaturalpools.com

Howard Roberts
Liquid Inc., Landscape Architects and Designers Inc.
Pittstown, New Jersey
www.liquidscapes.net

Shelley Rodner
Decorating Den Interiors
Bethany Beach, Delaware
www.decdens.com/srodner

Leslie Rohrer
The Carter Rohrer Company
Canton, Georgia
www.carterrohrer.com

Arthur Ruebel
The Pond Guys
Saint Peters, Missouri
www.thepondguys.com

Greg Schaumburg
Bertog Landscape Co.
Wheeling, Illinois
www.bertoglandscape.com

P. Allen Smith
P. Allen Smith Co.
Little Rock, Arkansas
www.pallensmith.com

Ethan Roland Solaviev and Dyami Solaviev
AppleSeed Permaculture LLC
High Falls, New York
www.appleseedpermaculture.com

Carrie Stanker
Garden Gate Design Studio
Mansfield, New Jersey
www.gardengatenj.com

Barbara Stock
Stock & Hill Landscapes Inc.
Seattle (Lake Stevens), Washington
www.stockandhill.com

Stephen J. Suzman
Zeterre Lanscape Architecture
San Francisco, California
www.zeterre.com

Barbara Tabak
Decorating Den Interiors
Harrisburg, Pennsylvania
www.barbaratabak.decoratingden.com

Terry TerHaar
TerHaar Garden Design
Chicago, Illinois
www.terhaargardendesign.com

Deidre E. Toner
DT Design
Oak Mill Creek, Illinois
www.dt-landscapedesign.com

Tony Tradewell
Tony Tradewell Landscape Architecture
Deville, Louisiana
www.tonytradewell.com

Troon Pacific
San Francisco, California
www.troonpacific.com

John S. Troy
John S. Troy Landscape Architecture
San Antonio, Texas
www.johnstroylandarch.com

Judy Underwood
Decorating Den Interiors
Bonita Springs, Florida
www.decden.net

Laurie Van Zandt
The Ardent Gardener Landscape Design
and Project Coordination
Huntsville, Utah
www.theardentgardener.net

Amy Wax
Your Color Source Studios, Inc.
Montclair, New Jersey
www.amywax.com

Bob Wilhelm
Poynter Landscape Architecture & Construction (ASLA)
Ballwin, Missouri
www.poynterlandscape.com

Fred Wilson
Morgante-Wilson
Chicago, Illinois
www.morgantewilson.com

Winn Wittman
Winn Wittman Architecture
Austin, Texas
www.winnwitman.com

Stephen Wlodarczyk
Botanical Gardens
Olney, Maryland
www.botanicaldecorators.com

Scott Yarnell
Arterra Landscape Architects
San Francisco, California
www.arterrasf.com

Barbara Ballinger and Michael Glassman, 2015

PHOTOGRAPHY CREDITS

Front Cover

MMGI / Marianne Majerus; design: Shades of Green Landscape Architecture, San Francisco, California

Back Cover (left to right)

James Hughes Landscaping; Howard Roberts, Liquid Inc., www.liquidscapes.net; Marion Brenner; Greg Schaumburg, Hursthouse Landscape Architects and Contractors

Foreword

James Hughes Landscaping 7

Roger Foley Photography 8

Nick Novelli 9

Introduction

Don Zinteck/Photographics 2 11

Rick Elezi 12–13

Howard Roberts, Liquid Inc. 13 (top left)

Marc Nissim, Harmony Design Group 13 (top right)

Chapter 1: Understand Your Site and Climate

Michael Glassman, Michael Glassman & Associates 15, 17 (left), 19

Sarah Barnard, Sarah Barnard Design 16

Laurie Van Zandt, The Arden Gardener Landscape Design 17 (right)

Chris Cooper 18 (left)

John Cowen. John D. Cowen Landscape Associates Ltd 18 (right)

Chapter 2: Develop a Budget and Stick to It

Howard Roberts, Liquid Inc., www.liquidscapes.net 21

John Algozzini, K&D Landscape Management, Inc. 22 (top)

Carrie Stanker, Garden Gate Design Studio 22 (bottom)

Stephen Wlodarczyk, Botanical Decorators Inc. 23 (top)

Amber Freda, Amber Freda Home & Garden Design 23 (bottom)

Michele Lee Willson Photography 24–5

Michael Glassman, Michael Glassman & Associates 26

Sarah Barnard, Sarah Barnard Design 27 (left)

Amy Gallo 27 (right)

BioNova Natural Pools 28–9

Chapter 3: Hire the Best Professionals

Michael Glassman, Michael Glassman & Associates 31, 34, 35

Arthur Ruebel, The Pond Guys 32 (top left)

Werner Straube 32 (top right)

Brian Hahn, Botanical Decorators Inc. 32 (bottom)

Amber Freda, Amber Freda Home & Garden Design 33

Don Zinteck/Photographics 2 37

Chapter 4: Find Your Garden Style

Marion Brenner 39 (top)

Amy Gallo 39 (bottom left)

Westhauser Photography 39 (bottom right), 43 (top left)

Michael Glassman, Michael Glassman & Associates 41 (left, center)

Stephen Suzman, Zeterre Landscape Architecture 40, 41 (right), 43 (top right), 44 (left), 45 (top)

Ronni Hock, Ronni Hock Garden and Landscape 42 (top)

Robert Benson 42 (bottom)

Torrey Ferrell Creative 43 (bottom left)

Henry Doll 43 (bottom right), 54

Greg Weiner 44 (right)

Greg Schaumburg, Hursthouse Landscape Architects and Contractors 45 (bottom), 55

Dave Lawrie, Kettelkamp & Kettelkamp Landscape Architecture 46

Mark Darley 47 (top left)

T. Daktyl 47 (top right, bottom)

Ethan Roland Soloviev, Appleseed Permaculture LLC 49 (top, bottom)

Dyami Soloviev, Appleseed Permaculture LLC 49 (center)

Steven Mays Photography 50 (top left, top right)

Michele Lee Willson Photography 50 (bottom), 51

Jarrod R. Baumann, Zeterre Landscape Architecture 52

Douglas Hill Photography 53

Chapter 5: Design Principles for a Functional and Aesthetic Outdoor Environment

Howard Roberts, Liquid Inc., www.liquidscapes.net 57, 61 (bottom), 62 (bottom left, right), 66–7 (top)

John Algozzini, K&D Landscape Management, Inc. 58 (top), 64, 65 (top left, top right)

Westhauser Photography 58 (bottom), 67 (bottom left), 67 (bottom right), 68, 69 (top left)

Design by Brian Hahn, Botanical Decorators, Inc. 59 (top left)

Henry Doll 59 (bottom)

Hoffman Landscapes, Inc. 59 (top right)

Poynter Landscape Architecture and Construction 60 (left), 69 (bottom right)

Michael Glassman, Michael Glassman & Associates 61 (top left), 61 (top right), 63 (bottom left), 69 (top right)

222

Renee Mercer, Mercer Landscape Design, Kankakee, Illinois 60 (top right)

Danielle Quigley 60 (bottom right)

Carol Heffernan 62 (top left)

Troon Pacific Inc.; Shades of Green Landscape Architecture 63 (top left)

Dave Lawrie, Kettelkamp & Kettelkamp Landscape Architecture 63 (top right)

Laurie Van Zandt, The Ardent Gardener Landscape Architecture 63 (bottom right), 69 (bottom left)

Carrie Stanker, Garden Gate Design Studio 65 (bottom)

John Martinelli 66 (bottom left, bottom right)

Cipriano Landscape Design 67 (top)

Amy Wax, Your Color Source 70 (left)

Philip Liss 70–1 (center), 71

Chapter 6: Recognize Problems Before You Start

Elaine Waetjen 73 (top right, bottom right), 74 (right), 75 (top left), 76 (midde left, center right, bottom right)

Jennifer Wait, Michael Glassman & Associates 73 (top left, center left, center right, bottom left), 74 (left), 75 (top right, bottom left, bottom right), 76 (top right)

Michael Glassman, Michael Glassman & Associates 76 (top left, bottom left)

Chapter 7: Great Gardens to Inspire

Michael Glassman, Michael Glassman & Associates 78–9

Zen Garden

Jennifer Wait, Michael Glassman & Associates 80, 82 (top left)

Michael Glassman, Michael Glassman & Associates 80 (top right, bottom), 82 (top center, top right, plan, center right, bottom right)

The Eclectic Outdoor Room

Elaine Waetjen 84 (top), 86 (right)

Mary Waetjen 84 (bottom left, bottom right), 86 (bottom left)

Michael Glassman, Michael Glassman & Associates 86 (top left)

Plan by Michael Glassman, Michael Glassman & Associates 87

Adios Snakes

Jennifer Wait, Michael Glassman & Associates 88 (top left, top right)

Michael Glassman, Michael Glassman & Associates 88 (bottom), 90 (left), 91 (left, top right, bottom right)

Plan by Michael Glassman, Michael Glassman & Associates 90 (right)

Artist's Retreat

Jennifer Wait, Michael Glassman & Associates 92 (top left, top right)

Michael Glassman, Michael Glassman & Associates 92 (bottom), 94 (top left, center left, bottom left), 95

Plan by Michael Glassman, Michael Glassman & Associates 94

Savoring a View

Richard Poynter 96, 98, 99

Reclaimed Haven

Greg Schaumburg, Hursthouse Landscapes Architects and Contractors 100, 102, 103

Design Is in the Details

Michael Glassman, Michael Glassman & Associates 104 (top, bottom right), 106 (top center, top right, bottom), 107 (top right, bottom right)

Jennifer Wait, Michael Glassman & Associates 104 (bottom left), 106 (top left)

Plan by Michael Glassman, Michael Glassman & Associates 107

Bucolic Farm Redo

Susanne Fyffe 108, 110, 111

Waterfall Fantasy

Cipriano Landscape Design 112, 114, 115

Experimental Lab

William Renninger 116, 118, 119

Look: No Lawn

Jim Fogarty 120, 122, 123

Spanish Colonial Revival Muse

Anthony Exter 124 (top left, top right), 126 (top right)

George Zarour 124 (bottom), 126 (top left, bottom), 127 (top left, top center, top right)

Plan by Jeff Roberts Engineering Associates 127

Water Right

Darla Tradewell 128, 130 (top left, top right), 131

Plan by Tony Tradewell 130

Serenity Evolved, Water Banished

Laurie van Zandt 132, 134, 135

Multitiered Maximizer

Laurie van Zandt 136, 138, 139

Evolved Landscape, from Barren to Mature

Howard Roberts 140, 142, 143

Staycation Showcase

Linda Oyama Bryan 144 (top), 146 (top), 147

Jim Bertrand 144 (bottom left, bottom right), 146 (bottom right)

Plan by Jim Bertrand 146

Cohesive Clarity

Jim Bertrand 148, 151 (bottom)

Linda Oyama Bryan 150, 151 (top left, top right)

Trifecta of Delights

Brian Hahn 152 (top left, top center, top right)

Stacy Zarin Goldbert 152 (bottom), 154, 155 (top left, top right)

Plan by Brian Hahn 155

Hip Revival

Coles Hairston 156, 158 (top left, top right), 159

Plan by Winn Wittman Architecture 158

Natural Wildness Balances Cultural Turf

Terrence Parker 160, 162 (top right, bottom), 163

Eric Roth 162 (top left)

Woodlands Star

Danielle Quigley 164, 166 (top right, bottom left, bottom right), 167

Plan by Plusen Designs 166

Historic Inspirations for Food, Flowers, Company

Jeff Allen 168, 170 (top center, top right, bottom)

Torrey Ferrell Creative 170 (top left)

Plan by Jeff Allen 171

Rule No 1: Bag the Master Plan

Jarrod Baumann 172 (top left, top right)

Mitchell Maher 172 (bottom), 174 (top, bottom right), 175

Plan by Zeterre Landscape Architecture 174

Celebrating the Land

Michele Lee Willson Photography 176, 178

Plans by Arterra Landscape Architects 179

Family Fun

Hursthouse Landscape Architects and Contractors 180, 182, 183

Water Times Three

Marc Nissim 184, 186, 187

Minimalist Signature

Stephen Suzman 188 (top left, right), 190 (top left), 191 (top right)

Mark Darley 188 (bottom left), 190 (center left, bottom left, right), 191 (top left)

Plan by Suzman Design Associates 191

Nuts Inspire a Home Resort

Michael Glassman, Michael Glassman & Associates 192 (top), 194, 195 (top right, bottom right)

Jennifer Wait, Michael Glassman & Associates 192 (bottom left, bottom right)

Plan by Michael Glassman, Michael Glassman & Associates 195

Chapter 8: Find Inspiration—Garden Tours, Community Gardens, and Gardens Around the World

Jim Charlier 197 (top left, right), 201 (bottom left)

Don Zinteck/Photographics 2 197 (bottom left), 198–9, 200, 201 (top left, top right, bottom right)

Michael Glassman, Michael Glassman & Associates 202, 205, 206–7

Chapter 9: Dig into Garden Blogs and Books

Tre Dunham 209 (top left)

Thomas McConnell 209 (top right)

Leslie Rohrer, Carter Rohrer Co. 209 (bottom)

Jay Rosenblatt 210

Morgan Washburn, Botanical Decorators 211

Afterword—A Personalized Garden Teaches a Final Lesson: Remember to Pick up Clues

Courtesy P. Allen Smith 213

Authors

Courtesy Barbara Ballinger 214 (left)

Jeffrey Milstein 214 (right)

Michael Glassman, Michael Glassman & Associates 215 (left)

Elaine Waetjen 215 (right)

Acknowledgments

Cipriano Landscape Design 218–19

Jim Fogarty 220